HELLO!
MY NAME IS
Phil and I am...

Addicted to
REAL ESTATE

Why I Can't Stop and Why You Should Start

A $12,000,000 Portfolio with a 7% Annual Increase is $840,000 in equity

Phil! Honey! Are you listening?

Includes free downloadable investor forms

Phil Falcone

No part of this publication ....

LIMIT OF LIABILITY/DISCLAIMER OF WARRANTY: WHILE THE PUBLISHER AND AUTHOR HAVE USED THEIR BEST EFFORTS IN PREPARING THIS BOOK, **THEY MAKE NO REPRESENTATIONS OR WARRANTIES WITH RESPECT TO THE ACCURACY OR COMPLETENESS OF THE CONTENTS OF THIS WORK WITH SPECIFIC DISCLAIMER OF ALL WARRANTIES, INCLUDING WITHOUT LIMITATION WARRANTIES OF FITNESS FOR A PARTICULAR PURPOSE. NO WARRANTY MAY BE CREATED OR EXTENDED BY SALES REPRESENTATIVES OR WRITTEN SALES MATERIALS.** THE ADVICE AND STRATEGIES CONTAINED HEREIN MAY NOT BE SUITABLE FOR YOUR SITUATION. THE PUBLISHER IS NOT ENGAGED IN RENDERING LEGAL, ACCOUNTING, MEDICAL, OR OTHER PROFESSIONAL SERVICES. IF PROFESSIONAL ASSISTANCE OR ADVICE IS SOUGHT, IT WOULD BE NECESSARY TO HIRE THE APPROPRIATE PROFESSIONALS FOR SUCH ADVICE. ANY TRADEMARKS, SERVICE MARKS, PRODUCT NAMES OR NAMED FEATURES ARE ASSUMED TO BE THE PROPERTY OF THEIR RESPECTIVE OWNERS, AND ARE USED ONLY FOR REFERENCE. THERE IS NO IMPLIED ENDORSEMENT IF WE USE ONE OF THESE TERMS. ANY LINKS TO OUTSIDE WEBSITES OR ORGANIZATIONS DOES NOT MEAN THAT THE AUTHOR OR THE PUBLISHER ENDORSE THE INFORMATION THAT THESE SITES OR ORGANIZATIONS PROVIDE OR RECOMMEND. **NEITHER THE PUBLISHER NOR THE AUTHOR SHALL BE LIABLE FOR ANY LOSS OF PROFIT OR ANY COMMERCIAL DAMAGES, INCLUDING BUT NOT LIMITED TO SPECIAL, INCIDENTAL, CONSEQUENTIAL, OR OTHER DAMAGES.**

I HAVE TRIED TO RECREATE EVENTS, LOCALES AND CONVERSATIONS FROM MY MEMORIES. IN ORDER TO MAINTAIN THEIR ANONYMITY, SOME NAMES AND IDENTIFYING DETAILS HAVE BEEN CHANGED TO PROTECT THE PRIVACY OF INDIVIDUALS.

Copyright © 2010 Phil Falcone
All rights reserved.

ISBN: 1451544413
ISBN-13: 9781451544411
Library of Congress Control Number: 2010903912

TABLE OF CONTENTS

PART 1   HOW I GOT STARTED

Chapter 1	My Family's Attitude toward Business	1
Chapter 2	An Early Introduction to Real Estate	5
Chapter 3	I Made My First Purchase	11
Chapter 4	I Purchase My Second Property	15
Chapter 5	The Audiotape That Changed My Life	17
Chapter 6	The All-Money-Down Technique	21
Chapter 7	The Crash in the Summer of 2000	25
Chapter 8	Erdrick Street	27
Chapter 9	Laclede Avenue	29
Chapter 10	Getting My Real Estate License	33
Chapter 11	Realty Professionals of America	35

PART 2   MAKING THE TRANSITION TO COMMERCIAL

Chapter 12	Alignment of the Mind	39
Chapter 13	Fifty-Thousand-Square-Foot Building in Reading	45
Chapter 14	Forty-Unit Apartment Building in Trenton NJ	51
Chapter 15	The Hatboro Project	55
Chapter 16	Your Odds of Success Dramatically Improve with Each Attempt	59
Chapter 17	Finding Executec Suites	63
Chapter 18	The 1600 Building	85
Chapter 19	Expanding Executec Suites	109
Chapter 20	Bucks County Suites	113
Chapter 21	The Anatomy of a Commercial Deal	129
Chapter 22	The Thin Line between Success and Failure	133
Chapter 23	What Is an Executive Suite Center?	135
Chapter 24	The Simplicity of Real Estate	143
Chapter 25	Every Time I Deviate	147

PART 3 — CORE BELIEFS OF A FULL-TIME REAL ESTATE INVESTOR

Chapter 26	Buy and Hold in a Rising Market	151
Chapter 27	Liquidate at the Peak	153
Chapter 28	What Do You Do with All That Equity?	155
Chapter 29	Flipping Is Not Investing	157
Chapter 30	Falling Market, Go Fishing	161
Chapter 31	The Accumulation of Property	163
Chapter 32	Commercial if I Can Do Something with It	167
Chapter 33	Commercial Cash Cows	171
Chapter 34	Leveraged to the Hilt	173
Chapter 35	Partnership Only When	175
Chapter 36	Know Your Market	177
Chapter 37	Timing the Market	183
Chapter 38	Get Your Real Estate License	187
Chapter 39	Learn Construction	189
Chapter 40	Tools in the Toolbox	193
Chapter 41	I Don't Like Anyone Knowing Anything I Don't Know	195
Chapter 42	Get Started Young	197
Chapter 43	Manage Your Own Properties	201
Chapter 44	Don't Fall in Love	205
Chapter 45	Buyer's Anxiety	207
Chapter 46	Torture Yourself	209
Chapter 47	What Makes an Investor?	211
Chapter 48	Internet Marketing	213
Chapter 49	Get Rich Slow	217
Chapter 50	Transforming a Portfolio	219
Chapter 51	Pick a Sector	221
Chapter 52	Protect the Downside	227
Chapter 53	Seven Figures Easily	229
Chapter 54	Enhance the Location	237

PART 4 — OUTSIDE THE BOX IDEAS

Chapter 55	Sometimes the Move Is to Overpay	243
Chapter 56	Create Multiple Profit Generators	245
Chapter 57	Hi, My Name Is Phil and I'm Addicted to Real Estate	249

Chapter 58	Honor among Investors	251
Chapter 59	My Pet Peeves	255
Chapter 60	Everything Is Always for Sale All the Time	263
Chapter 61	Developing the Entrepreneurial Spirit in Children	267
Chapter 62	Overreaching Government Involvement	271
Chapter 63	Keep It Personal without Corporations	273
Chapter 64	Carry Paper to Make It Happen	279
Chapter 65	Workaholic, OCD and Insomnia	283
Chapter 66	Twenty-Something-Year Olds	285
Chapter 67	Sometimes You Win and Sometimes You Learn	287
Chapter 68	The Difference between Me and Most	291
Chapter 69	Sell the People Who Are Trying to Sell You	295
Chapter 70	Never Lower the Rent	297
Chapter 71	Barter Services to Keep the Machine Moving	299
Chapter 72	Don't Make Too Much Money	305

PART 5   WRAPPING IT ALL UP

Chapter 73	How I Run My Operation	311
Chapter 74	From Rags to Riches, and Maybe Rags Again	317
Chapter 75	What Did You Say I Cannot Do?	319
Chapter 76	How Can I Help You?	321
Chapter 77	The Coveted Phil Falcone Seal of Approval	323

ACKNOWLEDGMENTS

After twenty years in the real estate business, many people have formulated my thoughts related to this industry over the years. Some of the people who've helped me went out of their way to support me, and many were involved in the moments of my education without realizing it. Whether they meant to or not, they all have my appreciation for the assistance that they provided in bringing me to this point of my life financially.

So many people have helped me it will be impossible to name them all, so I apologize in advance if I missed anyone. Sincere thanks goes to the unknown realtor who took me around to look at duplexes in the 1980s, the guy I met in a bar who drove me around to show me his portfolio, Joe Rice, Steve Phares, Warren Matz, Tom Phares, Paul Bondy, Marty Ryan, Steve Martino, Andrea Carroll, Mike DeNoia, Raymond Lemire, Matt Falcone, Jeremy Ricci, Chris Smith, Michael Klein, Todd Lowell, Patty Burgess, Paul Luff, Mark Sherby, Marc Halpern, Dick Blum, Peter Gilbert, Justin Stranere, Gus Magazzeni, Vince & Arlene Falcone and Vladamir.

I would like to thank my wife, Terry, for her insights and a willingness to be a sounding board for my sometimes unconventional projects and for being a partner in our greatest project ever, Stone.

Finally I'd like to thank my parents for instilling in me the entrepreneurial spirit that still lives with me today.

DEDICATION

I dedicate this book to my now 12 year old son, Stone Falcone. Part of the reason I wrote this book is I had thoughts about my own mortality. I figured if I were to somehow fall off the face of the earth tomorrow who would communicate to my now un-interested son all my real estate philosophies? By writing this manuscript I document my real estate theories forever with the hopes that someday Stone may pick this book up voluntarily and absorb the information inside.

I love the real estate business that has enriched my life and empowered me to become a person in complete control of my own destiny. I hope that one day in the future he too will enjoy the freedoms all successful real estate entrepreneurs enjoy.

AN OPENING WORD

Keeping it simple is something I find myself saying more and more often whenever a problem or decision arises. It seems to me that the answers to most problems really are simple if you just break them down and don't let all the minute details cloud your judgment. While writing this book, I tried to simplify things as I really see them, allowing the reader to understand that the world of real estate investing is not as difficult as it seems. I hope to inspire you to roll the dice on real estate and take the chance of a lifetime when it presents itself.

> **"Create your own destiny or someone else will create one for you."**
>
> ~ MARSHALL SYLVER

Getting rich is hard and getting rich fast is even harder, but getting rich slow the way I describe in this book is very possible if you take your time step-by-step to make it happen. You realize that you're most likely going to be making the journey to 2022 whether you execute my plan or not. One day twelve years from now, 2022 will creep up on you pretty quickly, and you may find yourself in a situation where you didn't do anything, which is much worse than trying my plan. Since you will be going to 2022 anyway, you might as well try by buying one house and see how it works out for you. I always say sometimes you win and sometimes you learn. The worst thing that can happen is you're going to learn a lesson about real estate on your first house.

One of my favorite things about real estate in general is that there's any one of a dozen ways to go with it to end up getting what you want. I'm not foolish enough to think that every reader who grabs this book should take the path I chose. All I can do is explain to you how I did it, and you can draw from the stories which parts pertain to your plan.

As I write this book, it is taking shape more like a story of my life's real estate deals rather than a how-to book to invest in real estate. God knows I've read enough of those boring how-to books. My writing style is a lot like my method of investing. I do my investing with a lot of emotion and feeling. I only buy buildings that I think I will feel good about owning and be proud of the profit that I'm now making from them. I don't sit around and do fifty mathematical equations about whether or not this building will work under every potential scenario. I like to think simple and I believe that's the way you have to analyze real estate.

You don't want the greatest investment of your life to become your biggest nightmare. You want it to be a monument to your success in life and something you can't wait to drive your friends over to see, showing them what an amazing accomplishment you made. You want your quality of life to be improved from the intelligent decisions that you made in real estate, so that as the years go on, instead of beating yourself up, you'll be patting yourself on the back. It's an amazing feeling of accomplishment when you've reached a point where all you'll have to do for a living is manage your portfolio. Your intelligent commercial real estate purchases along with your management of those properties will allow you to be in a position of comfort in life. I put a great deal of brain power into this manuscript so the reader may one day be able to be in that exact position.

PART 1

How I Got Started

CHAPTER 1
My Family's Attitude toward Business

My family's attitude toward business was a perfect building block for becoming an entrepreneur in the real estate business. My great, great grandfather, Nicola Falcone, came to America in the 1880s. This was a good decade earlier than Italian immigrants were coming to this country. He was a stonemason and arrived in this country enthusiastic about picking up that trade in America. That's exactly what he did.

My great, great grandfather, Nicola, found a lot of prejudice in this country toward Italians. He determined that one of the best ways to succeed is to take the things that are against you and turn them into positives. The prejudice he experienced made it difficult to get a well-paying job, so he went out and started his own business. His success awarded him contracts to build facilities in the city of Philadelphia as well as the suburbs. My father has put considerable effort into determining what bridges, schools, and churches Nicola may have built in the areas we live in today. Unfortunately, much of that information died with Nicola.

He had five sons who all ultimately became stonemasons and worked in this company for part of their lives. The idea of being a strong proud entrepreneur who runs his own business started within Nicola and filtered its way down through five generations to me. The entrepreneurial spirit of the Falcone family made its way to my grandmother, who owned her own bridal shop that she successfully ran for many decades in Philadelphia. While some of my family members took jobs in the real world, I won't be glorifying them here, as I view these individuals as the shame of the family. I am just half kidding around with you.

"My great, great grandfather, Nicola Falcone"

My parents owned a printing company, Falcone Printing Service, which they ran successfully for most of their lives. I remember looking at their business cards and thinking what a big deal it was to have a company with your name on it. I was proud to see the words "Falcone Printing Service," as in my mind it sent a message to the world. Hey, look at this—we are smart enough to create our own business to produce the money we need, and we don't need to answer to anyone. I remember thinking like that as a young man and answering people quickly when they wanted to know what my father did for a living.

Our neighborhood was one of the best in Philadelphia, and there was a clear difference between the career paths the people in each family had chosen. Our area was filled with doctors, lawyers, pharmacists, and jewelers. My parents were the only printers, but I saw them as entrepreneurs and business owners. I was proud of the fact that they could raise themselves up with their business skills.

By the age of ten, I was the company's second best typesetter who would spend time in the darkroom of our basement setting display type. My father paid me to set type for new brochures and documents that he was producing. It was my first job. My mother was involved with the sales and accounting side of the printing company as well as running several successful side businesses. Since I grew up in an environment surrounded by entrepreneurs, the path to success was subliminally planted in my mind. There's no doubt in my mind that by the time I was an early teenager I had already made up my mind to be an entrepreneur. The only question was what kind of business was in my future.

In the early 1980s, many people encouraged their children to go to college and get a good job working for a large company that will take care of them most of their lives. I went to a summer camp around the age of fifteen where we took on a project of building a bridge over a creek in the nearby woods. I was put in charge of building a long stairway down a hill that approached one side of the bridge. I spent many days digging out steps from the dirt and placing stones that were perfectly flat to make the best staircase possible. I also built a railing over fifty feet long down both sides of the staircase made of logs, twigs, and sticks from the nearby trees. This project was extremely satisfying for me when it was completed. I found a great sense of satisfaction and accomplishment out of my finished product. Even though most of the kids in the camp worked on other aspects of the bridge, I was proud of my staircase. I learned something about myself that summer. I discovered that I had an interest in engineering and enjoyed using my hands to fix things.

It's difficult to become a full-time real estate investor from the beginning of one's career. Everybody has to have a way to earn a living. It takes a lot of money to be a real estate investor and a lot of time, so although at this point in my life I hadn't decided to be a real estate investor, I had determined that I was interested in engineering and would most likely go to college for it. That's exactly what I did receiving an associate's degree from the American Institute of Design in Philadelphia in 1985. I immediately went into the business of being a draftsman and an engineer for a company in Warminster, Pennsylvania, called the Pennwalt Corporation.

My degree was in mechanical engineering, which was used primarily to work for equipment manufacturers. When I first started college, I had to decide whether to go into mechanical engineering or architectural engineering. At that time, interest rates were very high, so construction was nonexistent. Knowing nothing about cycles, I chose to go into mechanical rather than architectural. In hindsight I wish that I would have chosen architectural engineering, but at that point in my life, I had no idea that real estate would be the business I would choose for life. It would be beneficial to have that architectural background to fit in perfectly with the business I'm in today, but it just didn't work out that way. I am still capable of making my own drawings and doing my own engineering work when the need arises, although that hasn't happened often in my career. There's definitely a few things that I would've spent years learning that I don't know now about how to produce a specific architectural drawing.

I worked as an engineer for over ten years, staying with Pennwalt for three years and then moving on to a company called Empire Abrasive Equipment Corporation. They produced sandblasting equipment that I engineered for four years. During that time I worked at Empire, a certain set of circumstances set me up to buy my first piece of real estate. The company was doing very well, and it had offered an amazing deal to several of its key employees, including me. The offer was unlimited overtime to help knock out the backlog of work that they had. As a single guy in my early twenties living at home with my parents, I gladly took this offer and ran with it to the bank. I worked twelve hours a day seven days a week. My salary at the time was around $24,000 a year, but with the unlimited overtime I had earned over $50,000 in a year, literally doubling my take-home pay. That was a lot of money for a kid with a grand total of $100 a month expenses for student loans. I saved very quickly $15,000 from the unlimited overtime arrangement, which lasted about a year. This first $15,000 I saved was the key to buying my first piece of property, which happened in 1989.

CHAPTER 2

An Early Introduction to Real Estate

But before we get on to my first property, I need to explain how I first decided to become a real estate investor. Sometime around 1984 while I was still in college, I got a job working as a cleaner for a guy named Joe Rice. Joe is a terrific guy who was about ten years older than I was and was starting his own cleaning business. I had worked for another cleaning company primarily stripping and waxing floors, and a friend of mine in college knew that and hooked me up with Joe. I had one ten-minute conversation with Joe on the phone where he informed me that he had a hair salon in the main line section of Philadelphia as a client and that he needed to strip and wax the floors. There was one little problem with Joe's plan. He never stripped and waxed a floor in his life although he had already accepted this job. The main line section of Philadelphia was a high-end area, and the salon that contracted Joe was a very expensive one. I told Joe in our first conversation what equipment he had to purchase so we could accomplish this job. Joe showed up at my house with a pickup truck full of cleaning equipment, and at our first meeting, he asked me if we had everything we needed in the truck to complete his job. It was the only time in my life where the first day on the job I was in charge of the company's business. The project worked out perfectly, and Joe and I began a lifelong friendship.

During my travels with Joe, we would go around to many homes and businesses doing cleaning work, and there was a property that we went to more than once, which was a duplex that Joe owned. At the time, I had no idea what a duplex was or why somebody would want to own one. Because we spent a lot of time together driving from one job to another, we had plenty of time to discuss the duplex and why somebody would want to own one. I vaguely remember discussing many aspects of real estate, including things like depreciation, even though I had never even filed my own tax return. A couple things became apparent to me about this duplex. It was making Joe money, and since I was with him most of the time, I was certain he didn't spend much time there. When he did, he had me or others who worked for him help do the necessary work.

It's funny that I can't remember where this duplex was or what it looked like. All I remember was that it was in Philadelphia and it was key to helping me decide what business I would be in. Somehow the idea of real estate investing resonated with me, and I began to think about it more and more. I started building on the idea of real estate through many different people that I knew at the time.

A friend of mine named Steve was going to college and had just gotten a job offer for a mortgage company. I spent a lot of time with Steve talking about mortgages, down money, and credit lines that were required to purchase real estate. Steve's knowledge of the subject as the years went on helped me to fill in all the blanks about the real estate business that I wasn't aware of. Concepts of using other people's money to purchase real estate and the strategy of leverage helped me to appreciate the investment aspects of a piece of property.

My parents took the bulk of their money and invested in the stock market and did so for most of their lives. In October of 1987, the stock market crash—or as some people called Black Monday—was something I found very interesting. How could so many assets from thousands of successful corporations just evaporate overnight for unrelated reasons? It was scary to watch 30 to 40 percent of one's life savings disappear overnight. I could see the stress and anguish in my parents' faces after that trying day. This helped strengthen my belief in real estate, as I was learning more about cycles and how they affect every investment vehicle. I was beginning to learn that real estate had its ups and downs, but they happen on a much lower speed than the stock market. Around this time, someone had said to me that the first word in real estate investing is *real*. You can touch a piece of real estate and you can live in it. You can rent it out and fix it up. My parents' stock investments seemed to be nothing more than a sentence on a statement that they received in the mail once a month. I knew that the corporations they invested in were real companies, but the actual ownership that my parents had in these businesses was the part that I had trouble grasping.

"Vincent and Arlene Falcone"

My mother, being the entrepreneur that she was, decided to spend a day with me going around with a realtor looking at duplexes to learn more about the business I was beginning to show some interest in. Around 1988, we stopped by a local real estate office and met a Russian woman handling floor time who took us to see a few duplexes local to my parents' home in Northeast Philadelphia. Afterward the realtor took us back to her office where she went over the basic mathematical formulas that make a piece of real estate profitable. My mother told the realtor prior to our visit that her son was the one who intended to invest in real estate. It must've looked kind of funny to this realtor, as I remember being the one asking the most questions and being intrigued by the discussion about profits back at the office. I remember having left that realtor's office completely sure that this was the business I would enter. Unfortunately I never saved this woman's name, phone number, or business card so that I could ultimately do business with her later. It would have been nice to tell her how she had such a positive impact in my life and how that one meeting turned into a guy buying millions and millions of dollars worth of real estate. What further makes this day interesting is that my mother has no recollection of ever doing this with me. I probably never brought it up until twenty years later when I began to think of writing this book. When I finally did mention it to my mother, she doesn't deny that it happened but claims to have no memory whatsoever of this Saturday afternoon that became so pivotal in my career.

Another individual that had a positive impact on me before I bought my first piece of real estate was a neighbor across the street who owned a jewelry store and a number of pieces of real estate. He explained to me the basics of real estate investing in a simple way that I could understand that still holds true today. The neighbor's name was Warren, and he told me that over time real estate will accrue equity that can ultimately be exchanged from one property to another to build a larger real estate portfolio. I didn't know it at the time, but Warren was explaining to me the basic idea behind a 1031 exchange. This conversation turned out to be one of the most valuable tools to a real estate investor and something that I used numerous times in my life. Why is this so important? This book is supposed to be about the transition from residential to commercial real estate. That can never be accomplished easily without the 1031 tax exchange program offered by the government. As I later describe the real estate deals that started the transition, you will begin to see how critical this really is.

The actual conversations I had with Warren about real estate were short and sweet. It wasn't that he taught me anything incredibly brilliant. Sometimes people can say the simplest things to you, but it sticks in your mind like a seed that was planted and grows into something much bigger. That's all that happened with Warren. He communicated to me in a simple way that if you hold on to real estate long enough you can exchange it for larger pieces of property much like the game Monopoly.

I used to play a lot of Monopoly with my family when I was a kid, so I understood that the acquisition of real estate could be traded for something else. Even to this day when I play Monopoly with my twelve-year-old son and my wife, I buy every piece of property that I land on regardless of what it is. Then I take my collection of eight different types of real estate and trade for the pieces that I want to complete a set. Trading four green houses for a red hotel is very similar to trading residential real estate for commercial real estate using a 1031 exchange. Now that I own three pieces that are all on the same block that all have the same color, I can begin to develop a large piece of commercial real estate by building large buildings on the set. Isn't it funny that the games I played as a child ended up becoming the games I play as an adult?

Another person whose name escapes me I met through a mutual friend in the neighborhood while I was at a bar at the age of twenty using my fake identification to pose as a twenty-one-year-old. I began to have a real estate conversation with the guy who owned several pieces of real estate in the neighborhood. After having a few drinks with him, we jumped in his car so he could show me his small portfolio. Luckily we survived an afternoon of drinking and driving as he showed me several of his duplexes and explained his strategy of buy-and-hold investing. Just like in the case of the realtor, I failed to remember this gentleman's name and number or any other information about him. I don't even have a visual image in my mind of what he looked like. I only know that the meeting happened and that I ended up buying a piece of property close to one that he had shown me.

CHAPTER 3
I Made My First Purchase

By the year 1989, I had a basic knowledge of real estate, and because of my unlimited overtime at Empire, I had the money to make my first purchase. My friend Steve, who was in the mortgage business for a year now and out of college, had met a woman named Laurie who was working as an assistant to a realtor. Laurie and the realtor she worked with took me to see several properties, and I purchased my first duplex in the Holmesburg section of Northeast Philadelphia for $79,900. When I talk about this investment in this book, I will refer to it as Arthur Street. It was built as a duplex with one bedroom and one bathroom in each apartment that was currently renting for $350 a month on one floor and the other floor was vacant. While this investment on Arthur Street was the beginning of my real estate career and ultimately turned out to be a building I sold and 1031 exchanged into the best piece of real estate I ever owned, you'll find that this Arthur Street investment was nothing short of a mistake.

Just some of the mistakes I made on Arthur Street were that I overpaid for the building in a market that was at the top of the cycle and ready to crash. I also paid full price for the property without any negotiations. For some reason, I was under the impression that this building would fly off the market if I didn't bite quickly. I happened to think that it's a trait of successful people that when they make a mistake they torture themselves. Ultimately, I overcame the mistakes that I made on Arthur Street, turning this building into a profitable venture on its own, but that didn't ease the pain during the tough years.

My father was not a man who did work around the house. Whenever improvements needed to be made to our primary residence, hired professionals were brought in to do the work. My dad was way too busy with his printing business and his full-time job to work on the house. So I had no idea how to fix a single thing in a piece of real estate. I didn't own a tool and had never painted a wall before in my life, but I was about to tackle my first vacant apartment in Arthur Street. My mom came over to help me do some caulking in the bathroom and some cleaning, and I painted my first wall including the kitchen cabinets, which were made of metal from the 1950s. Again considering the price I paid for this duplex, I made poor decisions as far as the shape and quality the kitchen was in. It was also quite comical when people came around to look at the apartment and they were ten years my senior. I remember the look on one potential client's face when I told her I was the owner of the property.

Showing the apartment in this property was also one of the first times I remember being a salesman and having the responsibility of closing the deal on my shoulders. Real estate investors don't really consider themselves salesmen, but I have always considered that being a successful salesman is one of the greatest skills a real estate investor needs. When I worked as an engineer and the word *engineer* was on my business card for ten years, people always assumed I was some kind of genius. People generally perceive engineers as extremely detail-oriented, intelligent individuals. When I made the transition from an engineer to a salesperson and the word *salesman* replaced *engineer* on my business card, I was shocked to see the perception individuals had of me changed for the negative. All of a sudden I went from this intelligent genius to a useless knucklehead who had no skills except to get the customer to sign on the dotted line. Of course, in reality nothing could be further from the truth. To be a good businessman and to be a good real estate investor, you must develop your sales skills. I do not agree with these negative perceptions as I have the highest regard for sales as an art form. I also find it hard to believe that you would ever be a successful commercial real estate investor without developing sales skills. Negotiating a commercial piece of real estate is, in its purest form, nothing more than sales and a basic knowledge of real estate.

On the first floor of Arthur Street was an older woman who was paying $350 a month for an apartment that probably should have been in the $400 a month range. Since I was already upside down on this building with a negative cash flow because I overpaid for it and because I had a vacancy, this woman had no chance at all of staying in this apartment for $350 a month. Her lease was a month-to-month lease, so one of the first things I did as a professional landlord was evict my one and only tenant from the building in the first month of my real estate career. Unfortunately for me, evictions would become much more commonplace than I ever thought they would. Managing real estate in a primarily Democratic city like Philadelphia with the judicial system with a very liberal attitude would become a challenge I would have to deal with my entire life. It seemed that the tenants were often perceived as the victims and the landlord was usually perceived as a multimillion-dollar rich investor. I wish I could show the judge sometimes how poor I was at this period of my real estate investing career and how many times I had risked my entire life savings to buy the Arthur Street building.

After fixing the second-floor apartment and renting it to an individual as well as renting the first-floor apartment after tossing the existing tenant, I was able to generate a small profit per month from this duplex regardless of the mistakes I made purchasing. My friend Steve knew that I was going to be a professional real estate investor or at least he knew that was my dream. At the time, the financial guidelines in the mortgage business allowed an individual to use a low down payment mortgage offered to investors through the FHA program only once. Steve had advised me to purchase the Arthur Street building by using conventional financing so that I could use this FHA program to purchase my second more expensive larger building. This building will later be described as Ellie Drive.

Ellie Drive was a beautiful modern duplex in the Torresdale section of Northeast Philadelphia. I purchased this duplex for $122,000 in 1990, approximately eleven months after I purchased Arthur Street. My friend Steve's assistance utilizing the FHA program allowed me to put approximately $12,000 down to purchase this building. While I had Ellie Drive under agreement of sale, the offer from Empire of unlimited overtime had come to an end. I was stretching myself so thin to purchase this building that I had to borrow $3000 from my parents to complete the transaction. Steve came up with some creative way to use that money in a form of a gift letter so that we could complete the transaction for my second building.

CHAPTER 4

I Purchase My Second Property

At the age of twenty-four, now my plan was to move into Ellie Drive as it was a condition of my mortgage through the FHA program, although I really wasn't concerned about getting caught on that technicality. In addition to the problem of moving into the building, I was broke and $3000 in the hole. I knew a guy who was in serious financial trouble living in a trailer park to whom I gave $1000 to purchase all of his furniture. I moved into a beautiful two-bedroom apartment on the second floor of Ellie Drive with 1200 sq. ft. of living space combined with a breakfast bar, backyard, and garage. I lived in this property for nine years spending some time on each floor, including the basement that I later on turned into an apartment that I lived in for five years. Ellie Drive became a triplex illegally giving me five units or five rental apartments from my first two pieces of real estate.

The Ellie Drive property had a 1200-square-foot basement completely unfinished except that somebody for whatever reasons had chosen to put a door in the back of the house in the hole of one of the garage doors. All of the properties on this block had two garage doors leading to a two-car garage. The previous owner had taken out one of the garages on my property, replaced it with a man door, and bricked up the hole where the other garage door was. I can only assume that someone had considered turning Ellie Drive into a triplex. I had that same idea and with the financial situation looking bleaker all the time, the move down the basement was a clear decision. When I moved down to Ellie Drive's basement and gave up my beautiful second-floor apartment, it was in the dead of winter. My new apartment had cement floors with cinderblock walls and no bathroom. The first thing I did was build a wall separating the basement from the bottom of the staircase where I had a washer and dryer for the existing tenants. For several months

I had to take showers at the local gym while I built myself a bathroom in the basement. The project of building an apartment in Ellie Drive's basement was the most challenging construction project I had taken on at that point. I knew the apartment in the basement was illegal, so I didn't spend a lot of money on the renovation. I'd build it as cheaply as I could while I lived in the basement. This move seemed crazy at the time but turned out to be one of the most important financial decisions of my life. All of a sudden my real estate portfolio began to turn a handsome profit as my living expenses were practically zero. For five years I lived in the basement saving a great deal of money and using those funds to buy more investment properties as well as my primary residence that I still live in today.

Let's talk about the cycles of real estate and how it affected my early decisions to buy real estate. As I mentioned earlier, 1989 was a hot year for real estate with prices soaring and the market clearly at its top. In 1990 when I purchased Ellie Drive, the market was beginning to slow then, but I wasn't intelligent enough on real estate cycles at this time to understand market conditions. My mind was focused on acquiring more and more buildings as quickly as I could and as creatively as I could figure out how to finance more real estate with almost no money. In the fall of 1991, approximately one year after buying Ellie Drive the local real estate market in Philadelphia began to drop.

From 1991 to 1995, Philadelphia's residential real estate market was in decline. By 1995 my Arthur Street property was appraised at $57,000 putting me significantly upside down on my equity position of Arthur Street. I had done a much better job of purchasing Ellie Drive, but the value of the building was still worth less than I paid for it. By 1995 it may have been worth $110,000 or even $100,000. So I think it's safe to say that my real estate investing career was off to a very rocky start, and I had made numerous mistakes up to this point. The positive thing that happened by 1995 is that after owning five rental units for over five years I had become a landlord. Although I choose the path of learning from my own mistakes, I did, in fact, learn how to be a landlord by the age of twenty-eight.

CHAPTER 5

The Audiotape That Changed My Life

Sometime around 1995, my aunt who lived in Florida named Andrea had sent me an inspirational audiotape for a business she was involved with called prepaid legal. It was an interesting business that I'm still involved with today, but it was the audiotape that came with the package that had an amazing impact on my life. The tape was several hours long in a cassette form that I listened to in my car while driving around working as a salesman. I had made the transition from engineering to sales around the same time and was beginning to spend a lot of time in the car driving all over the country. During this time, I listened to the tape and first heard the theory of association.

You become the average of the five people you spend the most time with is the basis of the theory of association. The idea is really simple. If you spend time with people who read books and are successful business individuals, chances are you will read more books and strive harder to be a successful businessperson. If you hang around with people who spend most of their time bowling and drinking beer, chances are your average will go up as well as your weight from all the beer you'll be consuming. The tape was suggesting that I search out some new friends who were more successful than I was so that I could learn from them and hopefully allow some of their positive characteristics to rub off on me.

The hardest part about the theory of association is the disassociation with individuals who don't have a positive impact on you. You can still associate with these individuals, but the tape suggested that you put a conscious effort into spending less time with people who have a negative impact in your life. Around this time I took a long hard look at the people I was associating with and determined that I would have to disassociate with almost every person I knew. I found myself with a list of only one friend whom I mentioned earlier in this book. It was my friend Steve from the mortgage business. If the theory of association suggested you become the average of the five people you spend the most time with, then I needed to find four other people to associate with. I decided to accomplish this task by looking for some new friends.

My buddy Steve had his own set of friends he should disassociate with. In fact, he probably should have run away from some of them. I told Steve about the theory of association, but it didn't seem to resonate with him the way it did with me. After looking at Steve's friends, I realized he had only one person in his entire collection of friends whom I was interested in associating with. His name was Paul, and he was a realtor. I decided to search out Paul's friendship, and I did it in a way Paul thought was quite comical. I simply came out and told him about the theory of association and the fact that I would like to associate with him. I was also in the market to buy another piece of property, and since Paul was a good realtor, we had a perfect avenue to develop a friendship. I began immediately working with Paul to acquire another property. It was a duplex on Benson Street, which I purchased in the Rhawnhurst section of Northeast Philadelphia. Shortly after the purchase of Benson Street, I had another life-changing moment in my real estate career.

After the purchase of Benson Street, Paul wanted to thank me for doing business with him by taking my wife and I out to dinner. At this dinner, Paul mentioned that he knew of another property that he'd like to show me. I pointed out that he was well aware that I was completely broke so I didn't know how or when I would be able to purchase any more properties. He said, "What makes you think you need money to buy real estate?" And at this dinner, Paul began to explain a technique for purchasing real estate that would accelerate my real estate career dramatically.

It was a little to no money down technique that I later coined the phrase "the all-money-down technique." It was a simple technique that started with getting a home equity line of credit secured against your existing piece of real estate and then using that money to purchase homes for cash. Don't be confused by the phrase "purchase a home for cash." I had no cash and no probability that a lot of it would be coming anytime soon. I was all bricks and mortar, and the only money I had was the equity in my real estate that I owned. I was able to secure a home equity line of credit, what I commonly call a HELOC as available funds to purchase my next piece of real estate.

I had been dating the love of my life, Terry, for several years now. She owned her own home in the Tacony section of Philadelphia and was intrigued by my real estate investment business that was growing. While I was applying for a home-equity line of credit on some of the buildings that I owned, Terry did the same on her home, freeing up an additional $25,000 to be used for real estate investment purposes as well as other things. Terry offered to allow me to use her $25,000 home equity line of credit to purchase more real estate that we would be partners on. I was never surer I had found the woman for me when she told me that. If you want to be a successful entrepreneur in the real estate business, you're going to need a lot of help, and I don't think you'll ever accomplish it if your spouse is not on board with the program. Terry was not only on board with the program, but she was taking aggressive steps to make it possible for us to achieve more in a quicker period of time.

I can today look back on the day I received the audiotape with the theory of association and I count that day as a turning point in my life moving me in a positive direction towards my dream. I hope that readers of this book will apply the ideas here and experience the same epiphany as I did.

CHAPTER 6

The All-Money-Down Technique

So how does the all-money-down technique work by purchasing a home with cash? First of all, let me repeat that I really didn't have any cash, but I had a significant amount of equity from Terry's home and several homes that I owned put together to give me a substantial cash down payment. Banks and mortgage companies alike will accept money from a home-equity line of credit as cash to purchase a home. At least they did in 1997 under the financial guidelines of the day. What you must remember about mortgages and lending is that the guidelines change constantly, so this technique I used in 1997 may or may not be able to be used in the future. Whether it is or isn't able to be used again doesn't really matter to me as I believe that there will always be a way to buy real estate with limited money down sooner or later. There will always be a technique to acquire real estate but exactly how that will be done in the future I'm not completely sure.

I began purchasing homes in the Mayfair section of Philadelphia with the prices in the $30,000 to $40,000 per home price range. I would purchase a home with three bedrooms and one bathroom on the second floor with a kitchen, dining room, and living room on the first floor and a basement. What we call a row home in Philadelphia would consist of a porch out front and a backyard the width of the home. Most row homes in Philadelphia are less than twenty-two feet wide. For those of you who are not from Philadelphia and can't picture what a Philadelphia row home looks like, I suggest you watch the movie *Rocky*. Twenty-two homes on each side of every block will really test your ability to be a neighbor. Things that will usually cause an argument with your Philadelphia neighbors often stem from parking, noise your children make, where you leave your trash cans, parties, and the appearance of your home.

In 1998 my girlfriend and I moved in together and to the suburbs of Philadelphia called Warminster. After living on a street in Tacony, much like Rocky did, I really looked forward to having space between my home and my next-door neighbor. I told Terry not to even think about talking with the people who lived next door to us. I told her if one of them comes over with a fruitcake I am going to take it and punt it like a football right into their backyard. I believe I was suffering from Philadelphia row home syndrome. My new neighbors in Warminster turned out to be wonderful people, but it took me eighteen months before I was willing to learn that.

So you just bought your row home for $35,000 in Mayfair, and after $2000 in closing costs and $5000 in repair costs, you find yourself a good tenant who wants to rent the home. After renting the home with a positive cash flow of $200 a month, you now have an outstanding debt of $42,000 on your home equity line of credit that will have to be paid off. When purchasing the home, I did not get a mortgage as I just purchased a home for cash as it is said in the business. All monies I spent on this house were spent from the home-equity line of credit.

The move now is to pay off your home-equity line of credit so you can go do it again. We now go to a bank with your fixed-up property and tell the mortgage department that you want to do a cash-out refinancing of your real estate investment. It helps to explain that the neighborhood you purchase your property in should have a wider range of pricing as the neighborhood of Mayfair did in the mid-90s. The pricing of homes in Mayfair is quite unusual as you would see a $3000 difference in home values from one block to the next. This was important when doing a cash-out refinancing because it's pretty easy for the bank to see that I just bought my property for $35,000 regardless of the fact that I did many repairs. I could justify the fact that I've spent more money on my home to fix it up, and by putting a tenant in, it was now a profitable piece of real estate from an investment standpoint.

If I was lucky like I was many times over doing this system of purchasing homes in Mayfair, when the appraiser would use homes a block or two away and come back with an appraisal of $45,000. Back then there were programs allowing an investor to purchase a home for 10 percent down or left in as equity doing a 90 percent cash out refinance giving me back roughly $40,500. Utilizing this technique allowed me to get back most of the money I put down on the property. I basically paid just $1,500 down for this new home. Why did the mortgage companies and the appraisers keep giving me the numbers I wanted? I assume because they wanted the business. I would only tell the bank I need this to come in at $45,000 or I am just keeping it financed as is. They always seemed to give me what I wanted within reason.

This whole process took three to four months during which time I may have saved a few thousand dollars. Between the money I saved from my job and my investments and cash out refinancing, I had replenished most or all of my funds from my home-equity line of credit that was now almost back to zero to begin the process again. And that is exactly what I intended to do. I used this system to purchase four to six homes a year utilizing the same money to purchase home after home after home over and over again. In reality, the technique is a no-money down or little money down technique. At the time maybe I had $60,000 in available funds to use to buy homes off of my HELOC, so I would buy a home and then replenish the money. It was a terrific technique that was legal, and I could see my dream of being a real estate investor full-time coming to an eventual reality even though I wasn't there yet.

During the years from 1995 to 2002, the real estate market in Philadelphia made gradual increases of maybe 6 percent as each year went on. I began to track my net worth that was 100 percent equity, meaning I had no other forms of investments to look at when calculating my net worth. Generally speaking, the first five years of my real estate career did not go well because of the bad decisions I made purchasing buildings and the decline in the market. Furthermore, my lack of knowledge and experience in repairs made it rough. The second five years of my real estate career that I just finished explaining didn't make much money either. I supported myself primarily through my career as a salesman, but I could definitely see the writing on the wall that down the road real estate was going to be my full-time gig.

CHAPTER 7

The Crash in the Summer of 2000

The high-tech companies of the NASDAQ in the era of day trading attracted many young people like me in the late 90s. I too fell victim to thinking I could pick stocks and make money trading individual stocks almost on a daily basis. I only did it for about a year, and in the summer of 2000 when the bubble burst on the high-tech stocks in the NASDAQ, I learned yet another valuable lesson. What the hell was I doing investing in stocks anyway? I'd learned from my parents' problems in 1987 that the stock market could do this, but again I didn't pay attention to the cycles and strictly focused on acquiring more, more, and more. The time to torture myself was here again, as successful people don't allow themselves to get away with screwing up. I believe truly successful people have to be honest with themselves and admit their mistakes. Why would a guy who loves the real estate business and wants to do nothing more than be a full-time real estate investor, spend time trying to be a stock market guy? In hindsight, I don't know what I was thinking. I think I lost somewhere around $25,000 in the stock market in the summer of 2000. I was disgusted with myself and the way that I allowed my plans to be diverted. It turned out to be one of the best things that could have ever happened to me. I found myself in a position to be completely focused on nothing but the real estate business. I kept telling myself I was an expert in the real estate business so my best chance of success is by no other way but real estate.

I began the most aggressive buying spree of my life purchasing a home every three months nonstop for about five years. My frustration with the stock market fueled my appetite for buying homes. I didn't know it at the time, but the bulk of the money I made in my thirties was acquired during this time frame of aggressive buying. I could see my net worth going up weekly as I read the Sunday newspaper real estate transactions. It wasn't uncommon for me to see my net worth up $5000 a week as an estimate each Sunday. The timing for acquiring real estate couldn't be any better for me as 2005 approached, but I got ready to stop on a dime and start selling.

Between 2002 and 2005, the real estate market went completely insane in many parts of the country. Philadelphia was no different as we experienced good gains in our real estate values, but as compared to the rest of the country, our gains here were about average. Many of the buildings I purchased during this time were higher-end properties with multiple tenants living in each building. The days of the $30,000 loan in Mayfair were long gone. I was beginning to see that I was addicted to real estate.

CHAPTER 8

Erdrick Street

My first venture into a small apartment building was a property on Erdrick Street. I purchased this quad, or as some people say a four-plex, in 2003 for $130,000. This building made over $1000 a month in profit. The building was a unique single with four tiny apartments, each approximately 400 sq. ft. When I first looked at the units, I thought there was no way anybody would ever rent these apartments. They were so small that the heating and air-conditioning units were just like the type you would see in a hotel room. There was no thermostat in the apartments. One simply went to the wall unit and set the heat or air-conditioning to the temperature desired, and in two minutes the whole house had conditioned air. Each apartment had its own water heater in the clothes closet of the bedroom. The dishwasher was eighteen inches wide, and the stove was twenty-four inches wide. The narrow appliances made the kitchen look a little more normal than the tiny cooking area that it was. In the hall on the first floor was a coin-operated washer and dryer that made some nice money, and upstairs where two more apartments identical to the lower level. This building was a tremendous way for me to become familiar with the management of apartment buildings. The problems experienced in a forty-unit apartment building are not that different from the ones encountered with a four-unit quad. Issues like parking complaints exist in both types of buildings. Mailbox issues, trash, and noise issues are just a few more of the things you will hear in any apartment building regardless of its size.

"Erdrick Street Quad"

I would put an advertisement in the paper for a one-bedroom apartment at $595 per month, and the phone rang off the wall in Philadelphia making this building a large success. I started to spend a lot of time looking to make improvements to the building. First thing I did was turn the entire parking lot 90° allowing me to squeeze in one more parking spot. I improved many of the features of this building such as the mailboxes, trash area, doorbell system, and put in a new fire alarm system, bringing the building up to code.

My purchases were getting much better, and my decisions were getting smarter all the time. A big part of the reason I was doing better was I had joined the local real estate groups DIG and HAPCO. The name DIG, Diversified Investors Group, was a learning organization for real estate investors. HAPCO, Home Owners of Philadelphia County was as well. I was also reading real estate books and constantly absorbing as much information as possible on the business I loved.

CHAPTER 9
Laclede Avenue

I purchased a building in Trenton with seven apartments in an area called the Island in Trenton, New Jersey. I've read in books over the years that if you buy an apartment building with one common heater, a great way to give the place more value is to eliminate the heater and put an electric baseboard heat tied to each apartment's electrical panel, making the tenants pay their own electric. That is exactly what I did with the Laclede Avenue building. The original system was costing me $6000 to $8000 a year to provide heat for all the apartments in this building, and the project to replace all the electrical panels and new electric heaters to every apartment was at a cost of $15,000. Therefore the money I put into this building would be paid for in heating bills within two years. Furthermore, the heater was going to need a replacement anyway, so if I just replaced it, I would have spent $6000.00 anyway. If you think of the cost of a new heater, the project paid for itself in about a year. Another thing I liked about it was that these new electric baseboard heaters with tubes of a gel-like substance that would get heated by the electrodes. The purpose of this design was to avoid a toaster-like smell that old electric radiators would provide and give you a feeling of a much softer heat. Another benefit to the new heaters was that a tenant could keep the heaters in their bedroom off during the day and vice versa during the night in the living room. The tenants' electric bill was more efficient because they were only heating rooms that they would use.

"Laclede Avenue seven-unit apartment building"

The Island in Trenton, New Jersey, is an attractive one mile long by one block wide strip of land on the Delaware River. If you have never been to Trenton, it's not exactly a beautiful place to live. However the Island is a very attractive small neighborhood in Trenton. Many cops live there as they must feel it's one of the better neighborhoods in town. But like all good things, there has to be flip side. The Island floods out during massive rainstorms if the Delaware River exceeds twenty-two feet. When I bought the building, it hadn't flooded for forty-nine years and then it flooded twice in the last three years prior to me buying. I got the building at a deep discount and felt like any businessman that if the building flooded my flood insurance would reimburse me the expenses.

In October of 2006, another flood wiped out the lower level of Laclede doing what would cost me about $25,000 in damage. The insurance company paid me $40,000. So financially I was correct that I was reimbursed for the trouble. The part I didn't understand was the emotional strain I would have when people who lived in my building had no place to live. I found one of my tenants in a Red Cross shelter that was set up in a nearby elementary school. I spent days at the building cleaning up the mess and met the mayor of Trenton.

The experience left me emotionally drained as I decided to take the money and run. I was already working on a new commercial project, and the forty grand would come in handy making that deal happen, so I decided to leave the lower level of Laclede empty. There were three apartments in the lower level that flooded with two apartments on the first floor and two apartments on the second floor. I decided the best bet for me was to take the money for a new deal and rebuild Laclede years later when I had the chance. I just recently reapplied for the license to reconstruct the lower level.

The equity in my real estate portfolio went absolutely haywire during this time frame. Every time I opened a newspaper I could see my net worth going up $5,000 a week. I couldn't buy real estate fast enough as I bought all the way up to the summer of 2005 where I believe the market stopped rising approximately Labor Day of 2005.

As easy as it to see now that the summer of 2005 was the top of the market, it wasn't so easy to see then, but I'd definitely had a good idea that we were at the top of the cliff with nowhere to go but down. I began making serious plans to start selling buildings and doing a massive 1031 exchange into commercial property. I can't stress enough how difficult this decision was to make. Every time someone talked to me back then, the question was how many homes I owned then, and every time they saw me that number kept going north. My real estate portfolio was fueling my net worth, my confidence, and my ego all at the same time. Selling those properties would not be easy, especially since so much hard work went into acquiring them. But that was exactly what I was going to have to do as this time I was finally going to pay attention to the real estate cycles and make the necessary moves needed to become a wealthy man.

After spending ten years as an engineer and ten years as a professional salesman with a large portfolio of real estate, it was becoming impossible to be good at both. I didn't waste a lot of time trying to figure out which direction I wanted to go. I knew I wanted to be a full-time real estate investor, but giving up a salary at that time of $107,000 a year wouldn't be easy. I was a fairly successful salesman in my spare time. After getting a job designing bakery equipment to be used in some of the largest bakeries in the country, I made the transition to being a salesman of that bakery equipment. While earning about $60,000 a year as an engineer, I worked on a project where the salesman's commission was double my yearly salary. I told the owner of the company that I wanted to be a salesman. He tried to deter me saying engineers make lousy salespeople, but I told him I was never that good of an engineer anyway. Engineers tend to be geeks, and I noticed on the first day of college I didn't completely fit in. But for ten years, engineering provided me a good way to earn a living while I chased my real dream of real estate. During the ten years that I was a salesman, I don't know how I would've ever built up a large portfolio like mine if I had to work forty hours a week. I worked hard as a salesman for bakery equipment companies, but I was able to set my own schedule, which allowed me to give real estate its due time when needed.

The company I worked for was aware that I owned real estate as I found myself incapable of lying. I sold 3.5 million dollars worth of equipment in my last year as a bakery equipment salesman at a 55 percent profit margin for the company. They were pleased with these numbers but not happy with my lack of traveling. I had so many buildings to take care of I was traveling less, and they were concerned I was not out in front of the customers as much as needed. They fired me in the summer of 2005. I too had reached a crossroads and couldn't continue as a salesman and a real estate entrepreneur. I made the transition without any grudges and all the enthusiasm to become a full-time real estate investor in the summer of 2005 while the market was just about to drop off a cliff.

CHAPTER 10

Getting My Real Estate License

One of the things that I did in the summer of 2005 after leaving my full-time job was to make plans to get my real estate license. Getting my real estate license was something I always wanted to do but never seemed to have the time to do it. I'm sure you've heard that excuse a thousand times. People always say that they're going to do something soon as they find the time to do it, but they never seem to find the time, do they? I try not to let myself make excuses for anything. So I'd made up my mind before I ever left my full-time job that one of the first things I would do was to get my real estate license. I enrolled in a school called the American Real Estate Institute for a two-week full-time program to obtain my license to sell real estate in the state of Pennsylvania. Two terrific guys with a world of experience taught the class, and I enjoyed the time I spent there. Immediately after completing the course at the American Real Estate Institute, I booked the next available day offered by the state to take the state exam. My teachers' advice to take the exam immediately after the class turned out to be an excellent suggestion. I passed the exam with flying colors and have used my license many times since to buy real estate and reduce the expenses. If you are going to be a full-time real estate investor or a commercial real estate investor, then you almost have to get a license. While I know a few people who don't believe this, I'm convinced it's the only way.

I worked on one deal at $3 million where the commission to the buyer's real estate agent was $75,000. By the time my broker took a share, I walked with $63,000 commission on that deal alone. With the average cost per year of being a realtor running about $1000 per year, this one deal alone would've paid for my real estate license for fifty-three years. Not to mention all the other fringe benefits like having access to the multiple listing service offered to many realtors in this country. While there are other ways to get access to the multiple listing services or another program similar to it, a real estate license is a great way to go.

Some of the negatives I hear over and over again about having your real estate license is the fact that you have to disclose that you are realtor when buying a home if you're representing yourself. Maybe I'm missing something, but I don't see this as a negative at all. If you're skilled in the art of negotiation, it's just another hurdle that you have to deal with. I suppose you could end up in a lawsuit where a court of law could assume because you are realtor you should know all these things. I don't spend my life worrying about the million ways I can be sued any more than I worry about getting hit by a car every time I cross the street.

CHAPTER 11
Realty Professionals of America

I own an office building that has a real estate company as a tenant called Realty Professionals of America. The company has a terrific plan where a new agent receives 75 percent of the commission and the broker gets only 25 percent. If you don't know it, this is a pretty good deal, especially for a new real estate agent. The company also offers a 5 percent sponsorship fee to the agent who sponsors them on every deal they do. If you bring an individual who is a realtor in to the company that you have sponsored, the broker will pay you a 5 percent sponsorship out of the broker's end so that the new realtor you sponsored can still earn 75 percent commissions. In addition to the above, Realty Professionals of America offers to increase the realtor's commission by 5 percent after achieving cumulative commission benchmarks, up to a maximum of 90 percent. Once a commission benchmark is reached, an agent's commission rate is only decreased if commissions in the following year do not reach a lower baseline amount. I currently keep 85 percent of all my deals' commissions; plus I receive sponsorship checks of 5 percent from the commissions that the agents I sponsored earn. If you'd like to learn more about being sponsored into Realty Professionals of America's wonderful plan, please call me directly at 267-988-2000.

PART 2

Making the Transition to Commercial

CHAPTER 12
Alignment of the Mind

I believe that I have the ability to accomplish any task I set my mind to with ease and comfort. I'm not afraid of making a fool of myself or being laughed at if an idea that I have appears funny to some. I have to be confident in my plan to the point that I sound arrogant. I have to be brave enough to throw large deposit checks at a dream that may or may not ever come to fruition. I have to accept that there is a chance that I would lose my down money or end up in a legal battle fighting for it costing me even more cash. I call this type of thinking the alignment of the mind. Much like the way an athlete prepares himself for a big game, you have to prepare yourself to enter the commercial real estate world. As you discuss your plans with your family and friends, my guess is you're going to experience a lot of negativity and pessimism. I can hear myself arguing with people who care about me, talking about my plans; while I may not have been able to convince them that the plans make sense, I was convincing myself with every comment I made.

I think it's important to say your plans out loud to whoever will listen, and if you're in a situation where no one will listen, then say them to yourself. That's correct. I am saying to talk to yourself. You might find your talking to the most intelligent person in the building anyway. Sometimes an idea in your brain may make sense, but when you try to explain it to someone intelligent, it doesn't come out so well. So keep saying it until it does. This process will help you come up with a plan that has a great chance of success. Talk it out. When people ask me about real estate, I tell them to go get a pillow. If you get me started talking about real estate, you'd better make yourself comfortable because I'm going to go on for quite a while. Keep telling yourself you can be the best at real estate. Remember half of all landlords graduated in the bottom half of their class.

When you go to buy a duplex and your family tells you one floor is vacant and the other floor isn't rented for much. Somebody already owned that building, and that person was not able to rent it. What makes you think you can? Just tell them half of all landlords graduated in the bottom half of their class. Show them your arrogant side and tell them because you are a hell of a lot smarter than that person. That's how you are going to do it. Even if you don't completely believe it, you'll be convincing yourself every time you say it.

Thinking big is an idea I first heard of fifteen years ago, and it resonated with me immediately. If you're going to be thinking anyway, you might as well be thinking big. I think in order to be successful at anything you need to be having fun, and dreaming or chasing building deals I have no right to be trying to purchase is fun for me. I say that because I always seem to be undercapitalized on deals I am following. Is it because I have no money, or is it due to the fact that I think big and I am always going after projects over my head? Thinking big is to me like looking to hit the home run. You're going to strike out often trying, but when you crack one, it's worth the wait.

Most of the people close to me have an enormous amount of faith that when I throw an idea out there they know by now I mean it. Like me, they believe in people more than they believe in ideas. When someone pitches an idea to me asking for my opinion, while the idea is important, I am paying more attention to how much that person who's pitching it to me believes in the idea. If the right person believes in a mediocre idea, then I think the success rate is very high. Some people, I think, will succeed at almost anything they do if they have the right attitude toward business. If they have the proper alignment of the mind, they can tackle the task at hand.

Other people have the uncanny ability to find the negative angle to every possible scenario in a split second. Excuses are like a virus of the mind to poison a good plan before it's ever had a chance to get off the ground. Much like the theory of association, you need to distance yourself from people who are always pulling out the negative angle and those who always have an excuse for something.

Trouble always comes in waves in this business. I cringe every time I hear of a large storm coming. Roofs usually leak after massive storms, and heaters always break in winter. The only people who can control utility bills are the provider and the end user. Handling tenants complaining is a big part of this business. Every business has its problems, and all clients complain at one time or another to the businesses they use. You sometimes go though a dark patch. Here are just a few of mine.

I have had an apartment building flood with eight feet of water where the fire department evacuated and shut down all the power, and I had tenants living in a shelter while everything they owned was destroyed. Then the town required me to rebuild the place to ADA compliance. That building is still not rebuilt.

I had another guy die in my unit from a drug overdose and was in there for four days until someone found him. The police broke into my unit destroying the door, and the smell took two months to leave. His crazy girlfriend threatened to kill me if I did not give her the security. I gave her nothing, so she had her new boyfriend call me every day with threats.

Prepare yourself for the inevitable dark patches that will come your way in this business. Align your mind to know and expect that they will come preparing yourself to handle them properly. I have seen businesses panic and make bad decisions in a dark patch that cost them dearly. Dark patches can make you semi-depressed if you let it and take out the fun of real estate. I always expect that every year or so some dark patches are coming and just push my way through it with the proper mindset.

I once worked with the realtor early in my career who found some decent investment properties that I purchased. He asked me a lot of questions about how I was doing it and eventually understood the all-money-down technique and how it worked. As I got to know him better, I began to question why he wasn't doing these things for himself as he was watching me get rich slowly, right before his eyes. In my opinion, he had everything he needed to make it happen except the proper alignment of the mind. Instead of planning to make these aggressive real estate investments himself, he chose to use excuses, such as "I am too old," "I don't have enough money," "I'm too busy," or "I have to take care of my children." I would've told him about my theories of brain power at that time, had I thought of that myself. Just because I was doing it didn't mean I understood what I was doing. I didn't believe in the power of positive thinking even though that's exactly what I was doing. Anyway the point to all of this is you need to prepare yourself mentally for entering the world of commercial real estate. If you do this, you will increase your chances of success, and all I'm trying to do here is increase your ability to make money.

I have some other guidelines I try to follow and I would like to share them with you below.

Health:
Drink plenty of water.
Eat breakfast like a king, lunch like a prince, and dinner like a pauper.
Eat more foods that grow on trees and plants and eat less food that is manufactured in plants.
Live with the three E's—Energy, Enthusiasm, and Empathy
Play more games. I play poker often.
Go to the gym every day; don't stay longer than an hour.
Read more books.
Sit in silence for at least ten minutes each day.
Take a twenty-minute walk daily.

Personality:
Don't compare your life to others. You have no idea what their journey is all about.
Don't have negative thoughts about things you cannot control. Instead invest your energy in the positive present moment.
Don't take yourself so seriously. No one else does.
Don't waste your precious energy on gossip.
Dream more while you are awake

Envy is a waste of time. You already have all you need.
Life is too short to waste time hating anyone.
Make peace with your past so it won't spoil the present.
No one is in charge of your happiness except you.
Realize that life is a school and you are here to learn. Problems are simply part of the curriculum.
Smile and laugh more.
You don't have to win every argument. Agree to disagree.

Society:
Call your family often.
Each day give something good to others.
Spend time with people over the age of seventy and under the age of ten.
Try to make at least three people smile each day.
What other people think of you is none of your business.
Your job won't take care of you when you are sick. Your friends and family will.

Country:
Respect and support the founding fathers of the United States of America.
Support the troops of the United States military.
Support democracies all over the world.
Beware of socialist and communists who want to change the USA.
Own a gun and be prepared to defend your country with your life if necessary.
Defend your freedoms at all cost.

Life:
Do the right thing!
Get rid of anything that isn't useful, beautiful, or joyful.
However bad a situation is, your brain has the way out if you just use it.
No matter how you feel, get up, dress up, and show up.
The best is yet to come.

Our company philosophy is "sales and service." That's not exactly a slogan you can put on the back of a business card and call it your mission statement. But what it means to me is to always be thinking like a prospective tenant. Would I want to rent an apartment with dirty carpets? No is the answer. You never want to blow a sales call because you were too cheap to clean the apartment. When I say sales and service, I am wondering as I walk down the hallways of my building if a prospective tenant would notice that mark on the wall. If the answer is yes, then go find a paintbrush.

The service end keeps me and my people thinking about how much easier it is to keep a current tenant happy than it is to go find a new one after renovating the apartment or office. I do cartwheels if that is what it takes to keep my current tenants serviced the way they need to be taken care of. I don't care if they are wrong or have high expectations. I don't care if they always complain or even if they have a few mental deficiencies. All I care about is sales and service.

Sales and service gets me on the roof a day after a big snowstorm to shovel snow away from drains. Sales and service gets me to an apartment twelve times to show it until it's rented. It all comes down to your alignment of the mind. What are you prepared to do to succeed? The world is full of snake oil salesmen who will tell you how to get rich overnight in the real estate business. I am here to tell you that's bull. This is a tough business, and only the strong will survive in it.

That's why I preach the get rich slow strategy is the way to go. My marketing guy will tell you that won't sell books. I would be better off preaching a get rich quick plan to millions overnight. Unfortunately for me, I cannot write a book about something I don't believe. I am not wired that way. I am incapable of lying to people except when I am playing poker. When it comes to this book, I wrote it with the proper mindset that if I broke even on it that was fine because it was fun to write. It was more of something I wanted to accomplish than a business that had to make money. If it sells or not won't take away from the goal that I may be helping a few people and doing something I always wanted to accomplish while having fun.

CHAPTER 13

Fifty-Thousand-Square-Foot Building in Reading

By this time, my real estate portfolio on paper was at a pretty substantial profit level that was good enough for most people to live off of, but things would have been tight with too many repairs or vacancies. I decided the only move was to sell a series of buildings and transition that money through the 1031 tax exchange program into a commercial piece of real estate. I started looking for that piece and immediately buying, or should I say getting under agreement of sale, many multimillion-dollar properties that I later chose not to settle on. The first was a 50,000 sq. ft. building in downtown Reading, Pennsylvania, that I got under agreement of sale and then backed out of due to a dispute over a poorly maintained elevator. Elevators cost a fortune to maintain, so if you're going to buy a building that has one, do your homework. The cost of maintaining an elevator can only be truly understood by people who own buildings with elevators in them. I advocate when I say doing your homework that you seek these individuals out and ask them to explain what you're going to be looking at when it comes to the cost of an elevator.

The Reading building was actually four stories of 10,000 sq. ft. per story with a ten-thousand-square-foot basement and two elevators. One of the elevators was a passenger elevator, and the other one was a freight elevator. It was an old building of seventy to eighty years old that was in good shape. The contract price for this building was only $300,000, which to me was a reason I became interested in Reading in the first place. The building would've broken even at purchase with about 20,000 sq. ft. of empty space, so if I could even rent a small portion of it, I would've easily been positive. I had plans to turn the top floor into ten individual one-thousand-square-foot apartments if I could get the zoning for it. It was one of the reasons I wanted to speak to the mayor of Reading. I made plans to visit the mayor's office.

Just in front of the mayor's office is metered street parking, and the road is a one-way road with three lanes of cars going in the same direction. In order to get into one of these metered street parking spots, you have to pull in front of it and back into the spot, parallel parking. I pulled in front of a spot and put my car in reverse to back up when I noticed another vehicle had pulled close to the back of mine. He realized I was parking and started to back up, and just as he did this another car smashed into him. Nobody hit my car, so I moved forward and took another spot. As I entered the front of the building of the mayor's office, I walked by this accident, and the woman who smashed into the car behind me was screaming bloody murder at me and accusing me of causing the accident. I told the crazy nut there wasn't a scratch on my car as I didn't have an accident. I went upstairs to the mayor's office, and I just thought it was classic as I was waiting to talk to the mayor's assistant and maybe even the mayor, the police were outside trying to identify me from my vehicle. Later I received a citation and had to go to court to fight it. Since there was no proof I had ever had an accident, I easily won. I always thought it was comical, as I probably was showing a little sweat on my brow as I entered the mayor's office. Maybe it was an omen that I shouldn't be investing in Reading.

After my meeting with the mayor's assistant, I did not have a good feeling that the zoning for that building turning into residential was ever going to happen, and other things occurred in this meeting that gave me great concern. One of the questions the assistant asked was what has brought me to Reading. I told him mostly price, as I was investing primarily in Philadelphia at the time, and I also told him I was getting frustrated with the way Philadelphia was treating landlords. All of my experiences with the court system in Philadelphia always seemed to be leaning in favor of the tenants. After having this happen over and over again in the course of many years, I began to get disillusioned with the city of Philadelphia.

In addition, we as landlords were getting taxed to death and bombarded with additional fees. To be a landlord in the city of Philadelphia, you first are required to have a business privilege license that will cost you several hundred dollars followed by a landlord license at a rate of $50 a unit. As I told some of these reasons to the Reading mayor's assistant, I noticed he was jotting down notes and acted like it was the first time he ever heard of a landlord license. I got the feeling he was going to run into his boss to suggest that he just found a new way to generate funds in Reading. One of these days, I should ask my Reading investor friends if in fact they have a license today and when it was initiated. I may be partially responsible for that fee.

The elevator was the technical reason I backed out of the deal in Reading but far from the only reason. During my due diligence of the Reading building, I made appointments to meet with a member of the mayor's office as well as separate meetings with the historical society. My 50,000 sq. ft. building was in the historical district, and the city would scrutinize any revisions I would make to the building's exterior. I didn't like that, but I did like the fact that some local government programs were offering tax breaks to certain types of companies that operated their businesses in the historical district. Some kind of urban development program I assume.

**"Fifty-Thousand-Square-Foot
Building in Reading"**

Another thing that came up in this meeting was I kept hearing of an individual who was a major player, or as we will call him, Mr. Big, in commercial real estate in Reading. I started taking drives around the city calling many of the signs that I saw on vacant buildings, and I began to learn that the same company owned and operated most of them. All these commercial buildings were controlled by a small company run by one man. While this major player made himself accessible to me and I could even go as far to say I found him helpful, he scared me terribly. My ability to acquire tenants in this building would require me to compete with a man whose portfolio was twenty times my size. I felt like a pipsqueak locked in a room with a nine hundred pound gorilla. As much as I liked him, as nice as he was, business is business, and he would've easily crushed me in any competitive scenario. In fact, I couldn't think of a scenario where I would get tenants to sign on the dotted line without them at least talking to him and if they were going to talk to him, the odds of me getting the deal were slim to none. Being a capitalist, I've never had a problem with competition in a free market society, but this situation was unique. He lived in Reading and had connections directly to the mayor's office, so if someone was going to consider moving to that city, chances were between Mr. Big and the mayor's office I didn't have that much of a chance.

Shortly after I spoke to Mr. Big, I was back in the building and took some time to have conversations with the tenants about the possibility of them staying in this building. I heard what I wanted to hear from all of them but one. It was a computer company on the first floor who had already made arrangements to move into one of Mr. Big's buildings, and that was the last straw.

All of these things in combination made me feel that it was a mistake to look in the city of Reading at all. It happens to be about an hour from my home in Warminster, Pennsylvania, and the wasted time driving back and forth to this building was going to be a real issue. Just in case I needed another reason not to buy this property, it had been for sale for many years in Reading with no takers in a hot market, so my chances of selling anytime soon were not good.

Know your market is something I constantly tell people now. I had learned this lesson at the time of the Reading building—maybe that's what I got out of the deal. Over the years, I've learned that every time I deviate from my area I usually make a mistake. So pick an area and force yourself to become an expert in that area.

I had this building under agreement of sale with a down payment of approximately $30,000. When I went to officially request my money back, the owners accused me of talking too much to the tenants and causing the computer company to vacate. I told them this was completely ridiculous as I was simply doing my due diligence. I had every right to talk to the tenants about their future intentions of staying in the building. The owners were attorneys, so I had some concerns that getting my down money back would be a problem. After a few weeks of silence, I received a check in the mail. I have not returned to Reading since that time.

Sometimes you win and sometimes you learn is what I always say. I was concerned about receiving back my down money and many other issues with this deal. I spent a lot of time and money working on the building in Reading. One way to look at this would be to say that it was a complete waste of time and money. After all, I went through a great deal of work and stress to come out with no building and no profit. But as you can probably guess by now, that's not how I think of the Reading building at all. I learned some valuable lessons on this deal that I would carry with me to every real estate purchase I worked on since. Let's take a minute to discuss them.

Always go to the top was one thing I learned from the Reading deal. When I drove around town and called all the competitors' signs and spoke to the largest commercial real estate owner in that city, that was a key moment in understanding what I was about to do. When I spoke to the mayor's assistant and began to see where his head was and how getting the zoning changed for that building was never going to happen, there was another key moment. When I spoke to all the tenants about their future prospects for staying in the building that was an exercise I would repeat many times in my real estate career. Finally, the due diligence that I did on the elevators provided some great lessons about the issues elevators can create. I've since looked at many buildings that had elevators in them but have always treaded cautiously when dealing with the vertical people movers.

You don't always need to settle on a building to gain experience in the commercial real estate world. But you can't learn about this business without being out in the trenches scratching, crawling, and fighting your way to the finish line, which ultimately is a settlement. If I work on a deal that doesn't get to settlement, I don't consider it a failure as long as I've learned valuable lessons that can be used on future deals. As you read further about the commercial deals I've worked on, I could confidently sit in meetings as if I was a man with $15 million to purchase dozens of commercial buildings when the truth was far from those numbers. Working on deals like the Reading building gave me the confidence and the skills to evaluate and negotiate real estate properly as if I had done it for decades.

CHAPTER 14

Forty-Unit Apartment Building in Trenton, NJ

I then tried to buy a forty-unit apartment building in Trenton, New Jersey. I was much more familiar with this area of Trenton since I already owned a successful apartment building just a few blocks away from this one. I was introduced to this building by a commercial realtor I had a relationship with who specialized in apartment buildings in Trenton. I lived only about a half an hour away from Trenton, and the properties there were quite cheap, making it possible for me to buy a large apartment building I normally couldn't afford. As usual, I didn't have enough money to buy this building, but I did have the seller who was creative and willing to carry paper to make this deal happen. The realtor who brought me to this building was also its listing agent and gave me a good feeling about his ability to broker a deal.

"Forty-Unit Apartment Building in Trenton, NJ"

I found quite a few things about this building appealing. The forty units were spread out with approximately seven apartments on each floor and six stories high. A six-story building looked like a massive monument to help fuel my ego as I found it mesmerizing. Structurally speaking, it was in excellent condition with an age of about thirty years old. It was described as a class "C" piece of commercial real estate. It was positioned across the street from a beautiful park and approximately two blocks away from the Delaware River. It also had a nice lobby with a waiting area and mailboxes for all the clients. I was also impressed with the maintenance room with all the tools and supplies the person who would take care of this building needed right there on site. I planned on spending a lot of time in the room if I were to buy this building.

The elevator was recently rebuilt and appeared to be in excellent condition, so I planned on not having to deal with it for several years. The roof was also in excellent shape, and I felt like king of the world walking around on the top of this building. Sometimes you have to be careful of what emotional feelings you get or what visions you may have of your future. Do not let a dream cloud your judgment of what's really going on. I felt terrific walking around on this roof, but a small part of me was cautious of such feelings.

A friend of mine bought himself a million-dollar home in 2006 because he had always had a dream of living in a mansion with a large backyard. He actually described to me that he had a vision in his mind for decades about his children and his dogs running around in his huge backyard. In 2009 when his home was now worth six hundred grand, he told me he felt quite stupid for allowing this dream or vision to cloud his view of reality. I think it's somewhat more complicated than that.

While I admire his honesty in explaining to me how this vision clouded his judgment and I agree with his assessment, what he really did wrong was ignore the timing of the real estate market. He paid no attention whatsoever to the fact that in 2006 we had just gone over the peak of real estate prices. Now he is not a real estate expert or even a real estate investor, but you still have to know these things if you are going to spend $1 million on a home. I tried to comfort him by explaining that I had made this mistake more than once myself. The mistake I refer to is ignoring the cycles of the real estate market. Although I can't ever blame a mistake in real estate on a vision that I've had, I definitely think that I too could be open to such a problem. I definitely had dreams of me standing on top of that building six stories high the day of settlement, on the roof pounding my chest like Tarzan. I found myself staring at the photos of this building as if it was somehow a monument to my massive ego. When I think about it now, it's actually kind of funny that my friend envisioned his dogs running in his backyard or me acting like Tarzan. I guess the lesson learned is that sometimes you have to protect yourself from yourself.

This building had a wide variety of things that concerned me, including a poor quality of residents. One thing I love about office buildings is that everyone goes home at five o'clock. One of the things I've hated about apartment buildings is that everyone goes home at five o'clock. I am a family man, and I prefer to be at home with my family in the late afternoon and evening concerning myself with my wife and son. When you own an office building, you can have many problems during the day, but things usually cool down by five o'clock and go completely silent as everyone has left the building or at least almost everyone. In an apartment building, the exact opposite thing happens as all the tenants come home after five o'clock and all the problems begin to surface. It only takes one bad tenant to screw up an apartment building and cause a world of trouble for the owner. As I went through many of the apartments in this forty-unit building, I began to have my concerns about the clientele renting this building. It didn't take a genius to see that we were dealing with poor individuals, and I wasn't quite sure what I was getting myself into.

Obtaining financing for this building was also difficult due to the fact that it was in a flood zone and it had experienced a fire recently. In addition, my lack of down money made it almost a requirement finding a partner, and while I was willing to invest in an apartment building in Trenton, I knew of almost no one else who was interested. Most of my real estate investor friends had no intention or interest in ever investing in Trenton even though they hadn't been there in twenty years. Anyway people's perceptions are important, and if I couldn't get them to look at the building, I did not have a chance of getting them to be my partner.. I had this deal under an agreement of sale, and they had my hundred thousand dollar usual down payment, but I was pretty sure it wasn't going to last.

Of all the commercial buildings that I tried to purchase, I went into this deal as unsure myself as ever and fell out of favor with it quicker than any deal before. In the end all I can do is say sometimes you win and sometimes you learn. This was definitely a sometimes you learn kind of deal.

CHAPTER 15

The Hatboro Project

By this time I was beginning to drive my wife and family crazy with the huge real estate ventures I was moving into and out of what seemed like every three or four months. Regardless I continued to move on to the next property. I spent six months working on the next property which was a $3 million retail shopping center with a seven-unit apartment building directly behind it and three industrial warehouses behind the apartment building in Hatboro, Pennsylvania. I called it the Hatboro project. One of the most appealing things about the Hatboro project was it was only three miles from my home. In the shopping center portion of the project, we had the lamp shade company that had been there forever and a state owned and operated liquor store. You couldn't get much more security than a state liquor store with a history of twenty-seven years in the same location. There was one vacancy in the shopping center, but I wasn't really concerned about it. In general the shopping center was in excellent shape with great road exposure. I always thought if I owned a shopping center, I would have constant ideas on businesses to start and test in vacant stores. This owner had a coin-operated laundromat that was a very successful business. At least I thought it was successful. When a business collects all cash, sometimes it's not so easy to verify what it makes but it seemed busy as I inspected it regularly. The laundromat business came with the real estate, making the overall Hatboro project fairly successful.

The three warehouses in the back of the development were rented for storage in two locations, and another was rented to a kitchen cabinet manufacturer. The apartment building was filled except for one unit and needed a lot of work. The work didn't concern me too much, as I would be able to renovate the apartments as they became vacant a few per year until the building was taken care of.

The main reasons I found the Hatboro project so appealing was its location to my home and the fact that it came with a laundromat business. I also loved the way that it's mixed use layout was broken up amongst retail, residential apartments, and warehouse space. I also felt strongly that the long-term tenants of the liquor store, laundromat, and a shady lamp company would be the base tenants to support this business for many years. The apartment building was appealing to low-income tenants in the town of Hatboro. There were several apartment buildings nearby with larger more expensive units. I felt a clientele for the apartment building would be young people looking for a small inexpensive one-bedroom apartment. This was an area I already considered myself to be an expert in, so managing and renting out a seven-unit apartment building gave me no concerns at all. After all, the Laclede Avenue building is a seven-unit apartment building of similar size and shape.

The warehouse space was even something I liked because it was positioned behind the retail stores so neighbors would not complain about trucks and noise. It also had all three spaces rented to long-term tenants who I didn't think were going anywhere.

It also fueled my ego very well to be able to say that I owned an entire block of downtown Hatboro. I was very excited about becoming the owner of the Hatboro project. By now, I had spent a lot of time spinning wheels on commercial deals that hadn't gone through, and I was really getting tired of it. I was determined as ever to make the Hatboro project become mine.

"The Hatboro Project"

As the summer of 2006 began to approach, I had what I like to call a dark patch that comes around every once in a while in the real estate business. On July 4 weekend in 2006, a torrential downpour of rain caused the Delaware River to flood and destroyed the entire lower level of the Laclede Avenue apartments. I had just finished renovating one of the apartments on the lower level and was in the process of renovating a second one when the flood happened. It was a very trying time for me as I completely underestimated the emotional strain the flood would have on me.

While trying to purchase the Hatboro project and dealing with the Laclede flood, I also had planned a two-week vacation for my family to go to Florida for one week and Puerto Vallarta, Mexico, for another week. I love the business so much that going on a one-week vacation is enough to drive me crazy, let alone two weeks in another country. I went to my vacation and tried to have the best time I could regardless of everything that was going on.

When I got back, I had a very difficult time negotiating the final portions of the Hatboro project. The largest problem was that the owner was just close-minded. Every time I asked for a meeting with him, he acted like he was doing me a favor. He wanted $3 million for his building, and I was willing to pay him that, but I needed him to help me out a little. Possibly carrying some paper for me would have been enough to get the deal done, but he kept playing hardball. I eventually decided I wasn't going to win on this deal either. I didn't think of what I was doing as walking away from the deal. My mindset at that time was let him sweat it out for a while and we'll come back later. I never got this building under an agreement of sale, but I worked hard to do so. The main stumbling block on this deal was the seller of this building was unrealistic about the value of his property.

Every time I drive by this building now, I think it would have been a struggle for me to make real money from this property. Today in early 2010, this building has some serious vacancies including one of its largest tenants, a lamp company that took three retail stores as its home for many years. I'm sure if I bought this building for $3 million, I would be upside down on it today in equity. The building would be still generating cash flow, but it would not be worth $3 million dollars. So in hindsight it was a good move not to buy this building.

CHAPTER 16
Your Odds of Success Dramatically Improve with Each Attempt

One thing you will learn about me as you read this book is I am a guy who is out there really doing deals. Not just someone talking about it. As I look back on the Hatboro project, the apartment building in Trenton, and the 50,000 sq. ft. building in Reading, I think I made a good move walking away from all three of these deals. While I don't think any one of them would have been a loser, I think all three would have been a real struggle to make money. I also think that the values of these buildings today are not worth anywhere near the values I was willing to pay for them in 2005 and 2006. Sometimes in real estate, dodging a bullet or avoiding a mistake is the best move you will ever make. You could make an argument that I spent over a year working on these three projects with nothing to show for it. I would say the lessons learned during this year were priceless, as they set me up to understand commercial real estate negotiating and how to identify a really successful property to purchase.

> **"Elegant persuasion is when the other person thought it was their idea."**
>
> ~ MARSHALL SYLVER

People ask me often how to get started in commercial real estate. My standard answer is on your way to work tomorrow morning call the number on the commercial real estate sign that you driven past fifteen times a week. Get the realtor to give you a showing, and if you're interested in the property, tell the realtor you want to meet the owner. You have questions only the owner can answer. Usually most realtors will do everything possible to stop that meeting from occurring, but I implore you that you don't dare buy a commercial piece of real estate until you've done exactly that. That is to sit down with the owner of that building and discuss with him every possible question and answer scenario you can think of. You never know the particulars of the building until you dive in and learn about them. How do you know what the financial situation of the seller is unless you've met him and had a chance to understand where his head is? When the realtor tells you "I don't think that's a good idea to put you together with the owner of this building," you simply say "do you really think I would spend $3 million on a building without meeting the man who's run it for years?"

I met a guy named Vladamir who seriously considered being my partner on several ventures. Vladamir was a guy with a lot of money that he had wrapped up in a trust fund, and he was looking for a place to put some of that money, which could only be invested in so-called prudent investments. He didn't know a great deal about real estate, so the marriage between us worked very well. We have not to date bought a building together, but we sure as hell tried to make some big deals work for the both of us. Commercial real estate is like that. Working a very long time on a building with nothing to show for it at the end happens more than I like it to. If your heart is really in it and your mind is focused on the eventual dream of owning a large commercial piece, you'll go through all these battles until you ultimately achieve your objective.

Vladamir brought something to the table though that I learned while hanging around with him that has proven to be a tremendous skill for me now. Vladamir would sit at that table with the owner of a building and ask question after question to the point of aggravating the hell out of the seller. He would even aggravate me as he would go on and on about every little detail in every situation. The more information that the seller gave Vladamir, the more questions came out of his mouth, but there was a method to his madness.

We would get back in the car together and begin to discuss the answers to the questions that the seller gave, and if we believed them or not. You're about to spend millions of dollars on a piece of real estate, so you'd better be damn sure that you believe this guy. If you can't believe him, you really need to reconsider if this is a deal for you. The due diligence portions of a commercial real estate project can last a very long time. You can ask for his tax returns, QuickBooks files, leases, talk to tenants, review escrow accounts, bank statements showing monthly deposits to prove the income from a specific property is all part of the due diligence. Vladamir and I would talk for hours after the meeting about the answers the owner gave to every question until we were completely certain what his motives were and where we could go with our bidding on the property. Just like the art of sales, the art of negotiation became something that now was part of my skill set. If the owner of the building was an open individual who would sit there and talk to me, there would be times when he would say things that I could later use against him. However, if he didn't sit there and talk to me, there was little to no chance that I would ever buy his building, so his only option with me as the buyer is to tell me everything I want to know as many times as I want to hear it.

CHAPTER 17

Finding Executec Suites

In the summer of 2006 during my so-called dark patch, I found the commercial deal I'd been looking for. The building and business is called Executec Suites with forty-seven offices located in Huntington Valley, Pennsylvania. One of the ways to value a piece of real estate is what we call a *cap rate*. Basically speaking, a cap rate is figured on the net operating income divided by the sales price equals the cap rate. The higher the cap rate is the better the deal or the better the rate of return on the deal. In 2006 when looking at cap rates of commercial real estate, most were somewhere from 5 to 8. The deal for Executec Suites was a 12.5 cap, an astronomically high number for a piece of real estate at this time. I almost jumped out of my seat when I saw it on a commercial real estate Web site.

When I first saw the building come up for sale, I recognized it immediately because it was the same building I took my real estate license in at the American Real Estate Institute a year before. Working with a commercial real estate broker from the largest firm in Philadelphia called Marcus and Millichap, I received a tour and immediately bid on the building. The asking price was 2.3 million, but through negotiation I was able to get that number down to $2,150,000. Figuring out the value of a building like this wasn't so easy to do. I was buying a lot more than just a building. As in any other piece of real estate, I was buying the leases along with a lot of things that I wouldn't normally buy in a piece of real estate, such as the furniture, the artwork, the copier, printer, scanner, the mail stamping equipment, the telephones and telephone system, 250 telephone and fax numbers, vending machines, coffee makers, and dozens of fake plants and flowers.

The phone and Internet system was a major concern. I had become, by this time, a real estate expert, but one look in the phone could give someone nightmares as it was more equipment and wires that I've ever seen jammed in one room before.

You're providing for these companies everything that they need from the furniture to the Internet to the telephones to the air-conditioning in the office to the cleaning service to the receptionist and the list goes on and on. That means that everything that could possibly go wrong in their office is something they're going to come to talk to you about. As a landlord, I've been used to leaks in the roof as an issue to call the landlord about, but in an executive suite center everything that could possibly go wrong was my problem with plenty of things that could become serious.

Rather quickly, an agreement of sale was put together to allow me to purchase this building with a long period of due diligence and time before we actually settled. One thing you'll learn about commercial real estate is if you seriously dig into it, every deal has its own set of circumstances that are important to the seller and the buyer. In this case, the seller was not hurting for money in any way but was merely looking to take the equity in this building and roll it into a much bigger development project in another country. They furthermore were concerned about the tax money owed on the profits, so delaying the deal until January of the following year was actually what they wanted. You can't do a 1031 tax exchange from the United States to another country.

"The more you affirm what you want, the more you believe it. The more you believe it, the more you think and act as one who is getting what you want. And hence, the more it will happen for you."

~ MARSHALL SYLVER

This was perfect for me considering that I needed $475,000 cash to buy this building and I had approximately $10,000 in the bank. Some people laugh when I tell them something like the last sentence. You didn't think you needed to actually have the money to buy a piece commercial real estate, did you? If you seriously want to be a commercial real estate investor you must come to terms with what I just said. A rational person wants to go out and raise their money and sell their real estate and have $475,000 sitting in a bank account ready to go before they are even ready to begin the process of looking at a building worth $2,150,000, but I can assure you that the system doesn't work that way. If that's the way you conduct yourself, every commercial deal you do will cost you 15 percent capital gains tax on all the money you use to buy this building. You'll never successfully conduct a 1031 tax exchange program if you're selling the buildings prior to finding the ones you want. If you do accomplish this, you then end up purchasing a building you really didn't want to buy but you had to avoid paying the capital gains tax, which is just as bad as the first scenario or even worse.

There's no room for mistakes in commercial real estate. I talk in this book about all the dumb mistakes I made when I bought my first piece of real estate. I take a little risk as a writer of this book because I could easily see the reader thinking, "Why should I follow the advice of a guy who made a stupid move that I didn't even make?" It questions my credibility when I tell you about some of the dumb mistakes I've made in the past, but they were critical to developing to the level that I am at today. The mistakes I made on Arthur Street tortured me for years and helped me to avoid making similar mistakes in the future. Avoiding mistakes became a serious part of my thinking process.

I think the only way to do it successfully is to find the deal that works perfectly for you and figure out a way to finance it later. If the sellers of the building are not comfortable with that, then you need to go find another seller in another building. I certainly don't tell them I don't have all the money, and for some reason most of them don't ask. If I represented the seller as a realtor, you could bet your butt that would be the first question out of my mouth.

These kinds of challenges come up constantly when looking at commercial real estate, and your negotiation skills and your salesmanship will make the difference between this deal working or not. As I've mentioned in several deals in the past, the sellers weren't even astute enough to ask me where the down money was. If I were selling a building, it would be the first question I ask. Before I sat there and had a buyer asking me one thousand questions, I would need to know that he was qualified before going any further. If he wasn't qualified, he would have to do a lot of explaining. Details of his existing piece of real estate would be needed or how he was going to prove he had home equity lines of credit or some other source of financing that would make this deal possible. Otherwise the conversation was over. The flipside of that is that if somebody had hit me with that kind of attitude he may have never gotten the buildings sold, so unless I'm sitting at the table listening and looking into the eyes of the buyer, I can't possibly advise what to do except to say keep an open mind.

As I have written, if the sellers of this building or the realtors representing the seller had asked me just one simple question—can you show me the money before putting this building under agreement of sale?—then the deal would've never happened. Luckily for me, no one ever asked me for proof of funds so I wrote $100,000 down money check off a home equity line of credit, and I immediately put eight pieces of residential real estate up for sale to pay for this building. Because I had a real estate license, it took me all but three hours to list as much of my portfolio as necessary to raise the deposit money to purchase this building.

Much to my surprise, I sold four buildings rather quickly including handling both sides—buyers I found plus the listing for the seller, me, of two buildings' transactions, saving me even more money on the real estate commission side. One of the buildings I sold during this time was the very first duplex I ever bought, Arthur Street. Remember all the mistakes I discussed about that building and the regret I had from all the mistakes I made with it. During the early 90s, almost everyone I knew told me to sell the building and cut my losses, but I never listened to them. Now I was able to reap the rewards from not selling that building in the 90s. I was able to get Arthur Street under contract for $155,000 giving me a profit of $100,000. That money was critical in making Executec Suites a possible purchase for me.

I started thinking about the $10,000 down I put on that building some seventeen years earlier and how when you use a 1031 exchange, the down money you put into a property like Arthur Street simply gets moved to a property like Executec Suites. In a way it's like the $10,000 is still with me today, similar to ten thousand little soldiers working their tails off to make me rich. When I walked around my new office building, I would sometimes think about the fact that $10,000 dollars is still right there with me helping me advance financially. It somehow made all the trouble I went through with that first purchase suddenly worthwhile. I guess the moral to this story is sometimes it pays to hang in there when you've made a questionable investment.

Generally speaking, I raised approximately $100,000 cash from each of the four buildings within a matter of about ten weeks leaving me only short $75,000 to purchase the building. I had more than enough available funds on my credit line that I could proceed with buying the building now and putting up the rest of my buildings for sale necessary to pay off my home equity line of credit later.

The deal got better because when you buy a commercial piece of real estate that has a rent roll of over $40,000 a month, you also receive the security deposit and the last month's rent. Those security deposits and last month's rent totaled to approximately $60,000 leaving me only $15,000 of my own money to come up with to buy this building. Four separate pieces of real estate that I sold for approximately $100,000 a piece and did a 1031 exchange program from each of those four buildings into the new building, accepting all of that equity without paying a dime of tax money. That's $400,000 in monies sitting in my attorney's 1031 exchange account and $60,000 in last months or security deposits.

Now that I managed to raise the money for the building, I went back to the seller to try to move up the settlement date so I could settle on this building as quickly as possible. Since I already had it under agreement of sale, the profit that would be coming from this building would be something like $15–$20,000 a month. I didn't want to waste any more time waiting to get that money. Regardless of the fact that I had already agreed to wait until the end of the year to purchase the building, I needed to accelerate the sale so I invented some time constraints on my 1031 program.

Making an exchange through the 1031 program is not as easy as it sounds. You have only forty-five days to identify the property you intend to buy. You have a grand total of six months from the day you sell the original property to the day you actually settle on that property to make the deal happen. If there is any reason the deals that you've identified cannot be settled, which happens more than it can be settled, you will have to accept the money and pay the taxes. There's a lot of pressure doing at 1031 exchange because if you've got, like I had, $400,000 sitting in a 1031 exchange program from the four buildings I sold, the tax implication to me at 15 percent is $60,000. That's a lot of balls to have up in the air juggling at the same time.

The owner of the building understood the basics of the 1031 program and knew that as time ran out on my tax exchange program I would have to pay taxes on that money and have less money to buy the building. He did not ever ask me about down money, so he didn't know when I sold the buildings. Always ask as many questions as you can think of. Therefore he did not have much of a choice but to agree to settle more quickly, so in October of 2006 I settled on Executec Suites for $2,150,000. WOW!

"Well done is much better than well said."

~ **BENJAMIN FRANKLIN**

I spent the next three months trying to learn about the new building and business I just purchased. I felt absolutely fantastic about the decision I had made to buy this building. After spending so many years trying to buy buildings that I backed out of, not only was I successful in purchasing this building, but it was the best one by far of anything I have looked at to date. It may not have been a class "A" building, and it certainly wasn't the newest, but the rent roll and location was tremendous. The business also suited my skill set and was close to my home, only eight miles away. I was thrilled about what I had just accomplished.

I would often ask myself why would a building at 12.5 percent cap rate sit on the market and not be gobbled up by somebody who had a lot of money. I came to the conclusion that there's too much maintenance involved in a building with forty-seven smaller offices versus some larger retail operation with half a dozen big stores. Somebody who has millions of dollars to spend on a commercial piece of real estate wants to buy a piece of real estate and show up once a quarter to see how it's doing. This is not that kind of investment. Executec Suites is the kind of investment that requires a staff of individuals to operate it. Maybe a person who has that kind of money necessary to purchase this type of building doesn't want to deal with the work necessary to operate it properly. Therefore I concluded that I was the perfect individual to buy this building. A guy who barely had enough money to scrape together to make the purchase but was still hungry enough to work it into a success.

"Either make your money work for you or you will always have to work for your money."

~ MARSHALL SYLVER

For days I walked around the building on cloud nine thinking what an amazing move I just made. Then an interesting thing happened. Executec Suites is what we call an executive suite center that rents offices to individuals who have small companies and provides an answering service for those businesses by having two full-time receptionists answer the phones at the front desk. My new office was just an earshot away from the front desk, and I kept hearing the name of an individual named Joe Rice from the cleaning business in my building. Sure enough, my buddy Joe, who first told me about real estate and that duplex that he owned in Philadelphia, turned out to be a tenant in my new office building. The guy who first turned me on to the idea of real estate is a tenant. It's great to be reunited with my old friend who I see all the time now whenever I'm at my building. It doesn't get any better than that.

The location of Executec Suites is perfect for a number of different reasons. It's positioned approximately one mile outside of Philadelphia, and the city hammers its small business entrepreneurs with taxes and fees. Many young entrepreneurs want an office in our building because we're close to their home but out of the city saving the money. We are close to the Northeast Philadelphia area, where there's a large concentration of Russian and Jewish people. I have a great deal of respect for some of these young entrepreneurs who are second-generation immigrants to this country but who act more like Americans than the actual Americans.

What I mean by that is young Russians come here and start their own businesses where they struggle to try to make something of their lives. Some of them fail and some of them succeed, but they continue to try until it works. Most of their employees are Americans showing that the entrepreneurial spirit of the young people in this country is dying by the thousands. I have developed a great deal of respect for these young people who come here with this attitude. I think that the American spirit is most present in the heart of the entrepreneur. Wake up young Americans before you find yourselves working for first- or second-generation immigrants. Capitalism is alive and well in the hearts of hungry young entrepreneurs who want something more than a handout from the government.

Even with a real estate license when it comes to commercial real estate, you sometimes need to deal with the professionals. At least you need to deal with the professionals when you're the buyer because all the good commercial properties usually go through big commercial real estate brokerages. The way a lot of these large commercial brokerage houses work in Philadelphia is something like this. They have approximately fifty agents in the Philadelphia office, but each are assigned geographic territories as well as commercial real estate categories that they specialize in. Their job is to go out there and meet every commercial real estate owner in their category in their territory. Because of their aggressive telemarketing and sales strategies, they get a very large percentage of the commercial listings. While it's true that some commercial real estate owners may want to list the building with a realtor they know is residential, most who know the business well would not go that route. Putting a commercial piece of real estate on the residential multiple listing service can't hurt to get some marketing out there, but in most cases my experience has shown that this will not get the building sold.

What gets the building sold is a large commercial real estate brokerage that has a massive database of all the major commercial players in the area. If you were to give the listing to one of these brokerages, the first thing they would do is take your listing and make it firsthand knowledge to the individual agent's personal list of customers. The next thing he'll do is take your building to the personal list of customers that each of the other fifty agents in his office has. Some of these firms have fifty offices all over the country, so the third step would be to go to all the agents and all their list of clients throughout the country. While it's a long shot to expect that an investor from Chicago would buy a piece of property in Philadelphia, it does happen in the commercial world more than you think. Especially when the individual in Chicago has a 1031 exchange and he's pressed for time to identify a building to purchase, a guy in Chicago might just make such a move to avoid paying the 15 percent capital gains tax that will come with the sale of that building.

These large brokerage firms also work with real estate investment trusts purchasing class "A" properties all over the country for thousands of investors. If you're unfamiliar with this investment vehicle, it's similar to a stock fund owned by many individuals who put their money in and professional individuals manage the investment, or at least you hope. There is even a real estate investment trust (REIT) that can be used as a 1031 tax exchange. For example, let's say you just sold a building and you have many dollars of profit, and your time constraints are running out quickly as far as where you can invest the money. There are funds you can put the money into that will invest into real estate and qualify so that you don't have to pay the taxes on the money. As all good things, there is always a catch. Usually these funds require a minimum investment of $400,000 and a minimum time frame of five years. But it still beats paying 15 percent on $400,000 or $60,000 in taxes.

Anyway, in summary when it comes to selling a large piece of commercial real estate, what you're getting from the big brokerage house is their list of contacts as well as their experience. Mostly their valuable contacts is what I view you're paying for when you do business with them. I have my own real estate license and I can list my own buildings for sale. I can advertise my buildings on Web sites like Loopnet and Costar to inform investors my buildings are for sale, but these sites cost money to have access to them that many real estate investors are not willing to pay. I had a membership to both in the past, but my dues ran over $1000 a year for both. I eventually canceled my membership with these organizations, as there are other ways to find properties. If I was selling a large piece of real estate today, I'd be tempted to list it and market it myself, but in the end I feel I'd be calling the large firms to get the word out to their clients and they won't do that for you without an exclusive listing agreement.

For an executive suite center, the strategy is to own the building in one name and the business of running the building in another. This is for the purpose of separating them should you ever wish to sell the building or the business and keep the other. For example, one thing that some of my competitors have done over the years is the owner would keep the building and sell the business to somebody for several hundred thousand dollars. The person who buys the business would also agree to a long-term lease to pay rent back to the owner of the building. This is a terrific exit strategy where I would end up still owning the building, which is the place I believe all the real money is made in this business anyway.

I decided to name the business of running the building Falcone Real Estate Holding Corporation. I had given considerable thought to using this name prior to buying this building and have to say I love it. I don't think I am a narcissist, but much like Donald Trump, I have a strong desire to have the Falcone name associated with my real estate investments. Putting the word holding in the name explains what my company is really all about. I consider myself a buy and hold investor. I couldn't wait to get my business cards printed up and changed the sign out front so that I could see Falcone Real Estate Holding Corporation in bright lights as I've always dreamed. I was always impressed with my parents' name on the business of Falcone Printing Service, and I finally was able to have my name on my business cards and signs. I've had some interesting business cards in the past that I would like to share with you below.

My latest card for Executec Suites may not look like much to you, but I have put a tremendous amount of thought into every word on it. Your image is everything, and your business card is a big part of your image so don't cheap out when you make one and don't make quick decisions on what you will put on it. Every word you put on it along with the colors right down to the phone numbers and e-mail addresses say something about you. Don't take the production of your business card, your Web site, or any signs in front of your building lightly. These items are saying a lot about you, and they need to be thought out properly. I recommend hiring a marketing consultant to help you understand all the hidden secrets of that business. I recommend The Barlen Group in the last chapter of this book. You would be amazed at how different people react to different typefaces. You could spend an hour discussing with a marketing expert how certain typefaces appeal to women and how others appeal to men. How your color scheme and logo not only have to be planned properly but have to be duplicated on everything you do, helping your clients remember you when they see a truck roll down the road or clients see your business card while paging through their index. When they pass by your building and your sign out front, you create a subliminal image in your client's mind. Hey, I know that guy. I have been to that building before. They do a nice job there.

I look for things to inspire me to keep moving forward in life. The movie *Rudy* has always been an inspiration to me. I love the story of the guy who's five foot nothing and weighs one hundred and nothing but sacks the quarterback at the end because his heart will not allow him to fail. I feel a lot like Rudy and have felt a lot like him after I've done something like purchasing Executec Suites. To constantly remind me that I too can sack the quarterback, I made the music that callers hear when they're on hold at Executec Suites the theme from *Rudy*. I might call the office, and I'm temporarily put on hold so I can be reminded of the spirit of Rudy.

In most executive suite businesses, the building owners will charge a price for the office with additional cost for everything else that has ever been used. There's a price for the furniture and a price for the receptionist and a charge for use in the conference room until the client is nickel and dimed to death. The theory is to get the client in the building for a cheap price and bang him over the head of a thousand times with little small-ticket items to make a profit. My wife and I decided to change that immediately. We decided to go with the one price fits all for every office starting at $495 a month you get everything you need for our smallest office. Every office had a price that usually was a $595, $695, or a $795 type of number all the way up to several thousand dollars. This was the opposite approach to what people who own these kind of buildings did, but as a professional salesman, I believed I had an inside angle to a better idea than this. For starters, I didn't feel comfortable deceiving people I was going to be developing a relationship with. Lying to someone is a terrible way to start a business arrangement with him. While I agree if I did business that way I would make more money, I think in the long run I would be less successful. People want to do business with people who are successful and with people they like and trust. I like to think that I leave money on the table with my one-figure approach, but I keep my clients longer because they're happier and I keep the building more occupied. Another big reason for using this kind of approach is when you're in the sales presentation and the client has taken fifteen minutes of the day to come see your building, the window of opportunity you have to close the deal is small. If you have to explain to the client all of these items and everything that they cost, it gets very confusing. I could see it in the clients' faces as I did my first few sales presentations. Going to one price delivers a strategy for removing the questionable look on the client's face. A guy would sit in my office and say, "so tell me again what is included?" I would tell him, "It's easier to tell you what isn't included than what is included. Everything is included for $495 a month except your outgoing phones calls." Easy as can be.

"See how happy we look!"

My wife and I decided to upgrade the kitchen along with the landscaping until we got the building to a level we were proud of. Since we had an office building with a captive audience, we tried to come up with ways to provide services that we could also charge more money for. One of those things we came up with was the digital billboard in the lobby. I first got the idea while waiting to be seated at a restaurant; there was a flat screen television set along the wall, and every thirty seconds an advertisement would flip from one vendor to another. I thought it was a brilliant idea that would work in our building. Working together with a Web site designer in my building named Dennis, I began to create a plan. We first made half a dozen slides for our business of renting offices, mailboxes, and conference rooms as well as providing an answering service to the tenants. I will talk more about these features later that are additional profit centers within the building's walls. Every tenant was given the opportunity to advertise his or her business for free on the digital billboard. All they had to do was pay Dennis $100 to create a slide. This fee was a one-time fee, and advertising in the digital billboard was never charged again as long as they were tenants in the building. With fifty visitors a day coming to the building, we estimated thirteen thousand people a year would see each slide. Not bad advertising for $100 investment. Most of our tenants jumped at the chance to put their ad on the digital billboard. This program also helped Dennis; as he began to create slides for people, he also designed some Web sites and performed other marketing functions for the clients in the building. As Dennis was my client, I was helping him to build more business from his new landlord. I began to claim a phrase that is one of only a few original Phil Falcone quotes.

"Do business with the businesses that do business with your business."

~ PHIL FALCONE

Do you know what a virtual tenant is? A virtual tenant is somebody who uses your building in one way or another who doesn't actually reside in an office in your building. One way you can have a virtual tenant is by renting him a mailbox very similar to a P.O. Box but much better. A post office box is obvious to everyone that you work at home and have your mail delivered to a box. How does that help your image? My mailboxes provide addresses that create the appearance of having an office at our building. Instead of writing mailbox numbers on your business card, you can put Suite #B36. A mailbox in my building at Executec Suites cost $69 a month. Our clients can have their mail delivered to our building, giving them the appearance of a professional organization as opposed to a small company being run out of a residential home. It also keeps their clients from knowing where they live, which is as a landlord a pretty critical thing. Most of our people would stop by daily to get their mail, but some would have their mail delivered to their home. Others would call and ask for their mail to be opened and scanned or faxed to them. Large packages could also be accepted by our receptionists, who would put them in a closet. We even have people who don't even reside in the state of Pennsylvania utilizing our mailboxes as virtual tenants to present the image that they do in fact conduct a business in Pennsylvania.

When I bought this building, contracts were in place for signing people up for mailboxes as well as other virtual services. My experience in sales led me to constantly think, "What was the easiest way to close the deal and make the client feel comfortable?" We decided to offer no contracts on mailboxes. You would be shocked to learn how easy it is to convince people to pay you $69 a month when they don't have to sign a contract and they can back out at any time. It was a brilliant idea if I do say so myself. Another sales-related idea that helped close deals.

The perception of a salesman has always been negative in this country, but I think the exact opposite. I think the best businessmen you will encounter in your life are also terrific salespeople who have respect for other salespeople. Sales is an art form, and the more energy and effort you put into it, the more success you will have in business.

Another virtual tenant service we provide at Executec Suites is an answering service. If you remember that in the $495 deal as well as any other office deal, you get to a full-time receptionist to answer the phone in the name of your company and patch the calls to you regardless of whether you're in the office, your car, or at home sleeping on the couch. We were able to do this because we have a special program that identifies the telephone number as it comes into our building, and a screen pops up telling us how to answer this phone and who are the individuals in that company that we may patch the calls to. For $99 a month, our receptionists can answer the phone for businesses that are not even in our building. Did you ever call a painter for example during business hours and a cheesy voicemail box takes your message? When you look on his business card and see 123 Oak Lane, don't you know right away he is a one-man operation conducting business from his house? Now for only $99 a month, this one-man operation can utilize our receptionist to answer his calls, "ABC Painting Company, how can I help you? Would you like to speak to John Smith? Let me see if he's finished with his meeting." The girls would then page John Smith, who could be on the top of the ladder painting a wall, and ask him if he'd like to take the call from his potential client. If he says yes, the call is forwarded to him, and if he says no, the call is put into a computerized voice mail box that he can check remotely which is all part of his $99 fee.

Image is everything in business. People want to do business with successful people, and they feel more comfortable doing business with the corporation that is based somewhere as opposed to an individual working out of his home. The answering service we provide creates a valuable image for our clients and a stepping stone for them to move from a virtual client to an actual client. My wife and I also decided that the answering service would be provided with no contracts, making it very easy for the client to say yes, I will try your service.

Conference rooms are the last piece to the virtual tenant. If a client uses our mailbox, he presents the image of being located in our building, and the receptionists answer the phones for him, which also does the same. But now he needs to meet an important client, and he still works from his home, so he rents our conference rooms by the hour and sets up his appointment with the client at our building. He arrives early for his meeting and is waiting in the conference room for that important client. When the client arrives, he notices he has driven to the address on the business card. As he waits in the lobby, he hears the receptionists' voices and recognizes them, since he has called so many times before. The receptionist then brings the client to the conference room where our painter friend John Smith is waiting. This completes the illusion that John Smith and the ABC Painting Company are located at Executec Suites.

Virtual tenants make up about $3000 a month in income coming from thirty-five different companies. Some use just the answering service while others use just the conference room. Some ask for a package deal to use all three that we may provide for $200 a month as an example. Imagine that over time being a virtual tenant improves his image to a point where he's ready for an actual office. At that point a $495 office is less than $300 more and comes with a mailbox, answering service, and conference room included. This is how the virtual tenants slowly progress into actual tenants.

I've seen this happen many times before; a company begins to use the virtual services and immediately progresses. It's a great feeling when you're making money while helping other people. Too many individuals in this world are making money while screwing people.

At the time I bought Executec Suites, there was a push-button mechanism on all three doors, and every tenant who used our building had a code. If one of the tenants gave the exact code to friends or left the building, it was hard to keep track of all the codes. We decided to switch to an automatic key fob system that would not only provide security for the building but also be a source of revenue. The investment in the key fob system was $7000. We needed about one hundred key fobs to be given out to the existing tenants. At $35 a piece we were able to get back half the money we invested on the system from day one. As each new tenant moved into the building we would get to charge them for new key fobs. It took about two years to get back all of the money we put into it, and the safety of the building is now much better. If the tenant leaves the building, we can deactivate his key fob immediately. If a company in the building has a disgruntled employee, we can deactivate his key fob immediately. If a company wants to know what time their employee came to work, we can provide that information. The key fob system is a decision I am proud of implementing in my office building.

We also put together a deal with direct TV to wire many offices in our building. I wanted to provide a television set for my receptionist to lighten the load of answering eight thousand calls per month. I also wanted to put one in my personal office. Each additional receiver cost us five dollars a month that we are able to charge tenants $49 a month for. Some clients, like stockbrokers and limo dispatchers, who have to be in the building seven days a week, could easily justify the expense. This was just another idea that became an additional source of revenue.

The efficiency of an executive suite center is something I never counted on having. Because I do business with the businesses that do business with my business, I began to do a lot of business with the people in this building. Before I knew it, my real estate broker, my title company, attorney, Web site designer, the accountant, and staffing agency were all people in my building. You would be amazed at how efficient you can be when everyone you work with is located in the same building. It becomes like a networking group as all the people in the building are small companies and entrepreneurs who all have the same kinds of problems. I also constantly try to promote introducing people to one another so that they would do business with each other and strengthen the bonds they have in the building, hopefully getting them to stay longer.

If you like to learn more about Executec Suites, you can visit these Web sites listed below.

www.executecsuites.com
www.facebook.com/executecsuites
www.youtube.com/executecsuites
www.twitter.com/executecsuites
www.addicted2realestate.com

On my Web site I have many photos of the building and information about the services we provide, such as mailbox rentals, answering service, conference rooms, and office rentals. I also have a virtual tour that I made showing our building as I walk through it in an interesting five-minute video. If you're on Facebook, you can look me up and become a fan of executive suites as well as become a friend to me personally. I often post real estate related photographs of the properties that I'm dealing with as well as dates when I'll be traveling to do seminars on real estate. The same thing goes for YouTube and Twitter; information about my real estate holdings can be found there as well as a personal page I have on Twitter under the name Philly Phil.

"Victory belongs to the most persevering."

~ NAPOLEON BONAPARTE

You can also achieve great things in the commercial real estate world, but you have to believe that you can do it and keep reminding yourself that you can continue to do it. Life is not a journey to the grave with the intention of arriving safely in a pretty and well preserved body, but rather to skid in broad side, thoroughly used up, totally worn out, a vodka in one hand, a cigar in the other while loudly proclaiming—WOW! What a ride!

Thanks for reading this far to and for purchasing Addicted to Real Estate. Would you like a free copy of my office lease? If so just go to www.addicted2realestate.com/officelease and follow the instructions. Thanks again and good luck with your investments.

CHAPTER 18
The 1600 Building

Before I even settled on my new office building Executec Suites, I had already made up my mind that this building had the concept I wanted to duplicate somewhere else. If you look at the price per square foot an individual can earn in his business, it's much better than any other version of real estate with the exception of self storage. Also with so many offices to rent, it takes a real salesperson to keep the building filled by being out on the street working it. The executive suite center concept simply fits my skill set well.

Just a few months into running Executec Suites, I decided to start looking for a new building that could be used for the location of a new executive suite center. It didn't take me long to find a building that I called the 1600 Building. The 1600 Building is a 35,000 sq. ft. two-story facility located on a major road with great visibility and also just a few blocks from another very large road. This major intersection would be well known to anybody from the Bucks County, Pennsylvania, area making it easy to tell people the approximate location of my building.

You've probably heard it said a thousand times that location, location, location, is the most important thing in real estate. I'm not one of those guys who say that very often because I believe that an investor has the power to change the location. An investor has the power to purchase multiple homes on the block and improve the appearance of the exterior of those homes while at the same time upgrading the quality of the tenants who would live in such homes. Investors can have a positive impact on the neighborhood and on the lives of the people living there. I'd like to think that any building I ever bought was improved in more ways than one after I purchased it. I know I made the buildings more aesthetically pleasing. I also made the building more financially attractive on paper, and I tried to make the tenants an upgrade from the neighborhood's current residence.

That last part is not the easiest to accomplish. If I failed in any category of residential real estate in Philadelphia, I most likely failed in upgrading the tenants. My philosophy on finding tenants was very outside the box. I would advertise on the Internet or Craigslist like most landlords would, but I didn't spend a lot of time investigating their back rent paying histories, credit reports, or anything else for that matter. My motto was you needed three things to rent an apartment from me: a driver's license to prove you are who you say you are; a paystub to document the income that you claim to earn on this simple application I give out; and enough cash to pay three times the rent for the unit available. First month's, last month's, and one month security along with a beating heart pretty much got the deal done for me. I was always more interested in closing the deal and moving on to the next project than I was spending time investigating the qualifications of the people standing in front of me. I would have to tell you that most landlords don't conduct themselves like this when it comes to renting a residential apartment. They would spend more time than I would to investigate the qualifications of the individuals moving into the place. Most landlords would not have to deal with all the evictions that I had to deal with because of my loose renting style, but I can guarantee you that my apartments weren't vacant for very long and my cash requirement always made it easy to sign the lease, get the cash, and give him the keys.

I found the 1600 Building through a commercial real estate realtor I called from a sign on another building. He told me he had a building I might be interested in seeing. We immediately drove to the building to inspect it from the outside. He got me in to see it and I loved it. I thought it was perfect for me. They were asking $3,500,000 for the building, so I told him to throw a number at it of $2,500,000 and see what happens. They rejected the offer, and the realtor I was working with did not really think I was serious, so he sort of exited the picture.

I went back to the property and called the sign out front to find the young realtor who had the listing was the son of the owner of the building, and I immediately requested a meeting with the owner. As I've mentioned, realtors never want to put the buyers and sellers together in a room, as they fear it is the quickest way to destroy a deal. Don't ever let anybody feed you this line of garbage, as the only way you're ever going to learn anything about the real estate you'd like to buy is by sitting across the table from the man who owned it and looking in his eyes as you figure out exactly what is going on with this investment. The owner of the building was a nice man named Gerard. Gerard was a real gentleman who enjoyed very much talking about his real estate and was quite open to discuss anything I wanted to know about it. I liked him and thought we could really work together to make this deal happen.

In our first meeting, which took about two hours, Gerard made it clear that the number of $2,500,000 was not going to get it done. Since they were offering it at $3,500,000, I said let's split the difference and settle on $3 million. They were shocked, and we agreed verbally on that number. Based on my feelings at this meeting I quickly decided to just go for it and gave them a strong number quickly. As usual, I didn't have sufficient down money to buy this building, but at the same time I wanted to create the perception that I could easily purchase it if I wanted to. All I had to do was write an agreement of sale and get him to sign it so I could take the building off the market and evaluate it later using inspections to determine if it was suitable for my needs. My thought process at the time was the building was perfect for me and I could always bring up issues to lower the price later should I find any surprises. My mind was focused on locking up the building and gaining equitable title to the 1600 Building.

Normally I would've said something like, "If this building is worth $3 million, you will have plenty of opportunity to prove to me that that's correct." I don't waste time arguing over the price of a building I know nothing about. It's a complete waste of time. I prefer to pretend that a $3 million number could or could not be logical depending on a number of other circumstances, such as the appraisal, the rent roll, the age of the building, etc. In my opinion, the best way to get started in the negotiations is to begin to acquire as much information as possible about the building you are considering buying. Ask for everything you can possibly get, such as blueprints, QuickBooks profit and loss statements, tax returns, bank statements, and a list of the tenants' rents owed each month. Ask as many questions as humanly possible, and when the seller wants to talk about his building, sit back in your chair, put up your feet, and let him talk away. Then later analyze what he said and why he said it and determine how you can use that information to figure out what this building can be purchased for. Most of the information regarding the tenants didn't really apply to this building since it was empty.

This first meeting between Gerard and myself happened sometime early in 2007 with a series of several other casual meetings where we had agreed verbally that I would purchase the building for $3 million. How I came to this conclusion so quickly takes some explanation. For starters in order to buy a building worth $3 million, I would have to have something like $750,000 cash down to purchase a building, which incidentally I didn't have. Four months earlier I had purchased Executec Suites for $2,150,000, and I was completely broke when I looked at the 1600 Building. Regardless of my lack of funds, I was quite confident that I would figure out a way to purchase this building sooner rather than later. I still had enough home equity lines of credit secured against other existing pieces of real estate to put down a serious down payment of $100,000, and I also had enough buildings left that I could still raise about $300,000. I guess my mindset at that time was for $300,000 I could buy a 50 percent position in this $3 million building, but I really hadn't thought it through that well. The next step was to draft a contract that would normally be done through an attorney where a large down payment would be made upon signing of the contract. I decided not to draft a contract at all because I already had one from five months ago on my computer for Executec Suites that only needed to be changed in some small categories to make it a usable contract to purchase this new facility. I made the changes myself and consulted an attorney and issued it to Gerard so that he could send it to his attorney. No down money was provided in this agreement until the seller accepted it, and I made sure there were plenty of things in my favor that he wasn't going to accept anyway.

Gerard made it clear that $3 million was as low as he was willing to go, and since I was there to look in his eyes when he said it, as a experienced poker player I knew he meant it. Neither Gerard, his son the realtor, nor his son's broker, who was in some of the initial meetings, had thought to ask the magic question: "Do you have the money?" That's correct that once again no one asked me that question as I was about to take this building off the market and secure equitable title of a $3 million building without proving to them I had $.10 in the bank.

Some of the other interesting things in my contract included one of my favorite paragraphs of all time that says I can get out of this deal for any reason or no reason. I also put in to the contract four months of due diligence, giving me all the time I needed to go out and find the partner who was going to invest in this new and exciting venture. Because I felt so secure in my contract's legal powers to get my hundred thousand dollar deposit back for any reason or no reason over the course of a four-month period, I was quite comfortable moving forward with writing that check and signing the contract for the 1600 Building should he sign the agreement.

Now my biggest challenge was to go out and find a partner to buy this building with as well as the construction money required to make numerous changes and improvements to it as well as the carry cost money required for an executive suite center. Let's take a look at that for a second and analyze all the money required for a big move like this.

If the building is a $3 million property and I am going to have to come up with the 25 percent down payment than 25 percent of $3 million would be $750,000 plus closing costs, let's just call it $800,000. Construction was estimated by me as a complete and total shot in the dark of $500,000 required to do enough to the building to allow me to operate an executive suite center. This building already had been broken up in a manner similar to the needs I would have in order to run an executive suite center. Let's assume at this point that I could borrow 75 percent of the $3 million and I could borrow 100% of the $500,000 to do the construction. That left me with the carry cost money which would be the amount of money it would cost me to pay the mortgage, taxes, insurance, salaries etc. while I tried to rent out this building. I know of no scenario that any bank would allow me to borrow the carry cost money. Therefore I needed the $800,000 down money plus the $500,000 in carry cost money leaving me with a grand total of $1.3 million in cash required to do this deal. I had at best $300,000 but no one except me knew that.

The 1600 Building is in my opinion a class "B" piece of real estate, meaning that it is not a new modern building but is still in decent shape. The definitions of a class "B" piece of commercial real estate will be described later. The agreement was accepted as is and Gerard's son showed up at my office building, Executec Suites, to pick up the hundred thousand dollar deposit check. A few days later Gerard stopped by to talk and surprised me a little. He sat in my office and simply said, "Is this concept of breaking up offices as you have done here what you intend to do with my building?" I of course said, "Yes, I intend to duplicate the concept you see here in your building." I would never have told him that unless I had to until he signed the agreement of sale, which he had done by the time of this conversation.

It was about this time that he started asking me some questions instead of just answering mine and began learning information instead of just giving it away. He shocked me next by asking if I would consider allowing him and some of his partners who currently own The 1600 Building to become my partners in turning his building into an executive suite center. Without even trying to find a partner and still struggling with how in the hell I would ever put this deal together, I found myself maybe a month out from my initial meetings with Gerard not only having the building under contract but also having a wealthy set of partners in position who clearly had a knowledge of the building, second to none. They also had financing available to them that was probably out of my reach. I began to learn that of the three partners who own the 1600 Building, they had a combined net worth of somewhere around $70 million.

As a former engineer from what seemed like a lifetime ago, I began making engineering drawings for the changes I would make to The 1600 Building as well as numerous other Excel charts and calculations about my new venture. I had already done quite a bit of this prior to giving them an agreement of sale, but now I was doing it for different purposes. I was going to have to make a presentation to Gerard and his partners to get them to come along with this deal. We scheduled a meeting for a month out, and I began to get to work on what could be one of the most important sales presentations of my life. I put together a very solid package in the form of a binder about one inch thick with a confidentiality agreement on the first page to be signed by all individuals at my presentation and also to keep the binders in my possession until they would officially agree to become my partners. When the time came for the actual presentation, I was well prepared, and I believe I hit it out of the park. Shortly after that meeting, I had a full agreement with Gerard and his partners to proceed.

The agreement put together between me and my new partners consisted of an arrangement where we would form a new corporation to purchase the building in the name of the new corporation from the existing owners. The purchase price of the building would be $3 million, and I would be 50 percent owner of the building and 50 percent owner of the business that I would run in the building. The down money requirement for me that was a huge problem now seemed to be resolved. I would have to raise $325,000 to purchase half of the building. The money represented a 10 percent down payment of $300,000 on a $3 million building and roughly $25,000 for estimated closing costs giving me a grand total requirement of $325,000 down. All the remaining expenses for construction costs would be borrowed from a bank along with the mortgage to purchase the building by the new corporation. My new wealthy partners would pay the down money required on a construction loan, and 50 percent of that money would be considered a loan to me, and the business would pay it back out of my end of the profits. My new partners would completely pay for the carrying cost money, which couldn't be borrowed under any circumstances, and I would pay 50 percent of it from my end of the profits from the new business that I was planning to run.

This was a very exciting time for me as I began to drop just about everything I was doing in life and focus solely on making this a successful project. Of my new three partners, the only one I really worked with was Gerard, who was the managing partner of the three. The other two individuals did not live locally, and I had only met them on the one occasion where I did my dog and pony show hoping to convince them to join this venture. Gerard was a very intelligent and classy gentleman who was a pleasure to work with and who always seemed to have a good opinion on any subject. He took a lot of time to introduce me to individuals in the banking industry whom he had respected. Some of the contacts I made with these people were excellent individuals to help us with the problems of the time as well as future issues.

I worked almost every day for 2 1/2 months climbing over every inch of the building to understand the best way to spend the construction money we had in our budget as well as get the building as close to perfection as possible before our grand opening would occur. Keep in mind that at this point we were still in the due diligence and hadn't even settled on the building yet, but when you're setting up a business of this magnitude, a lot of these details have to be worked out prior to settlement. The name of the corporation and incorporating the new company, opening bank accounts, and putting funds in there to get the operation started were just some of the issues I was dealing with. All the loan money that I discussed earlier had to be worked out as well as contractors in place to get it moving quickly right after settlement so I could proceed with construction almost immediately. Time is of the essence when working on a big project like this, and I certainly didn't want to waste any time waiting for these things to happen while we were losing money with a new mortgage and an empty building.

The best-case scenario for the new project was several years down the road when the business was near 100 percent occupied and running smoothly we were planning for $100,000 a month gross income to be coming in with an estimated 50 percent of that going to profit. My end would be $25,000 a month, some of that of course being owed back to my partners in the form of repayment for the down money they put on the construction loan as well as any carry cost money that was required. But that wasn't the best part of the project. According to some basic cap rate calculations that I had done on the building, the amount of equity that could be accrued very quickly was outstanding. With the purchase price of $3 million, a construction loan of $500,000, and an estimated loss on the carry cost side of $500,000, we as partners would have roughly $4 million into this venture. But with a business grossing $1.2 million a year in income has an estimated value of the building and business together could potentially be sold for as much as $7 million based on a rate of 8.5 percent or 8.5 cap rate. There was an upside possibility that the building would be worth three million more than we had into it if I could fill it. That meant for me personally that besides having $25,000 a month in additional income, my net worth would've gone up by $1.5 million in the time frame it took me to take this empty building and fill it to capacity.

Being a positive guy that I am I don't spend a lot of time dwelling on the negative, but the worst-case scenario was something I could live with on this deal. I would lose my down payment of $325,000 plus run the risk of adding a lawsuit filed against me for some of the monies loaned to me to get this business going, but I've felt all these risks were worth taking. My new partners were asking me to sign personally for my half of the loans, and I agreed to do so. In my opinion, there was not a huge chance that this would happen. I found myself thrilled with the potential my future had for me with the 1600 Building.

Just like in the past when Gerard visited me to shock me with the positive news that he and his partners would like to join me in my new venture, he requested my presence at a meeting where he once again shocked me. After working so hard with me to make this new opportunity happen, I noticed that he got a little quiet over the last few weeks. It was at this meeting he informed me that he and his partners had changed their minds and decided not to be involved in this project. Damn! Not another commercial deal down the drain. Not this one. I was crushed.

Normally when an individual would have equitable title in the building that he has under agreement of sale, it would be quite difficult for the sellers of that building to back out of the deal. This case was not quite that simple. Since the owner and his partners were a week away from the requiring date to put their initial down payment into our new bank account and were now refusing to do so, there was little I could do to exercise my equitable title and force this deal to settlement. The sellers were the buyers as well. I took the only route I could and backpedaled three months to where I was when I first negotiated this deal, and I told Gerard, "Fine, give me three more months and I'll just go find some other partners and purchase the building from you in ninety days." Much to my surprise my request was refused, and I was told that my only option was to buy the building right now under the current agreement that was scheduled to settle in four weeks or walk away from the deal.

There was no way I was going to put this deal together in four weeks, so I had no choice but to back out of the deal and received back my hundred thousand dollars deposit money. I could have gone to the lawyers and started a war, but I chose not to take that route. I knew myself, and I was better suited to dreaming and working on large commercial opportunities than fighting with someone in court. Plus I had a feeling this deal was far from dead.

Gerard and I parted ways as gentlemen, but I told him he hadn't heard the last of me. I'd be back to buy this building in the future. I didn't know it at the time but what had happened to our deal was the township that the 1600 Building was located in made an offer to purchase the building straight up from Gerard and his partners for $3 million that required no partnership on no additional infusion of cash from the current owners. The partners decided that this deal with the township was a much safer, cleaner way to go for them, so they backed out of the deal they had with me as described.

It took me a few months to find out that the reason they had backed out of the deal was because of the offer made by the township to purchase the building. I felt completely rejuvenated when I heard it was the township because in my opinion townships move like frozen molasses, and if they were my competitor, I felt strongly I had a good shot to buy this building.

I took out the old one-inch binders from my brilliant dog and pony show I did for the partners and began interviewing people and presenting this package over and over again to many different individuals who may consider being my partner on this deal. I literally just about called everybody I knew who had a few bucks to invest. When I say a few bucks, I meant a minimum of $100,000 was where I set the bottom requirement for a partner. My quest went on for three or four months, and I must admit as positive as I can be, sometimes I found myself somewhat disillusioned.

I found an individual who was willing to match my $300,000. His name was Paul Luff, and he ran a successful business advisor group called Lamco LLC. This was not the same Paul I mentioned earlier in this book, but a new Paul I had been friends with for several years and had used his business advisor company to assist me in some ventures I was working on. Besides money, Paul brought an awful lot to the table. He was a smart and worldly man who was ten years my senior and had been involved in many different businesses throughout his life. He also had some excellent skills in financial analysis and of real estate opportunities. Paul could do things with a spreadsheet that would blow me away. He could lay out on a spreadsheet with month-to-month projections for years to come how every number in a business affected every other number and made it so simple to see what to focus on to make an operation work. One of the main things I learned from Paul that will stay with me forever is to not be afraid to ask for help. Sometimes when you're working a big commercial deal, you need to open up your wallet and spend some of your money to get the proper help. Commercial deals can make you rich and be extremely exciting, and you can also lose everything you've ever had if you make the wrong move.

As supportive and helpful as Paul was, between the two of us $600,000 was not enough to get this deal done, and I had decided quietly to slow down for a while. That's when my new friend Vladimir came out of the woodwork and started asking me about that deal I had pitched him recently. He was now renting office space from me at one of my buildings and was beginning to see what kind of operation I ran. When I first told Vladamir about my new building idea, he showed little interest, but sometimes planting a seed in an individual's mind will work for you, especially if they see it is a strong idea. Vladamir in a casual conversation approached me about becoming a partner in the deal and asked me to discuss everything that had occurred again. I got my second wind and became enthusiastic about bringing Vladamir into this project to be my only partner. Vladamir was a wealthy, successful businessman on his own with financial capabilities that far outweighed all three of my previous partners. Furthermore, Vladamir's business skills in negotiating were second to none as I briefly mentioned earlier. As an individual he had a positive impact on my life, and by watching him operate and working with him on the 1600 Building, I learned an awful lot.

By this time six months had passed since my last meeting with Gerard where I was told he and the other owners would not be my partners. Vladamir and I set up a meeting with Gerard and agreed before the meeting that Vladamir would take the more powerful position of our new partnership and I would sit back and try to be quiet. I set up a meeting between Gerard and Vladamir to get together and talk without me at Vladamir's request.

When I first set up the meeting, Gerard enthusiastically agreed, since just as I had projected, his township deal had come to life and died quickly. Gerard immediately began to discuss redeveloping this deal for the $3 million purchase price, but Vladamir would have a lot to say about that. I told Vladamir prior to the meeting exactly what Gerard would say. After the meeting, Vladamir admitted I had Gerard pegged all the way. As I mentioned earlier, Vladamir's amazing ability to ask thousands of questions and Gerard's willingness to answer them virtually gave Vladamir all the information needed to determine that a good place to start bidding on the 1600 Building would be roughly $2.1 million. Here we go again on the roller coaster of commercial real estate. If you're not having fun doing what you do, you may not be any good at it anyway. I have to admit I was having a great time.

Vladamir was able to reveal information about this deal that I had no idea about through his brilliant questioning of Gerard. Vladamir wanted to know why Gerard and his partners bought this building in the first place. The reason was they were actually partners in an insurance company that grew so large they needed a 35,000 sq. ft. building to run their business out of. Vladamir began to ask many questions about what happened with the insurance company and why they were no longer there. This uncovered a whole list of problems between the insurance company and the owners of the building over a long history of bad blood between the two of them. The insurance company was facing bankruptcy, and Vladamir had a great deal of knowledge on how to purchase businesses that were facing bankruptcy and how to purchase real estate from individuals as well as corporations that were facing bankruptcy.

Listening to Vladamir go on and on about every little question regarding the insurance company began to aggravate me. I sat there thinking, "Where in the hell is he going with all this, and why does he keep wasting time talking about it?" Furthermore Gerard just continued to answer everything as it went on forever. But then I started to see the method behind the madness that Vladamir was working on. He explained to me later about all the different avenues that could be taken with this newfound information. All of a sudden I felt this deal had a world of possibilities and many avenues that we could go down. It was a pleasure to watch Vladamir operate like a surgeon finding new and interesting ways to purchase this building.

The deal had taken on a new and more complicated way of trying to get to the settlement table. Vladamir and I met with the president of the insurance company with the approval of Gerard and looked at various ways that we could possibly buy out their position on the mortgage that they currently owned. We didn't last long in this meeting, as we were completely stone walled from discussing any possibilities. Since Vladamir's style was based completely on gaining information from individuals who are willing to talk to him, when he came across someone who wasn't willing to talk, the only option was to leave the room.

Does that mean that the president of the insurance company beat Vladamir? I don't think so. I think the president of the insurance company screwed himself from having an opportunity to get out of this deal. I viewed him after our meeting as one of the most close-minded men I've ever had the displeasure to meet. There's an important lesson to be learned here. As the owner of a building, a business, a mortgage, or anything else related to real estate, the answer you should have to anyone who has questions about buying a business is please come in and let's talk. Everything I own is always for sale all the time to everyone. Why would you possibly want to limit your ability to make a beautiful deal? The president of the insurance company barely gave Vladamir and me a chance to even open the discussion. He simply told us the price is what it is; if we wanted to buy them out here was the number. I can't even remember his name, but I can remember the stupid look on his face.

As time went on with Vladamir and I continuing to negotiate with Gerard as well as try to figure out how we would do the construction and carry cost portion of this deal we began to slowly raise our price to $2.2 million and then later to $2.3 million, both of which these offers were rejected by the owners.

Gerard and his partners had a first position mortgage of $1.5 million, and the insurance company that originally occupied the building had now moved to another location. Gerard owned a portion of this insurance company and at one point had taken out $1 million second mortgage. This insurance company was now on the verge of bankruptcy and was no longer paying their million-dollar second mortgage. Vladamir had all kinds of interesting ideas that included offering Gerard $1.5 million to buy out the first mortgage, taking over the building and then waiting for foreclosure on the insurance company. That idea was just brilliant. Let's discuss it for a minute.

If Gerard and his partners had $1,500,000 note on the building personally and another $1,000,000 note owed by the insurance company that Gerard and his partners owned, then they directly or indirectly owed $2,500,000 on the 1600 Building. The insurance company was heading to bankruptcy anyway, so the $1,000,000 was not going to get paid. If they sold the building to another buyer for $3,000,000, Gerard and his partners would have $500,000 in profit. But as time went on, that was looking like it was not going to happen. The building had been for sale for two years now, and we were the only interested parties. Our highest price was now $2,300,000. If we bought the first mortgage for $1.5 million, then Gerard would be out free and clear, and we would wait for foreclosure on the insurance company or paying them hopefully less than the total amount. We would end up owning the building for something under $2,500,000, and Gerard did not have to keep paying the first mortgage. They rejected our offer much to my surprise as I thought the idea was a real win-win for all involved.

He also had ideas of buying up the second mortgage at a reduced price and then making mortgage payments on it so that we couldn't be forced out of the deal. Vladamir and I would essentially own a piece of the 1600 Building. Vladamir even looked at buying the insurance company as another way to get the deal done.

After spending a great deal of time on the bankruptcy options that this deal presented, Vladamir and I decided that there was no viable plan going in this direction either. We decided to make a final offer of $2.5 million to Gerard and his partners. The funny thing about saying final offer with Vladamir was that as I got to know him nothing was final and nothing was ever solid. There was always the way to renegotiate the previous negotiation or adjust a previous decision no matter how solid it seemed. Gerard decided to shock me for a third time by calling me and accepting my offer of $2.5 million for the 1600 Building.

By this time, Vladamir and I had spent six months together working on this deal. I first looked at the 1600 Building early in 2007, and here I was in February of 2008, a year later, about to draft my second agreement of sale for the same building at a price $500,000 cheaper than I originally purchased it. You've really got to love this stuff to hang around that long trying to buy commercial. If you've read this story to this point, think about the fact that I've spent a year of my life working on a deal that still hasn't happened. There have been obstacles, partnerships, trials, and tribulations, and it's enough to make your head spin.

Just in case you forgot, we now had a verbal agreement to buy the 1600 Building for the same price I offered them on the first verbal offer before our first meeting a year earlier. This was the $2.5 million I had offered them verbally through the realtor that originally had shown me the building. Now a year later after all of this, we end up in the same exact place.

Vladamir and I immediately drafted an agreement of sale similar to the one I previously drafted with the exception that we would be putting no money down on the deal. We would simply show up at settlement with a check for $2.5 million to purchase the building on March 20, 2008. We estimated a six-month construction schedule along with some time to get our ducks in a row and schedule our grand opening for November 1, 2008. We continued to do our due diligence, interviewing construction individuals, electricians, and plumbers to help us with this massive construction project we were about to take on. Because of the additional funds that Vladamir had to invest and because of his demand to make this place 100 percent perfect for what we wanted before opening we increased the construction budget to $1.2 million.

Everything that could be improved would be with high-end granite countertops, beautiful carpet, top-shelf landscaping, and a new elevator. Since we got the building for $500,000 cheaper than my original partnership but we were going to be spending $700,000 more on construction, the typical profit range of this deal was similar to the first deal as far as my part was concerned. Vladamir was also willing to not only cover the down money required for this entire deal but also be the bank for the mortgage company bringing to deal to settlement. The only amount of money Vladamir asked me to put up was $250,000. With a $2,500,000 purchase price and a $1.2 million construction estimate plus $500,000 in carrying costs, the grand total of this project was now $4.2 million.

Vladamir also introduced me to a product he called the freedom mortgage. The freedom mortgage is similar in some ways to a home equity line of credit. Vladamir would be the bank on this deal financing all monies needed. After putting up my $250,000 when the business first opened its doors, it would owe Vladamir $3,950,000 and would make payments on it monthly just like a mortgage. But as time went on and the mortgage began to get paid down as well as the business began to have a large rent roll of say $50,000 a month, this would be simply kept in a bank account controlled by Vladamir's mortgage company. The $50,000 that would be coming in and out of the account each month would actually count as principal paid off on the loan of $3,950,000, so in theory the loan would already be under $3.9 million very quickly. The interest would be paid on it at an average daily balance of each day to determine the principal and interest paid off each month. The reason it had to be calculated daily was because the bank account or loan amount was changing constantly.

This was a wonderful way to take advantage of the income coming in from your business to reduce your monthly mortgage amount, but there were other benefits. The amount of money that Vladamir would make available to me in the beginning was $3,950,000, but as the money was paid off and I got the loan down to 3.7 million for example, I would still have an additional $250,000 to borrow back at any time. Much like the way a home equity line of credit works, Vladamir's company was allocating $3,950,000 for this new business to use as it sees fit over the years—hence the name freedom mortgage. The mortgage gave the business the freedom to use the money as it saw fit, and I absolutely loved the idea. Since the money was coming from a trust fund and needed to be spent on prudent investments, he almost did not want the money back. I could have possibly used the extra money down the road for other real estate deals as well.

Like all wonderful deals, there's always a catch. My new partner was an excellent negotiator, and he didn't limit his negotiation skills to owners of buildings. He also used his superior negotiating skills on me and made me agree to a very dangerous clause. He said if this venture loses money and falls apart, he retains the right to pull the building and sell it for whatever price he likes whenever he determines it's required if I miss payments. Furthermore, if he sells the building and the business would go under, I would have to cover not only my losses but also his. His business philosophy was that I could never do this deal without him, and he was taking the risk of losing all the money. He was not willing to lose a dime on this deal. It was my idea, and I found the building and the business concept to make this operation work. While he liked it and he believed that it had every chance of success, if by some chance it would not, the burden of all losses, which could be in the millions, would be all mine to bear. It gets worse.

If theoretically I lost $1 million of our money on this deal and I have to repay a million dollars, I would have absolutely no way to pay this man back. This was not a consignment loan and would not be stretched out over a fifty-year mortgage. Vladamir would be coming for my assets, and he made that very clear to me upfront. If something went wrong with this deal, I could lose everything I've ever earned in life, including my largest office building, Executec Suites, and my home. I took the deal. If you ever hear anyone say I don't have any guts, tell them to read this portion of the book again. While I found this deal with him to be disconcerting, I saw no possible way that I would fail.

I must admit that I had an awful lot of sleepless nights thinking about the 1600 Building but not particularly over the deal I made with Vladamir. Generally speaking, I'm a very positive man, and I just didn't see any way that this deal wouldn't at least breakeven. After all, I already owned a building that was an identical operation to this one that was currently running at 100 percent occupied. I wasn't turning people away from my other operation but steady streams of individuals were constantly ringing my doorbell.

Executec Suites was eight miles away or twenty minutes in the car. There was no executive suite center anywhere near the 1600 Building, and the location of my new building was far superior to my existing one. My existing operation was on a small road with one lane going in each direction; my new building was on two of the largest roads in the middle Bucks County. The traffic count was six times the size of my existing operation, and the building was only three times the size. During the year that I worked on the new building, I had inquiries all the time about how it was going and when it would be open. I had every reason to believe that success was the only option coming my way.

After I bought Executec Suites, I started to think that I was one big deal away from being a multimillionaire. Instead of looking for residential homes to invest in, I figured one more commercial deal would put me over the top and set me up for life. With the 1600 Building only three miles from my home and every aspect of this project reviewed thoroughly, I felt confident I had done everything possible. We prepared extensive marketing strategies with a budget of $75,000 to be used for brochures, direct mailing, e-mail blasts, Web sites, social media marketing, guerrilla marketing, and many other brilliant ideas. I began to have visions of changing my name from Phil Falcone to just Mr. Falcone.

Settlement was scheduled for March 20, 2008, and I was extremely excited to see a deal that I had worked on for over a year about to come to fruition. By early March we had already issued verbal contracts for the electricians, construction workers, HVAC, and other vendors to be prepared to start immediately on the construction of the 1600 Building. Vladamir had mentioned to me on several occasions that he had some health issues and that if he disappeared for a few days the chances were strong that his health issues had reoccurred. We scheduled a meeting to meet his attorney so that I could make the payments every month should Vladamir get sick again. He also set up points of contact to send accounting records for the building as well as phone calls to make when I needed business advice. I was not sure, but I had the feeling he was preparing me for his death. I had to contend with the fact that there was a possibility that Vladamir would not survive to see this building become a success. Although I didn't know the details of his illness, I knew it was serious. Vladamir once told me that the only way that he would invest in this deal is if I guaranteed him that there would be no losses on his end. If I wanted his money invested in this deal, this was the only way it was going to happen. Furthermore, I had to contend with the fact that my relationship with him could not be something that would bail me out because he might not even be around if I did get in trouble. Sometimes in life you have to roll the dice, and that's clearly what I was doing here. I figured only two possible things could come from this deal. I would either be a multimillionaire or completely broke. In my mind if I was forced to put a percentage on my chances, I clearly saw my chance of success was 95 percent.

I always had the attitude that I can't fail because I am willing to do anything necessary to make a project succeed. If I had to move into the 1600 Building and work there twenty hours a day, I would gladly have done it before going bankrupt. Besides working on my real estate empire, which I'm clearly addicted to, the only hobby I really had was going to the gym every day, which happened to be the building next door. I had visions of rolling the dice, but instead of actually having dice, my home and all the pieces of real estate I owned were the dice, and I was rolling them on down the sidewalk along with my self-respect and my family's security.

During the first week of March, his illness resurfaced. His health problems reoccurred, and Vladamir went into the hospital for five months straight. During the months of April, May, June, July, and August, I did the best I could to keep this deal alive and to keep the sellers interested. But by the time the August calendar was getting taken down from my wall, Gerard informed me that he was moving on to greener pastures. Could it be now in September of 2008 that I was destined to spend a year and a half on a building that would never happen? No, not again. I wanted to pull my teeth out with a pair of pliers. I really couldn't make up my mind if I wanted to cry, scream, or just beat something.

After complete silence for six months, my partner reappeared from his deathbed to meet with me about the 1600 Building. By the time the fall of 2008 rolled around, as Vladamir and I met in October of 2008 for the first time in seven months, the economy was starting to look very bad. Furthermore, the election of Barack Obama looked like it was going to happen, and his promise of change left businessmen like Vladamir and myself very concerned about what the future held for small businesses. Executive suite centers cater to small businesses, and liberal policies tend to destroy small businesses faster than a forest fire burns trees.

My partner and I decided that while we were both still interested in doing the deal, he was not the man he was seven months ago after going through such a great deal of health issues. I told him I was enthusiastically prepared to do everything we originally discussed, but both of us agreed that the building's value had definitely dropped over the last seven months. So we decided to rebid our offer on the project at $1.5 million. Would three times be a charm?

If I think back to my deal to partner with Gerard at a price of $3 million then my end of the deal would be half. We were now offering $1.5 million for the whole deal with no ownership to the existing owners. If the original deal were to have gone thru I think I would have had enough time to make it work before the economy tanked. It's a shame for me and for Gerard the first deal was squashed.

The answer to that question has yet to be revealed as my offer of $1,500,000 was rejected and the building has been sitting dormant, and Gerard has remained silent as I write this paragraph on New Year's Eve 2009/2010. At an operating cost of approximately $1000 a day, the 1600 Building still sits vacant some three years after I first looked at it. Hindsight always gives you the clearest image of a situation that you could ever receive. When Vladamir went in to the hospital, I was concerned for my friend's health and equally disappointed in the lack of a way to get this deal done, but in hindsight it may have been the best thing that's ever happened to me.

Specifically speaking of the carrying costs on this deal, I was estimating $500,000 in losses was based on a year and a half waiting for the building to breakeven. In this economy, I think it's safe to say that number could have been doubled or more. I also think it's safe to say that Vladamir would've pulled the plug at some point, and not being able to sell the building, he would have no choice but to come after me for my assets, which could never even cover the losses that would've been incurred by now. Vladamir would own Executec Suites and other buildings, and I would have nothing to show for twenty years in the real estate business. I really dodged a bullet because there's no doubt in my mind that if Vladamir did not have his health issues that I would be the owner of this building and in maybe in deep trouble by now.

There's a lesson to be learned here. Things happen for a reason. Every door that closes opens another. Luck has something to do with every successful business. Take your pick what lesson you choose to learn from this story. I still think one day I'm going to own that building, but with the economy being what it is today as we approach 2010, there is no amount of money I would be interested in investing in that building. Maybe later in 2010 when the political arena has changed and the economy begins to come back, we can then reconsider, but until then I want no part of it.

As I try to be positive about everything I'm involved with, I have to say that this building was the greatest learning experience I had as far as negotiating commercial real estate. I doubt I could've attended Harvard University for a year and a half and learned more about the trials and tribulations of a commercial real estate investor as I did on trying to purchase the 1600 Building. After this fiasco I truly feel like I have a Ph.D. in commercial real estate deal making. I am a professor of entrepreneurism. Maybe one day in the future I'll be writing a new ending to this chapter, but until then I'll keep looking for deals in the business of real estate that I truly love.

CHAPTER 19

Expanding Executec Suites

Connected to my existing operation in Huntingdon Valley is an 8000 sq. ft. facility on each side of the existing building. One side is owned and operated independently as a machine shop; the other side is chopped up into twenty different offices similar to the way that an executive suite would be laid out. My next-door neighbors are not running an executive suite center as they don't have the receptionist, the mailboxes, and many of the other services that I offer, but they do have twenty offices that they rent out separately. They run a chiropractor business, a mortgage business, and the title company that uses about thirteen of the twenty available offices. The remaining offices they rent out to a few people, and they have a few vacancies.

In the summer of 2008 when Vladimir was in the hospital and the 1600 Building wasn't looking good, I decided to approach both my neighbors and make an offer to buy them. Machine shop side told me that in three or four years he'd be interested in selling it and we could talk then, but until then he was going on with his business. The other side with the twenty offices gave me a number of $1,100,000. I thought the building was worth about $750,000, but because it was connected to my building, it increased its value maybe as high as $900,000 to me. So that's what I offered them, and using what I could, I was able to convince them to accept it. I wasn't really in a good negotiating situation since neither of these people was selling the buildings in the first place. The only way to really make it work was to overpay them, making them willing to sell.

I got the twenty-office portion of the building next to mine under agreement for $900,000 and began working on the construction drawings to do the engineering work required to merge their building of 8000 sq. ft. into my existing building. I had to move some existing tenants to pick up access to the other side, but in the end I had sixty-seven offices as well as access to a courtyard that came with the other building. The layout wasn't perfect, but knowing I wasn't going to be going anywhere soon, I thought it was a good move to turn Executec Suites into an even greater and more successful business.

With the sellers on board and the agreement of sale signed, down money received, and the layout finished, things were looking good except for one problem. By the fall of 2008, banks were starting to show signs of trouble, and lending money for commercial properties was the last thing on their minds. Through my connections with the Bucks County Economic Development Corporation, I was able to make business contacts with the Small Business Administration (SBA) for loans. After working hard with the lender, I was able to get approval for 10 percent down loan for half of the purchase price and all the construction money. The way an SBA loan works is I would get a bank to put up 40 percent of the money and take first position. The government or the SBA loan officer works out the details to get the financing for the remaining 50 percent. Ten percent comes from me, and an additional loan for $100,000 of construction money was granted if I meet certain criteria they require.

But they primarily require that you have to create jobs so that the Bucks County economic development will improve because of this project. An executive suite center is an approved idea by the SBA, and it is an allowable concept for lending money. I worked on this loan for over six months trying to get the financing, and I really didn't think I was going to ever get it. The agreement of sale with the sellers next door had gone over its time limit allowed to close the deal. Normally if the deal was hot, I would've extended the contract, but I simply didn't think it was ever going to get the financing. I also thought if I did get the financing there was no way they were going to turn down a $900,000 offer. Much to my surprise, I finally got the financing sometime around November of 2008, but the sellers had changed their mind.

Even if they were still under contract to sell me the building, I don't think it would've been that easy to force them to sell, nor do I believe that I would go the legal route and destroy good friendly relations with my next-door neighbor. Even if I had it under contract and they change their minds, I think I would have just let the whole deal die there. This was another deal that fell through, but I felt relatively comfortable that if anybody was going to buy this building or the one on the other side or even both, it was going to be me. I also made some great contacts with the SBA program loans director and learned a lot about how to get government financing for such projects. Furthermore I would say that now that I can look back and see what's happened to the economy in 2009 it's another "dodged a bullet" scenario. Renting offices certainly didn't get any easier in 2009, and having twenty extra offices would have been a boatload of problems. Once again the deal fell through and somehow seemed to help me.

Maybe when it comes to commercial real estate, I am one of the luckiest guys ever born, but I must admit I'm surprised they turned down a $900,000 offer for a building worth $750,000. The way things have been going in commercial real estate last year, I have to say that building is now worth more like $550,000 and dropping. With all these projects that I've worked on that didn't come to fruition, I certainly don't feel like I have to spend a lot of time going around looking for deals. I already have more than one building that I'm interested in buying when the time is right and the financing is in place. If I can have all my ducks in a row to make it happen, I will be ready for the right deal at the right time.

CHAPTER 20

Bucks County Suites

One of the first things I did when I first bought Executec Suites was call all of my competitors to ask for a sit down meeting. Most of the executive suite businesses in the Philadelphia area are owned by the nine-hundred-pound gorilla in this business. They rent about twelve hundred locations in the United States. The business model is actually to rent space from landlords and run their operations out of someone else's building.

After calling all my competitors, I received responses from two private owners and one of the gorilla's locations. One of the privately owned locations is called Bucks County Suites located in Bucks County, Pennsylvania. This location was less than five years old and was clearly a class "A" building.

Depending upon their age and physical condition, buildings are commonly classified A, B, C, or D properties in the commercial arena. Class A buildings will typically be newer properties less than twenty years old and in excellent condition. They may even be newly constructed buildings that are still being leased up. This type of building will command the highest price per unit for several reasons, one of which is the cost of new construction, building materials, and labor. Class B buildings are slightly older than class A buildings, usually between ten and fifty years old and are still in relatively good condition. Class C properties are those that range in each from twenty to one hundred years old and can be found in a variety of different conditions from fairly good to poor. Class C buildings are usually in fairly stable neighborhoods that are well established and have not suffered from deteriorating conditions in the surrounding area. Class D buildings are generally those in excess of thirty years old in range and then primarily poor condition. Class D buildings are likely to be found in declining neighborhoods, so improvements to the property may not result in that much added value because people who could afford higher rents will likely choose a similar property in a better community at comparable rates.

When I first met the owners of Bucks County Suites, buying a building was not on my mind as I had just purchased Executec Suites for $2,150,000 and I was already involved in the 1600 Building. I was mostly just going to check out the competition and to try to establish a friendly rapport with the people I competed with. Isn't that a radical idea? Instead of badmouthing each other and fighting for the same clients over and over again, maybe we could actually help each other. For example, if one of my competitors has a larger office available than I have, I could kick the client to my competitor and receive a commission. I once had a client who needed a conference room big enough to hold twenty people for a board meeting. He was willing to rent space from me, but he needed a place to have his board meetings once a month and my conference rooms could not hold twenty people. I thought I could work with my competitors on situations like these.

The people at Bucks County Suites were private owners just like me, with their first executive suite center. In our initial meeting, we just talked about helping one another, but about a year later I received a call and I was asked to come to a meeting. At that meeting, I was told that the building was going to be put up for sale, and I had hinted in my first meeting that if the sale was ever likely I would be interested. As usual I didn't have two nickels to scratch together when I made that suggestion. Just another case of me planting a seed in somebody's mind hoping they would later grow into something more. On the second meeting, numbers were being thrown around somewhere in the range of $4,500,000 for fifteen thousand square feet of the twenty-five-thousand-square-foot facility. I was so sure this price wasn't even close to justifiable I asked the following question. I asked them to explain to me how they could justify that kind of value for building that was significantly nicer than mine and slightly larger than mine but with a lower rent roll. It was an interesting meeting, and I really enjoyed meeting the people who own Bucks County

Suites, but considering I was already in my second stage of the 1600 Building by this time, there was no way I could even think about another building.

About three years after I bought Executec Suites and now fast forwarding to the fourth quarter of 2009, the owners had decided that running Bucks County Suites was something they didn't want to do anymore. We started having some creative conversations about a way that the deal could get done. Over the course of quite a few meetings, we banged around just about every crazy idea both of us could think of. We talked about everything from carrying paper to lowering the price of the building with a second mortgage to being partners. We even talked about the current owners renting back many offices from me to make the rent roll look better to a bank. We finally settled on the idea that may be the only way we could ever get this deal done. We negotiated out a complex lease with an option to buy the building.

The lease option was structured in a way where the owner could get the number he wanted, which was $4,200,000 for the full 25,000 sq. ft. facility. Fifteen thousand square feet of the facility consisted of fifty-five executive suites in a drop dead gorgeous facility. There was additional 10,000 sq. ft. of space connected but separated from the executive suite center. In the 10,000 sq. ft. of space, half of it was already fitted out into nice office space split up into three large suites. The remaining half of the building was about 5000 sq. ft. and was left as unfinished warehouse space. The executive suite center side was for sale for $3 million and the other side for an additional $1.2 million giving you a total of $4,200,000 for the entire facility. A much reduced price from the previous meeting. It also came with all the other items required to run a successful executive suite center. In an executive suite center, since you provide everything to the client from the telephones to the furniture to the pictures on the wall, all of these items must be included in the sale because I'm buying the business as well as the real estate. When you count every stitch of furniture, phone equipment, paintings, and anything else you can name, you're probably talking about $200,000 worth of extra items. All of these extra items were included in the $4.2 million.

We structured the deal where I would rent the facility from the current owners for a figure of approximately $25,000 a month that would be a breakeven number for him on his current mortgage taxes and insurance. He would be signing over the rights to his building as far as any future sales would go for the next five years, but he would also gain a breakeven position on a building he was now losing a little each month. The building currently was bringing in about $21,000 a month, so I was agreeing to cover the losses of about $4000 a month the minute I walked in. In exchange for covering the losses, the owner was allowing me to come into this lease with no money down. I also retain the right to walk from this deal at anytime, so if it lost money for ten months in a row and I decided that I had taken enough losses on this deal, I could simply walk away with ten days notice. I also got to keep all the profits should I be lucky enough to rent the facility up in a manner in which it would begin to turn a profit. I repeat that none of the profits would have to be shared with the current owner. I would be in a position where I could make an awful lot of profit off of the building I don't even own yet with the option to purchase anytime between day one and five years into the lease.

Normally this kind of deal would be virtually impossible to put together, but because the building was in such pristine condition, the fears of having any major repair work to do were almost nonexistent. The owner could be happy with breaking even in a month as he expected me to do any repairs to the building as long as they were under an amount of $2000 as stated in the contract.

Originally my plan was to only lease the executive suite center side with the 15,000 sq. ft., and as the other side began to be rented, I would then take over that portion as well all in the same contract. If the existing owner or I found tenants for the other ten-thousand-square-foot side, I could then lease that portion as well under the lease agreement. Going into it initially I only agreed to take over the executive suite side since all of the $21,000 in income was coming from that side. But I retained the right to, at anytime, grab the other side as well. I was merely waiting for some of it to get rented up so that it justified the additional $1.2 million in purchase price and the additional increase in the monthly rental fee I would pay the owner. Since I was only running the executive suite center when the deal started, he was going to continue to try to rent the other side. I made it very clear to him, and he completely understood that the goal would be to control both sides.

Another complex issue with the deal is the 5000 sq. ft. of unfinished space. What would happen if somebody came in and wanted the whole thing fitted out into office space or some kind of special design? We agreed that the existing owner would finance the operations, and if for example he spent $100,000 fitting out the last 5000 sq. ft., then the sale price of the building would go up $100,000 so that he would be compensated for his construction money upon settlement.

Another interesting part of the contract was that during the five years where I would essentially be paying his mortgage, taxes, and insurance, I asked for a little bonus. My little bonus was that I wanted the principal that was being paid off on the loan to be credited to me over the five years so that eventually if I were to buy the building I would be given that credit. I know that his existing mortgage on the entire facility was $3 million, so I was estimating that his principal pay off each month was somewhere in the range of $4000 a month or $50,000 a year. If I rented the building for five years, I would be owed a credit of $250,000 at the end. If you think about it, it almost doesn't make any sense to buy the building until the end of the five-year contract. If I just continue to lease the building, I end up getting all the profit anyway and the principal.

One of the things about this deal I was giving up is I was paying too much for the building. If you know anything about real estate, how in hell could a building that only makes $21,000 a month is worth $4,200,000? Quite frankly, it wouldn't be worth that money. Commercial real estate is valued on a lot of different things but primarily on how much money it makes. If it makes $21,000 a month, its value is nowhere near $4,200,000. It does have some correlation to comparable properties in the area, but that would put a value somewhere around $2.8 million for the whole kit and caboodle.

Evaluating real estate is typically looked at from the standpoint of the cap rate. The formula is the net operating income divided by the sales price to give you the cap rate. Net operating income or NOI is defined by the gross income subtracting the operating expenses.

Gross Income – Operating Expenses = NOI

NOI divided by the Sales Price = Cap Rate

In the case of Executec Suites, the net operating income was $268,000 a year divided by a sales price of $2,150,000 bringing the cap rate to something like a 12.5. What does all that mean? It means that you could expect to get a rate of return on your money of 12.5 percent. Cap rates can be a little confusing, but when you look at commercial real estate over and over again you begin to understand it's one of the better ways to determine the difference between one building and another. That's all it really is used for by me.

$268,000 divided by $2,150,000 = .1247 (or) 12.5 Cap Rate

I sometimes use a more sophisticated formula to determine what is called a derived cap rate to arrive at a maximum purchase price but for the purposes of most people this standard cap rate is a good way to measure each piece you evaluate. You can also take the net operating income and divide by the cap rate to give you the value of the building if you knew what the rates were going for in a particular area. For example, if there were a lot of similar buildings to the one you are considering buying in a certain area; you could take the net operating income and divide it by the cap rate the buildings were being offered at to determine a fair market value for the building.

$268,000 divided by .1247 = $2,149,157.97

In the case of Executec Suites, you would take $268,000, the net operating income, and divide by a rate that other buildings were selling for in the area at the time, which was about 8.0 cap rate, giving you a value of somewhere around $3.3 million.

$268,000 divided by .08 cap rate = $3,350,000

Now I don't believe that Executec is worth $3,350,000 and I don't believe that I could ever sell it for anywhere near that amount. What this calculation showed me at the time of purchasing it was that Executec Suites made a tremendous amount of profit compared to most buildings. It also took a tremendous amount of work to bring in net profit every month, so that was the trade-off.

Dave Lindahl is a nationally known speaker who uses a system he calls the "Times 10 Valuation Calculation". It is an easy way to determine a properties approximate value. NOI x 10 = Approximate Value of the property.

$268,000 x 10 = $2,680,000 for Executec Suites

If Dave is correct and in this case I hope he is, I purchased Executec Suites for $530,000 under market value. Another way to say it is I received $530,000 in equity at the time of purchase. WOW! I only put $475,000 of my own money into it.

When it comes to executive suite centers, it is such a unique operation that comparable rates or comparable buildings were virtually impossible to come up with. Another way to come up with a cap rate is to create it yourself. For example if you are getting 80 percent mortgage at 7 percent interest, you multiply those numbers by one another and come up with 5.6. Then you take a 20 percent down payment, and you're going to be getting a 15 percent return on your money and multiply them against one another for a number of 3.0. You then add 5.6 to 3.0 to get a cap rate of 8.6 for this particular building. This is a way to calculate what a cap rate for this building might be if you don't have any area caps to use.

80 percent mortgage x 7 percent interest = 5.6

20 percent down payment x 15 percent return on money = 3.0

5.6 + 3.0 = 8.6 Cap Rate

So back to why am I overpaying for this building at $4.2 million when it only makes $21,000 per month. I learned during my negotiations with the owner that there was only one thing he truly cared about and that was getting the number he wanted. If I didn't give him the number he wanted, then there was no way in hell that this deal was going to get done no matter how you slice it. So I had to find another way to make it be a win-win for both parties. I gave him the number he wanted, but if you take into consideration that the prices are going to come down $250,000 because the principal paid off; I'm really paying under $4 million now. So for sake of argument, let's say that the actual price I'm paying for the building now is $3,950,000. Over the next five years, this building is expected to make money or I am not going to be there. So let's just pick a number as an estimate of what this building could make over the next five years. Let's pick a safe number of $400,000 in profit over a five-year period. I'm basing that on making nothing the first year and making $100,000 for each of the following four years. Now the sales price of this building is dropped to $3,550,000 because I'm subtracting the $650,000 I am generating from having this lease. If I save all the profit that I make over the five years, I should have $400,000 in the bank with a $250,000 credit coming to me at settlement.

I can do this because I'm going to be paying myself a salary for running the building, which is taken out of the gross numbers before the hundred thousand dollars in profit. In order to buy a building for $4.2 million, I think it's safe to say you're going to need $1 million in cash to make it happen. I've already figured out a way to get $650,000 ready for settlement. Is the deal starting to make sense to you yet?

First we have to estimate the net operating income of $350,000. This number is the total shot in the dark, but I have to start somewhere. If my other building is doing $268,000 and this building is 12,000 sq. ft. larger, it seems like a reasonable goal to expect a net operating income of $350,000. Below I will do some rate calculations on what the cap rate would be at $4,200,000.

$350,000 divided by $4,200,000 = .0833 or 8.3 cap rate

What would it be worth at the $3,550,000 that I view I am actually paying for the building?

$350,000 divided by $3,550,000 = .0986 or 9.8 cap rate

So the real trick to making this building work is going to be my salesmanship abilities and my management skills. The owner of this building has operated it himself for almost five years with some real ups and downs. He actually grossed $630,000 in the year 2009 but lost a tenant that was paying him $200,000 a year in rent just recently. The massive upside potential to this building is it could have $1 million a year gross income making me a couple hundred thousand dollars a year just for running a building I don't even own. Furthermore, I'm going to have the rights to buy this building for the next five years, so if anybody were to come around and want to buy, they've got a talk to me. I could actually sell my contract to somebody for a few hundred thousand dollars in profit. I might even be able to get somebody to put up the remaining down money needed and get him to run the building. I'm just thinking outside the box now, but let's just say that my $250,000 credit plus my $400,000 in money saved and then an outsider who wanted to buy the building and the business came in and put down the remaining deposit money. I could walk from the deal and let him run it and move on to the next exciting arrangement. The possibilities for a deal like this are endless as I could go on and on about every way this thing could get done.

From the owner's standpoint and mine, it's really a win-win and that's what I like about this deal the most. His main concern is he wants to get out of this business as I think he underestimated the amount of work it takes to run an executive suites center.

He is also an older and more established guy financially than I am, and he has a lot of other interesting things he could be working on. He builds buildings and enjoys trying to develop areas, and this deal is far from a development project. He also has a successful family business that has the potential to make way more money than this particular piece of real estate does. So by doing this deal with me, he gets to free himself from a building that he views as a burden, and he breaks even every month for five years. If he could sell it today, he would in a heartbeat, but nobody is going to get financing for the deal let alone a buyer to pay him the money he wants. I am the only guy who can make it happen because I'm willing to overpay for his building to get this deal done. You have to admit that in this economy where people are buying buildings for $.40 on the dollar, paying $1.40 on the dollar seems ass backward. Maybe I'm crazy or maybe sometimes the move is to overpay.

Remember I'm not putting any of my own down money on this deal and I can walk at any time, so I just don't see how this deal is bad for me any way you look at it. I also think it's an excellent deal for the owner because he needs to get away from it to go work on other things. My deal allows him to do that, and at the end of the five years if I don't buy the building, we most likely will be in a much better economic scenario than we are today or somebody else will. Either way, he wins and he gets his $4.2 million.

How does he get his $4.2 million five years from now? If I run the building successfully, I'll stay there for five years because I am making money; therefore, it will have a much higher occupancy rate than it has now. Then it's going to be worth much more than it is now. I think the chances of this building being worth $4,000,000, five years from now is very possible. I can just take the money and run at the end of five years, but I know myself and that's not going to be a viable option.

It's a rare thing when you find a deal that wins for both parties, but of course a lot of things have to happen for this deal to work after we sign the papers. Right now as I write this paragraph the contracts are on his desk, and all he has to do is sign them. I think that's exactly what he'll do. What I don't know is if I'll be able to increase the rents fast enough to stop the bleeding and get the building into the black. His marketing of this facility has been weak as his heart really isn't in it. The effort he puts toward this building is nowhere near the effort that I intend to put into it.

People often ask me how I can have a building that's 95 percent rented when all around me are buildings that are empty. I'm able to do it because I don't do anything else. I wake up every morning and try to figure out how I can go find another tenant to fill my building, and when you think like that and you're excited about getting out of bed to make that happen, there's no way you can't be the best at it. There is a way to fail because I cannot create clients to come to the building, and I can guarantee you that there are significantly less of them today than there were in 2006 when I first entered this business. I'll tell you a little bit about some of the marketing plans I have.

I happen to be a local expert on how to market an executive suite center because I'm one of a few people in the Philadelphia area who actually own one. Most of the leads we get these days are a combination of either people who just walked in the building because they know us because it's been there so long or they come from the Internet leads. Internet Web sites are no mystery to the people who own Bucks County Suites, but I think that's where they stop. I am planning on a series of different ideas in order to get some beating hearts into this new building. There's a local radio station that I'm going to be working with doing a half hour radio show on a weekly basis and that should be a terrific way to get the word out. I love talking about real estate anyway, and most of the people who know me have just about had an ear full, so this radio show will be a terrific way for me to get the word out. I also plan on doing some traditional marketing where I produce brochures and postcards to be sent out to the people who occupy other office buildings in the area. One of the appeals of an executive suites center is we have smaller space at a much cheaper price to work going after the guys who are downsizing. There are people paying $3000 a month for 1500 sq. ft. who would gladly pay us $800 a month for 200 sq. ft. Our price per square foot is much higher, but we have a massive amount of common space that the client will use that they're not actually paying for, such as conference rooms, kitchen space, and the reception area. Another area that makes closing a deal for a downsizing customer fairly easy is if he has a receptionist answering his phones. I provide a full-time receptionist to answer the phone in the name of your company regardless of what size office you rent. For $495 a month, you have an office big enough for one person with the furniture in that office with the telephone on your desk and the telephone number and fax number and the Internet. You also get two full-time receptionists who answer the phone in the name of your company with the conference rooms, printer, copier, scanner, mailboxes, kitchen space, and a whole lot of extra stuff including free coffee. Sorry but I just can't talk about what I provide without spitting out that paragraph every time. That's how I got the nickname Mr. $495 all over town. I tell everybody I know what you can get for $495 a month at Executec Suites and soon to be the deal being offering at Bucks County Suites.

Another idea I plan to try at Bucks County Suites is a swap for service packages with people such as a computer company that may want space in my building. I always try to do business with the people who do business with my business, so I can offer a computer company coming into the building spending $8000 a year on rent 50 percent of the rent back in business. If I promise to spend $4000 a year on their computer services and I don't actually do it or maybe I only do some of it, I still owe them $2000. I give that back to them in the form of a credit after the one-year lease is up. Anyway I am giving free rent or cheaper rent, but I'm keeping live bodies in a building and still profiting, which is my main goal. If I had five vacant offices out of forty-seven executive suites, I would never offer this deal, but at Bucks County Suites I have over thirty empty offices out of the fifty-five so I'll be offering deals any way you can think of them. If a good negotiator comes walking into my building looking for office space, the chances of me uttering the word *no* is about 0 percent. The answer will be *yes* to any deal proposed to me as long as it makes sense for both parties.

If you think about the lease option I negotiated for Bucks County Suites, it's one of the most intelligent deals I've ever put together. This deal does what I've always hoped every deal would do. It protects the downside, and the upside takes care of itself. While it's true I can walk into this deal losing $4000 a month and I could do that for an entire year, it is still a small amount of money compared to the amount of funds one can lose on a big commercial deal. For a deal half this size, I would need $500,000 down to make it happen, much like I did for my existing buildings. You need $1 million cash to actually purchase this building, and there's no way that's going to happen right now. I can go into this deal feeling quite comfortable and give it the best effort I possibly have. If I get to break even soon, then my fears are over. Spring is coming as I am writing this book in the first quarter of 2010. Spring is usually a very good time for renting offices, so I expect to get this building to breakeven by May or June at the latest. If I do it like I think I can, the downside to this building is already over with, as soon as I rent any more space. I am in the black as opposed to losing money and being in the red. As long as I pay the owner his $25,000 month, there's no way he can get me out of the deal or out of this building. I will be in complete control of the facility for the next five years. Let me dream a little and give you some of the upside potential.

With thirty-something offices vacant and most of them being offices I would rent at Executec Suites for $700, $800, or $900 a month, my plan is as follows. I'm going to take all these empty offices and offer them at the $495 a month deal until the building is relatively filled. This is a dangerous concept as I might anger the people who are already paying as much as a thousand, but it's a chance I think I'm going to have to take since I have those people on a lease, their options are limited. If I rented thirty offices at $495 a month, my income stream would go up $15,000 month. Under that scenario, I'd be up $10,000 a month and $120,000 a year as soon as I could make that happen. Let's assume that I breakeven in the first year, losing money in the first six months and making money in the second six months to breakeven position and then in the second year I am up $120,000 year. Once I get to an 80 or 90 percent occupancy rate, I can start re-renting the offices at the price that they are worth. It may take me two or three years to correct the discounted numbers, and if the economy holds up, this system will be able to keep the building relatively filled making year five at the market value figures. If that could happen, I might be up as much as $25,000 a month. Now we're talking $300,000 a year in my last year as the best-case scenario. A lot can happen in five years. I like my chances of making this deal work, and I think my future looks brighter and sunnier than ever.

Let's continue to explore the upside for a minute. Let's say I breakeven in the first year, and I made $100,000 in the second year followed by $200,000 in the third and fourth year, and $300,000 in the fifth year. In that best-case scenario, I would have made and hopefully saved $800,000 plus the $250,000 in credit I would receive giving me $1,050,000 during the five years I ran this building. I already have all the money I need to survive from my other properties; plus I plan to take a small salary from this deal. While it will be difficult to save every penny I make in profit, it is potentially possible. Since we're exploring best-case scenarios, let's assume that's exactly what I do. I would have all the down money I need to buy Bucks County Suites for $4,200,000. You could almost make the argument that I used none of my own money to make the deal work. I could potentially get people who work for me to come over and help me get this deal to become a success and maybe even hand it over to one of my best people to run after I get through the first couple years. I could then run it from a distance as I do with a lot of my other buildings and take the money I have set aside and go buy something in a more conventional manner. The expansion of my real estate portfolio in the next five years could become an amazing thing.

What would the net operating income be of a building that was allowing me to pull $300,000 now in profit? Let's call it $500,000 a year in net operating income and see what the cap rate calculation looks like.

$500,000 divided by $4,200,000 = .1190 or 11.9 cap rate

With a $500,000 net operating income and a purchase price of a $4.2 million that puts the cap rate at 11.9. That's a very close number to what my other executive suite center operated at when I purchased it. I already know that formula works wonderfully, so I feel very comfortable if this scenario could be achieved. Furthermore I really didn't use any of my own down money to buy this deal which makes it even sweeter than any existing deal I've done before.

How many people have bought a $4.2 million building with no money down? I'm sure someone has done it before, but I'm not aware of one. Maybe that would be a good title for a new book. How I bought a $4.2 million building with none of my own money down. I might buy a book like that. That's what I love about the commercial real estate business. There's no limit to the amount of creativity that you can use to get a deal done. I use my personality and salesmanship along with the expertise I have in real estate to figure out a way where everybody wins, and I end up in this scenario as an extremely rich man. I envision myself in the future having a real estate portfolio north of eight figures, and in a rising market I make more money in equity in one year by managing my portfolio than most people could ever make in a lifetime.

CHAPTER 21

The Anatomy of a Commercial Deal

Breaking down the process of a commercial deal starts with knowing what you want to buy in the first place. You will probably never know that until you go out and look at a bunch of properties anyway, so it's kind of like a chicken before the egg scenario. Once you've made the decision about what type of real estate you're going to invest in, get right into it with the owner of the building. I'll take a look at a piece of real estate without meeting the owner first, but I prefer he or she be there the day I look at it so I can immediately begin dissecting the opportunity before me. Commercial deals don't happen quickly if they're going to happen at all, but if we're talking about the anatomy of a commercial deal, let's get right down to the heart of the matter. The heart of the patient or the heart of the commercial deal lies in your ability to negotiate with the owner of that property. So get started as soon as possible talking with him or her about the opportunity in front of you.

WE LIKE TO THINK OF US AS OLD FASHIONED!

WHEN YOU WANT THAT PERSONAL TOUCH THAT YOU GET FROM A PERSON ANSWERING YOUR CALLS. CALL US (866) 296-8405

Don't get discouraged if your first meeting doesn't go well, as many times I think you'll find they don't. One time I went to look at a diner in the Pocono Mountains of Pennsylvania with an investor friend of mind who intended to buy it. He asked me to go along for the ride and advise him of my opinions afterward. The owner was arrogant and began to get frustrated as we asked him question after question about his building and his mortgage and every other thing he didn't think was our business. His levels of aggravation grew to the point where we got up and walked out of the building. At the time we left the building, the price for his diner with everything in it was $2.1 million. He had roughly at the end taken the attitude that we could take it or leave it, and we kindly said we would leave it.

With a 2 1/2 hour ride home, I told my friend that in my humble opinion the facility was worth somewhere around $1.6 million give or take $100,000. By the time we had gotten back to the Philadelphia area, we stopped by my friend's office to see three voice mails from the diner owner with the last message naming a number of $1.7 million. We got quite a few laughs out of that voice mail, and we decided to ignore him for a week or two just to let him sweat it out. I had mostly negative things to say about the property and business deal that my friend mostly agreed with. He never did follow through with any further meetings, nor did he ever attempt to purchase the diner. I think my friend just lost interest in the diner after that day. That happens sometimes, especially to commercial real estate investors as another deal always comes down the road and takes the interest away from the first one.

The owner of the diner seriously misread the situation on the day we came up to talk to him. He knew we drove 2.5 hours to see him, so that should have proved we were serious and it also should send an alarm off in his head that he had this chance and this chance only to make this agreement happen. Watching him handle himself in this meeting was not a complete waste of time. Everything he did can always serve as a bad example. Needless to say, it was a good learning experience, as sometimes the best move in a negotiation is to get up and walk out the door. While

I admit it could lose a deal for you, it also can be a strong move if it's done at the right time in the right place.

Another technique that I like to use when negotiating a commercial deal is that I tried to get as much of the deal as I possibly can discussed and agreed upon verbally before I go to the lawyers to draft a contract. There's nothing I hate more than spending money to draft a contract with an attorney only to find out that the deal is not going to happen. It's a colossal waste of time and money, so you want to try to avoid it at all possibilities. Furthermore, if you spend the time to negotiate every little thing with the guy, you're going to get to know him well enough to give you a terrific sense of whether this deal will ever make it to settlement. Get right to the heart of the matter and start talking to the owner and keep talking as long as it takes.

I've often had to tell realtors who were involved in a commercial deal and just wouldn't get out of the way that at this stage of the negotiation they are not needed. I have nothing against realtors as I am one, but a listing agent for a commercial piece of real estate is going to bring very little service to a guy like me after twenty years in the business. I want to deal directly with the owner and get the answer straight from him or her. A good commercial realtor will try to get in the way of that, but you must overcome that obstacle.

Another line I've used many times and hope I don't have to continue to use it is when the realtor tells me that I can't meet the owner. I can't even tell the story without laughing, as it happened to me more times than I can remember. I would raise my voice and say, "Do you really think that I would spend $2 million for this building without meeting the man selling it?" When it's tried on you, just make sure that the realtor knows that there is no way you would accept not meeting the principal individuals involved.

As I think back about the best deals I've done, I'm most proud of the ones I was patient on. I worked a year and a half on the 1600 Building. I probably worked six months on Executec Suites.

Bucks County Suites, which I'm hoping to have closed in a few days, has been a work in process for a year and a half. I took a lot of time off in between meetings. So take your time and have fun negotiating the deal you're trying to buy and don't ever fall in love with a piece of real estate. I probably learned just as much from the deals I didn't buy as the deals I did, so don't get too crazy about any particular deal. You'll be learning as you go negotiating one deal after another, developing this skill you can't really learn in school. Negotiating commercial real estate is learned in the school of hard knocks in a world of entrepreneurs, and they don't give degrees at the end. What they give you is much better than any degree you will ever get. What they give you is a multimillion dollar income-producing building.

CHAPTER 22

The Thin Line between Success and Failure

I think it's pretty clear as you read some of these stories about the commercial deals I've worked on that the line between success and failure is so thin it's practically invisible. As I look back on my career up to this point, I think I've taken too many chances and rolled the dice too many times. I also think if I hadn't taken those chances and rolled the dice I would've never bought the buildings I own and worked out the deals I currently have. So how do you go about doing something that is in its nature incredibly risky but somehow make it safe? Maybe you can hire people like me to look at your deals to help you analyze exactly how crazy they really are. Maybe you should hire a lot of people like me who come from different areas of real estate expertise and get as many opinions as you possibly can on each deal you look at. But from a practical standpoint, every new person you bring in will increase your costs as you should pay these people to assist you. Not only are you increasing your expenses but you're creating a lot of exposure on your deal. When I'm working on a commercial deal, I treat it the way World War II sailors would treat the secrets about their ship. They would say that loose lips sink ships. So I usually keep my mouth shut about any deal I am working on. Even my most trusted friends will know that when I am working on a deal they won't know the address or specific location of the building. If I tell one of my most trusted friends any specific details of the building, I don't think that they would reveal this information to harm me, but they might discuss it with someone who would.

People love to present themselves in a way that they're more than they really are. Everyone wants to pretend like he knows more than he really does, especially when it comes to rich people and big deals. I learned this early in my engineering career when I worked for this Philadelphia bakery equipment company. The owner of the bakery equipment business was a real player, and his hands were in all kinds of things with about seventy employees working for him. When I was training to become a salesman and when I was a salesman, I had a lot of exposure to him, and I had a lot of inside knowledge about the deals he was working on.

You would think that people would ask me about these things, but they very rarely ever did. Much to my surprise, what they did was try to tell me what was going on with the deals, and most of the time everything they said was completely wrong. Maybe it gave them a sense of importance when they could go around and talk about the direction the company was going and the ideas that the president had. Since most of the people they were talking to had no idea they were wrong, the cycle just continued. I suppose it's just human nature that people want to feel important and want to become something they are not.

The point is to be aware of the thin line and how invisible it may be. As I look at some of the moves I have made just a few short years ago I am not so sure I will be able to make these same kinds of moves again. As you have more success in life you also have more to lose. The older we get the more careful we become. If you are too careful in this business you may never take the chances needed to really achieve something amazing.

CHAPTER 23

What Is an Executive Suite Center?

There are many special characteristics that make a regular office building into an executive suite center. The first thing is that the size of the building would have to be a minimum of 12,000 sq. ft. This concept just doesn't work in a small building under that size because one-third of the building will be used just for hallways, reception area, and kitchen areas. When you take away all the common space, you are not left with much to work with. If you took a minimum size of 12,000 sq. ft., you could probably chop it up into forty-five offices of different sizes. The best possible layout you could ever make is forty-five different offices of different configurations, shapes, and sizes. Having a variety of offices to show your new tenants will be priceless in your success, and having many options for your existing tenants to move into as their business changes will be equally as powerful. The layout of the offices will be obvious to you based on things like the location of the windows, outside doors, and other permanent fixtures in the building. After your layout is done, take the drawing of the building into each individual office and leave no stone unturned. By figuring out the most logical place to put the furniture, you can then determine the location of your internet, telephone, and electrical receptacles. This is important as it relates to the furniture because you don't want wires all over the place in the office. Nothing looks worse in a beautiful office with gorgeous furniture than twenty wires running all along the walls and floors. The location of the outlets is critical to hiding the wires for all the required devices the office will need.

With so many offices, you could never have individual control in every office when it comes to heating and cooling. You cannot spend enough time thinking through the HVAC system design to ensure consistent temperatures from office to office. Even if you did a perfect job, humans will still like it hotter or colder and constant adjustment of thermostats will always be in your future.

Conference rooms should be positioned as close to the receptionist area as possible so that visitors are not walking all around your building during the day. It's also easier for the receptionist to walk visitors back as well as clean up after them when the meeting is over. I always want my receptionist to go into a conference room after a big meeting and straighten it up. My obsessive compulsive disorder requires all the chairs to be positioned in the right way with the height adjusted equally so that the arms of the chairs slide nicely under the table instead of bumping into the side of the table. Can you imagine how crazy I could make you if you worked for me?

The phone equipment used in an executive suite center is special to the industry and designed specifically for that type of building. The first thing you have to understand is you may have two hundred different phone numbers ringing into the building at any given time. So how does one deal with all those different phone numbers? We have a program that identifies the calls as they come into the building. The program identifies the call as it comes into the building and a screen pops up on the computer telling the receptionist exactly how to answer the call. She simply has to follow the instructions on the screen and then deal with the call accordingly. All of the individuals who work for a company will have an icon on the screen with their names on it. By clicking on the icon, the receptionist automatically comes up through the speakerphone in the person's office to announce the calls and allow the tenant to screen the call. If the tenant is not in the building, the receptionist can patch the call to an outside cell phone or home phone. To the client calling the tenant, it'll sound like he is in the office even if he's home sleeping on the couch.

This service of answering calls from people and patching it to them is a great value to new perspective clients. We have what we call virtual tenants in our building. Virtual tenants are people who use the building in one way or another who don't actually reside in the facility. We charge $99 a month for our answering service, and we have about thirty-five people who do not reside in the building who use the service monthly. It does a great deal to help individuals' image when they use the virtual answering service. It sounds like they are a larger company than they really are, and it puts the clients at ease knowing that when they call they reach an actual human being.

One of the worst things that can happen when you own an executive suite center is the telephones or the Internet going down. If the power goes down, both of these things go out simultaneously. Have you ever had one hundred people coming after you at the same time to rip your head off because their business telephones aren't working? You haven't lived till you've gone through that a couple times. I have never lost a tenant, at least none that I know about, because of the telephones or Internet going down, but it certainly has been a major source of stress for me as the owner of this kind of building.

I spent an immense amount of money, time, and energy to make sure that this type of thing would never happen. My telephones and Internet requires constant changes to keep up with technology and constant improvements to ensure redundancy. To avoid power outage issues, constant upgrading of battery sources and backup devices make sure everything from your databases to your phone voicemails are saved properly in the event of a catastrophe.

Another service we provide to virtual tenants is to rent conference rooms for $25 an hour. We have a few of our virtual tenants as well as a few individuals who don't use the building for anything other than the conference rooms. The people work on the road or from home, but once a quarter they need a place to have an actual meeting. They can call our receptionist and reserve the time with a credit card. We don't earn a great deal of money this way, but it tends to be a steppingstone into other virtual services. And those other virtual services tend to be a steppingstone for virtual tenants to become actual tenants.

And that, my friends, is a terrific way to fill a building. I'm giving you pearls here, so I hope you're paying attention.

The other virtual service we provide is mailbox rentals. These mailboxes don't look any different than the post-office boxes many people all over the country rent except for one big difference. A post office box says PO on it. Everyone knows it's a post office box. My addresses look like real addresses and that helps the image look more professional. At the post office, people have to go there every day to check their mail, but in our executive suite center, you can simply call and ask the receptionist if you have any mail. If you do, she can open it for you and fax it to you or scan it and e-mail it to you. She can also drop it in an envelope and mail it to you or overnight you a package once a week. We have people in Arizona rent mailboxes from us because they want to present the image that they have an office in Pennsylvania. In one case, we have an accountant in Arizona who flies in several weeks a year during tax season to see all her Pennsylvania clients. Every year they meet in the same building, ours, and they hear us answer our phones twelve months a year patching the calls to her in Arizona. They also know all of her mail goes to our location completing the image of her working from this location regardless where she actually resides.

The mailbox area itself has to be designed in a way where individuals who are virtual tenants can come in and grab their mail from the box and have a place to sit down and open it. We also use this area as a way for tenants to network with one another as it tends to be a gathering location. Furthermore, we allow tenants to put business cards on their mailboxes, which tend to develop networking in the building, which is a great thing for a landlord like me. Just think of it like this. I do business with the people who do business with my business. If I can get people in my building to do business with other people in my building, it strengthens relationships and makes them feel more comfortable and more at home. If they feel that way, hopefully they will both stay a long time, and now this is the reason to promote as much networking as possible in an executive suite center.

The reception area is a place you should spare no expense to make sure it looks as professional and classy as possible. Your clients are the tenants, and their clients will be waiting in the lobby too, so its appearance needs to be second to none. It is also designed in a way where the receptionist up front can control the visitors who come into the building so that they don't just wander through the place without being properly announced to your tenants. We also have television in the lobby for the tenants and receptionists enjoyment. I don't mind providing a television for receptionists to watch since they answer eight thousand phone calls a month. Anything I can do to make their lives a little easier and their job a little more bearable is something I strive to do.

Your tenants are going to expect to have twenty-four hour a day seven days a week access to an executive suites center. A great way to do that is utilizing electronic key fobs to open the doors after hours. I spent $7000 on a key fobs system that also controls electronic locks on the doors. We have three doors in my building, two that I locked all the time and one that is the front door. The side doors are used by the tenants only who have key fobs that they wave in front of the door and it unlocks. The front door is a little more complicated as a computer program opens and closes the door lock mechanism daily. Between the hours of nine to five Monday through Friday the front door is unlocked allowing visitors to freely walk in and be greeted by the receptionist. After hours the door automatically locks allowing only tenants who have key fobs to get into the building. When you rent an office to a tenant each key fob is $30 each. Sometimes the client will come in with four employee's total, and I am charging $120 for the fobs.

We also sold these to all of our existing tenants with very little static or complaints. Some people didn't like paying the money for the key fobs, but they liked the security. Prior to having this system we had a pushbutton mechanism, but the code could be given out to anybody, so it wasn't exactly very safe. Now if the tenant is in the building late at night and hears the door open, he or she can feel comfortable that that person has an authorized key fob. If a tenant's employee becomes disgruntled or a tenant doesn't pay the rent, I simply deactivate his key fob. It beats hell out of the eviction process that I used to do. I never bothered to figure out if it's legal or not as we really haven't had to deal with an eviction situation in the office business yet. We do have issues collecting money but not like we do in the residential real estate. Financially speaking, after selling key fobs to all the current tenants and to all the new tenants coming into the building, we recouped the $7000 investment in about two years. That timeframe is certainly an acceptable payback in my opinion.

The printer, copier, and scanner we have is leased for approximately $300 a month. This device has a digital screen that allows a tenant to put in a code before using a digital copier. It also prints a report every month that allows us to charge the tenants for using the copier, and we charge a rate of $.13 per copy. We charge five cents for every page that was scanned. These figures are calculated monthly and put on a separate bill we call the amenities invoice. The tenants would be billed for rent every month due on the first, and then they would receive an amenities bill that would have other things on it such as use of the printer, copier, and scanner, outgoing phone calls, secretarial services, UPS shipping that they may send out on our account, and many other things. By charging for the printer, we generally turn a profit on this device as we have a captured audience in our building that will usually not lease their own printer because we already have one there. Creating additional profit centers beyond the rent is a way to make your business really successful. The printer, copier, and scanner is also attached through the Internet to every office in the building. Anyone could drop a document in the scanner, and it would show up as an e-mail on his computer regardless of what office he was in or he could print from his computer to a printer when large packages need to be produced. If the client did large quantities of printing, say about $500 per month, the price of that printing per page would be reduced.

Another profit center in an executive suite center is the usage of the outgoing phone system. To set up a phone system in a large building, the cost can be as high six figures when you own hundreds of phones and all the equipment necessary to support it. The expenses on the phone side might consist of $1500 a month in the usage charges as well as a monthly fee required to pay off the cost of the actual phone equipment. The way to recoup this cost is by charging your tenants for all their outgoing phone calls on the pricing structure that you can get reimbursed for all of these costs and make a few bucks for yourself. All of these profit centers put together increase revenue including things like vending machines that you obviously can mark up at a rate of about four to one. Put them all together in addition to forty-seven offices to rent and you've got yourself a profitable business. The price per square foot you can obtain in an executive suite center is the highest I've ever seen. I have a building with 12,500 sq. ft. providing a gross income of $40,000 per month. Some of the offices price per square foot exceeds $70 a square foot in an area where traditional office space would rent for more like $15 a square foot. But of course, you have to take into consideration all the extra benefits that the small company gets in my type of building as opposed to a conventional building.

Nothing looks worse to prospective clients coming to your building and seeing five people out front smoking cigarettes. Nothing looks worse than having cigarette butts thrown on the ground, even though there's a cigarette smoking pot nearby. It's become somewhat of a pet peeve for me as I worked so hard to make the building look beautiful, and I have to go out and clean up trash and cigarette butts all the time. The only way I can think of to get around this problem is to design somewhere in your building an area surrounded by shrubs or fencing where cigarette smokers can go without destroying the integrity of the building.

Offering secretarial services to be performed by the receptionist for a rate of $35 an hour is another thing I've done to make money from this kind of business. After all, your receptionists are sitting there all day answering phones, and they will have down time so you might as well figure out a way to make some money off of it. We offer secretarial services to people who may need somebody five to ten hours a week, and it's a hell of a lot cheaper to hire us for a few hours than it is to hire somebody specifically for that task.

Another good idea to consider is developing a community area near the front of the building that I would call a cyber bar. A cyber bar could be used for people who need a place to hang their hat for a few hours a day but don't want the expense of an office. The cyber bar would have nice chairs and be lovely, but it would actually be in the middle of the hallway in your building that would allow them a place to plug in a lap top and access the Internet while they do some work. It could also be used as a place where tenants can begin to meet each other and to do business with one another. For example, say a new stockbroker moves into your building. Suggest to him that he hosts a free lunch for all the other tenants in the building at the site by the bar. He will get to meet everybody, talk about his business, and hopefully make some contacts with individuals in the building and vice versa. Some people have tried to make this kind of thing a private room along the lines of a hangout place, such as a Starbucks coffee shop. I know other building owners who've called it a touchdown zone or focus booth. It can also be used in a capacity where an existing actual tenant may have a part-time bookkeeper who could utilize the touchdown zone for a few hours a week at an extra cost to your actual tenant. For outside tenants who want to come in a few hours a day to use a common area like a focus booth, I would simply negotiate for a cheap but fair price to use the space.

CHAPTER 24

The Simplicity of Real Estate

People always ask me how to get started in commercial real estate. I usually tell him the same thing I've been saying for years, "Call the signs." Call the signs is the usual response. Call any signs you happen to be driving passed down the highway on your way to work tomorrow morning. Start making inquiries into the buildings you are most familiar with that you drive passed every day. Usually I'll hear a series of objections about "I don't have that kind of money" or "I don't know what to do." That's when I reach over to grab them by the ear and twist it and say, "Just call the signs." Your odds of success dramatically improve with each attempt. You don't need to be a genius to purchase commercial real estate. What you need is a backbone and half a brain as you call the signs. All the opportunity in the world is waiting right there for you as you drive back and forth to work every day right passed the signs for the commercial buildings on the highway.

Another objection I hear often is "I don't want to be deceiving people," and "I don't want to pretend to buy a building that I have no intention of buying." My answer has always been how do you know you're deceiving them and how do you know you have no intention of buying it if you haven't even taken the time to go see the building and the owner. When you talk to an owner, anything can happen. Just maybe you're capable of negotiating no money down 100 percent financing to acquire this building, or perhaps after you look at it, you find out it's a perfect location for someone you know. Maybe the owner of the building has been trying to sell for years, and he's upside down on his mortgage making it impossible for him to sell. When you find this information out it's a perfect scenario for lease option. Maybe he's tired of trying to rent this building, but he's involved in too many other things. Offer him a deal where you lease the building from him for minimal costs and retain the right to purchase it for years to come as you put effort into the building to rent it up. He will ultimately get his carrying costs money for the mortgage taxes and insurance, and you get to keep the profits. You don't need a lot of money to do this, and you don't need to be a rocket scientist. You need to have some guts and the ability to use creative thinking to make your dreams come true. It starts by finding out what the seller needs and then trying to figure if what you need and he needs works together to form a perfect marriage. It's easier than you think it will be so just go out and make it happen. Call the signs!

Once when I was doing a public speaking engagement to a commercial real estate group, I told the crowd to call the signs. More than that, I told the crowd that it was their homework assignment to call the signs. More than that, I told the crowd that next time I came around I wanted to hear from each and every one of them about their experiences when they called the signs.

What is really stopping people from buying commercial real estate? Most people drive by these large office buildings and think that the person who owns that building must be incredibly intelligent or born with a silver spoon in his mouth to be able to buy such an amazing building. Maybe he's an extremely successful individual whose family has been rich for a hundred years. Maybe he's an experienced realtor who gets the properties before the rest of us know about them. Maybe they come from a family of builders who constructed the building for 20 percent the cost of what it will cost me to buy it, and I certainly can't compete with that. In my opinion, while this may be true in some cases, for the most part these are just excuses.

In my life I've found the complete opposite in most scenarios when it comes to owners of large buildings. The people I've met are gutsy people and maybe even a little crazy. I've always in my life tried to take the negative things about me and turn them into positives, and that's what a lot of these people do when they're a little crazy. Maybe I'm a little crazy. Crazy people aren't afraid to try things because everyone they know already thinks they are crazy so what do they have to lose. If you take a long hard look at successful people you've meet in your life I bet you more than half of them are a little nuts. Nutty people take chances that a rational individual may never take.

The last engineering job I had before I became a salesman was for a bakery equipment company in Philadelphia. The guy who owned the business fancied himself a brilliant man and a great salesman. Sometimes he was every bit of those things and more, and at times he was also a complete fool. He was a real egomaniac so filled with himself that from time to time he would spend so much energy telling his workers how stupid they were he was only making a fool of himself. I saw this guy during sales presentations do things that if I had done them he would have fired me on the spot. He did things like showing up unprepared for sales meetings and then sending me as I sat in a meeting with him to run off and get a drawing or go get this or go get that. This was a sales call that he set up, and I was only there to assist him and to learn and mostly keep my mouth shut. If I had gone to a sales meeting without all the proper drawings and information available to do a professional presentation for a customer, he would've strung me up by my toenails. The guy was very intelligent and successful and also a little crazy.

My point is a completely rational individual would probably never have the guts to start a company the way he did and the determination to make it work the way he did. Maybe crazy people have no choice. They can't control their emotions long enough to work for somebody else, and they know it whether they're willing to admit it or not. I felt a little bit like that when I was younger. Feeling like I could try to pretend to be something I'm not, but sooner or later there were enough opportunities for them to find out who I really was—a guy who thought outside the box and liked to do things his own way.

My point to all of this is real estate entrepreneurs who own commercial buildings are by definition mavericks in their industry. If a guy owns a building worth $5 million, he must've gone through some pretty amazing hoops in life to make that happen. My guess would be the odds were in your favor that you would find this individual to be a very aggressive and clever outside the box kind of guy who's a little crazy. So don't be afraid to call the signs and take chances. If you really want to be a commercial real estate investor, sooner or later you're going to have to take a significant portion of your net worth and roll the dice. Sooner or later you're going to have to get a little crazy.

CHAPTER 25
Every Time I Deviate

If I look back on the mistakes that I've made over the course of twenty years, there's a similarity between them all. Every time I deviated from the area or strategy that I'm familiar with is generally when I made a mistake. Always thinking there's a better easier way to make money in real estate and deviating from your current strategy is the step we all have to take. I'm a big supporter of the real estate investor who learns every type of investment strategy available to use. I'm merely leaving you with a warning to be careful when you deviate from your current philosophy as this is usually when a screw-up will occur.

PART 3

Core Beliefs of a Full-Time Real Estate Investor

CHAPTER 26

Buy-and-Hold in a Rising Market

When people ask what kind of investor I am, I always say I'm a buy-and-hold investor. The truth is I haven't purchased a piece of real estate for buy-and-hold reasons since 2006. But that's because I don't buy real estate to hold in a falling market. I think the easiest way to get rich slow in the real estate market place is through the buy-and-hold process, but the market needs to be moving in an upward direction. I'm a firm believer that buy-and-hold investors work their tails off maintaining their real estate for very little profit. Regardless of what they will tell you, the real money in real estate is made from riding the cycle from bottom to top.

So if you believe what I'm saying above is true, then you don't want to be acquiring properties for a buy-and-hold strategy in a flat or declining market. You want to wait until the market has rebounded and values are moving in an upward direction before you start acquiring buy-and-hold properties in quantity. This is especially true if you're an experienced investor like me. We have the ability to buy many properties in one year as opposed to buying one per year. If you have the means and the knowledge to do so, you can wait until the market is clearly in an up surging direction and then aggressively acquire as many buildings as you can in a short period of time.

But I know that not everyone can do that, so to those people I say make the goal of buying one property a year. I would also say they don't need to wait until the market is surging upward to start buying. I am telling those individuals now, today, they should get started buying. As I write this book in early 2010, we are in a flat market, but if you're acquiring property slowly, it will make little to no difference. If a new investor is ready to get started now, I see little reason to wait if you're only going to buy one or two properties in the next twelve months. If you're an experienced investor and ready to buy six or eight a year, then I suggest that you wait until market conditions are in a rising position.

CHAPTER 27
Liquidate at Peak

One of the hardest things you'll ever have to do as a real estate investor is sell your properties at the top. If you're anything like me, you become very attached to the properties you own, and in many ways they become like your babies. I've worked hard for my buildings; converting them into the kind of properties I could be proud of today. It's not so easy to turn around and sell them just because it's the right time to let them go, but that's what the smart investor needs to do when you've determined we are at the top of the market. You shouldn't have to worry about this problem until around 2022, so I wouldn't lose sleep over it, but be aware that when the time is right you'll need to sell. Knowing that is very important, as it will affect the decisions you make as you own the building as far as what kind of money you're putting into it and what kind of longevity you're expecting to get from each improvement.

Timing the market is critical, and that's what I'm talking about here. Buying at the right time is terrific, but selling at the right time is even more important, and you need to understand that the best deals you will ever make in life are the ones you bought at the right time and sold at the right time. So the preparation of selling at the top is something you should be thinking about for years before you get there. By the time you get there, you should have your real estate license, especially if you're planning to sell an entire portfolio of buildings you own. Your real estate license will save you 3 percent of every building you sell. If you liquidate your entire portfolio over the course of a year or two at the top of the market and your portfolio is worth $5 million, then you saved yourself $150,000. With your real estate license costing around $1200 a year, you've justified the expense for three lifetimes. So now what do we do with all this money you are about to inherit? A 1031 tax exchange program into commercial real estate is my advice.

CHAPTER 28

What Do You Do with All That Equity?

Numerous times in this book I've discussed the 1031 tax exchange program and how I used it to convert capital gains without paying taxes. When you're able to do it and it works, it's the greatest feeling ever, and when you cant it's like getting kicked in the stomach by Uncle Sam. I've had large 1031 exchanges from four residential buildings when I bought Executec Suites that worked wonderfully, and other large 1031s I was forced to pay taxes on during the 1600 Building project. I think it's impossible to believe that you could convert every dime of capital gains money through the 1031 program into commercial real estate successfully. If somebody were able to do that, I'd be concerned that they were buying commercial real estate they maybe shouldn't have bought. As you read through the examples of the commercial real estate deals I worked on, you can see that I only ended up buying maybe one out of every five commercial real estate deals I worked on. Maybe I set my sites too high on properties that were too large, and my success rate for conversion would be better if I chose smaller commercial real estate such as an eight-unit apartment building. That's all fine and dandy if you want to end up owning a group of eight-unit apartment buildings. My dreams were bigger than that as I was chasing much larger properties primarily in the office arena. I am out there trying to hit the home run, and when you do that you often strike out.

I like to think simple, and that's the way I have to analyze real estate. You have to think simply what does this building bring in and what will this building cost and in the end of the day what will be left for me. I also want to own buildings that are going to last for decades beyond me, so I think a lot about my own immortality and how my son would feel about owning this building fifty years from now.

I also think about how my family would feel about working at this building. Is it in the neighborhood where I would want my wife and son to be spending their time? I often think of what type of business would be in this building? Would it be the kind of business that somebody would rob? Would it be the kind of business that somebody would come and stick a gun in your face? That certainly could be true in a piece of retail real estate in a questionable urban neighborhood.

"Either you don't know how to do something or you choose not to do something. There is no CAN'T!"

~ MARSHALL SYLVER

As I said earlier these are all things to consider as you don't want the greatest investment of your life to turn out to be your biggest nightmare. You want it to be a monument to your success in life. It's an amazing feeling of accomplishment when you've reached a point in your life where managing your portfolio is all you'll have to do, and your intelligent commercial real estate purchases along with your management of that real estate that allowed you to be in a position of comfort to live such a life. I hope one day this book will help you to be in that position.

CHAPTER 29

Flipping Is Not Investing

One of the things I'm preaching in this book is to buy and hold only in a rising market. But what do you do in a flat market? One of the things I recommend is to do flips in a flat market, but only if you need the money. If you have a job and you have sufficient income coming in to earn a living, then I wouldn't even bother. It's a good way to earn some extra income and learn about the real estate business, but it is not real estate investing. If you are doing it to earn extra money to raise a down payment to purchase a buy-and-hold piece of real estate, that makes sense to me. To me flipping is no different than if I went out and got a job making X amount of dollars for a certain period of time to help pay some bills or whatever I had at the time. If you have a need for that then it makes all the sense in the world, but if you have sufficient cash flow in your life, then I think that plan is not right for you.

If you have sufficient income and a down payment, I would suggest you start purchasing properties, one a year, and ride the cycle from bottom to top. It's the easiest way to make $1 million that I know of and something that I plan to do over and over again in my life in every upward climbing real estate cycle until the grave. For a full-time real estate investor a flat market is a wonderful time to make a few bucks by doing some flips and simultaneously learning more about the real estate market. If you're a beginner and you happen to be starting in this business in a flat market, then I would advocate buying one home a year minimum as a way of getting into the business. What I do in a flat market is flip only when I need the money and look for deals such as cash-flowing commercial properties that I can buy for a song. I don't need to start buying properties for a buy-and-hold strategy in a flat market because I know how to acquire them in large quantities quickly.

I'm going to sit back and wait until I'm absolutely certain the market has begun to return to positive increases each year. Then I will go on an aggressive buying spree acquiring many homes a year for several years until I've built up a substantial portfolio that I feel I can manage from afar with people to help me whose salaries are paid for by the profit from those properties. I will have to spend time managing these properties when I have a much larger portfolio of residential homes, but it will generate sufficient cash flow to support itself entirely. What will probably be left over for me is a small insignificant salary to call my own. The real payback will be in the year 2022 when I dump all thirty-six properties for $2 million in equity.

New legislation was recently approved that extends the First-Time Homebuyer Credit for homeowners through April 30, 2010, with a sixty-day cushion beyond that date to complete closing. The program broadens benefits to existing homeowners and now includes:

- $8,000 tax credit for first-time homebuyers
- $6,500 tax credit for existing homebuyers who have lived in their current residence for at least five years but want to relocate to a new primary residence.
- Increased income limits for individuals and couples

This puts time limitations on one's ability to do flips. The original first-time homebuyer's tax credit of $8000 was scheduled to end in November of 2009. I was deeply concerned when I saw the rush of buyers in September, October, and November hurrying out to take advantage of the $8000 tax credit before the program ran out. People have a tendency to be procrastinators, and clearly that was happening in the fourth quarter of last year. I thought with the program ending in November it probably made sense to let it die there. Winter around here is always usually a pretty dead real estate market anyway, and spring usually gives it a jump. By extending the program to April as you see above creates a false peak where every person who has any ability to buy a house will beg, borrow, and steal to get money to purchase before the deadline comes. I think it's reasonable to expect that after the deadline everybody who had any chance of buying a home in the first three quarters of 2010 will be long gone and had already done their deal. I fear that whenever this program stops—and sooner or later it's going to have to end—the market will experience an extremely dead zone. If I'm correct and the dead zone is coming no matter when this program ends, I suppose I'd rather just get it over with now and return to a normal market as soon as possible.

I know some people today who seem to have a problem with the word *flipping*. Apparently for them it conjures up an image of a scam or sales trick that the investor's doing. The word *sales* also has a stigma associated with it as people seem to think that if salesman is on your business card you're some kind of moron. I think nothing could be further from the truth. Sales and salesmanship abilities are key elements in the success of the real estate entrepreneur. I happen to think salesmanship ability is one of the strongest attributes you could ever have in the real estate business and definitely one of the skills that most commonly overlooked. As for people putting a bad karma on the word *flipping*, I say consider this. It's usually the people who aren't real estate investors who have a problem with the word in the first place, so I always tell them not to use words they really don't understand. If the word *flipping* bothers you so much, stick to something you know about. Just remember, flipping is not real estate investing.

CHAPTER 30

Falling Market, Go Fishing

In a falling real estate market, you don't want to be buying real estate. It's totally appropriate to be selling real estate. You want to try to predict when the market is going to fall and start selling before or into that falling market. Don't be worried that you're going to already be too late because you won't be if you move quickly. Unlike the stock market when the real estate market crashes, it happens very slowly, and the only people who know about it in the first six months are the professionals in the business. Newspapers and the general public are usually far behind in understanding what is going on. So if you just pay attention to real estate cycles, you will be able to time the market with a certain degree of accuracy. I knew as 2005 approached that the party was over and the real estate market was going to begin to fall. I started selling buildings in 2005 and continued the next three years until I've gotten rid of all the buildings I wanted to give up at that time. Of course, the buildings I sold in 2005 were sold at the highest possible prices, and the ones in 2006 were sold 5 or 10 percent less. The buildings I sold in 2007 were sold at an additional 5 or 10 percent less, but I still made out rather well on all of them. In hindsight, I would've made the largest amount of money if I dumped them all at once, but then I would have missed out on one of the greatest advantages available to a commercial real estate investor. Of course, I'm talking about the 1031 government exchange program.

If I dumped all the buildings I sold over three years in one shot at the top of 2005, I probably would've made an additional $50,000 to $100,000, but I also would've paid maybe that much in capital gains taxes, so in the end I think it was probably a wash. I think the lesson I learned is you could stretch yourselves out over three years and try to 1031 the money to other buildings or you could just dump them all when you're certain you're at the top.

You'll probably end up pretty close to the amount of money you made regardless of which approach you take. I've had about half the deals I tried to 1031 work and half of them not work. It's easy to say you should dump all your buildings, but when you put so much time and energy into them, I think you'll find it's pretty difficult to do. Next time around at the top of the cycle, I think I'll move quicker and just dump them all. Hopefully, they'll be such a large figure to earn I won't even care so much about the capital gains tax.

So my advice in a falling market is to sell your buildings at the beginning of this falling cycle and to try to find worthwhile projects to 1031 your money into. You have to expect that those projects will also drop in value, but the cash flow from commercial deals can be much more powerful than any residential deal you've ever seen. If you can't find the proper buildings to 1031 the money into them, go fishing. I mean go fishing for that perfect piece of real estate until you find it. Call the signs on every commercial building in your designated investment area, and I guarantee you something will happen. That's what I mean by going fishing, but if that plan doesn't suit you, I have an alternate plan. The alternate plan is to go fishing literally. When I say to go fishing literally, I mean doing nothing from an investment standpoint. Take some time and enjoy your life and the large amount of money you cashed in on and use it to buy back the same buildings you sold or similar buildings to it at sheriff sales for $.60 on the dollar what you sold them for. Sit on the money for years until you see the rising market begin to come back and aggressively go out and purchase properties. Of course, my advice is going to be using the money to buy real estate because I don't feel comfortable being an expert in any other area of financial investment. You may have skills that I don't have that will allow you to find other avenues to purchase such as gold or stocks. At this point in my life, I believe my investment strategies will be nothing but bricks and mortar. I think you will learn that as your second cycle approaches, you will be much more prepared to purchase large quantities of properties in a short period of time.

CHAPTER 31

The Accumulation of Property

During a rising market, I know of no better way to get rich through the accumulation of property—if you believe as I do that acquiring as many properties as possible while the real estate market increases in value is a terrific way to increase your net worth exponentially. As I write this book in the year 2010, the real estate market is clearly flat in the middle Bucks County, Pennsylvania, where I generally operate. I believe that after the elections of the Senate in particular in November of 2010 the Democrats should lose many seats. We should know by August of 2010 if it looks like that's going to happen, and if it will, I will begin to accumulate properties anticipating an increase in real estate values in the years 2011 going forward.

I would not buy stock in a corporation if I didn't think the value of that stock was going to go up, so why would I purchase properties without thinking the real estate market was going to be on the move upward. For the newbie out there who's probably not going to buy more than one property a year, it makes sense to get started now, but for the experienced investor with the ability to purchase many properties in a short period of time, I still think you need to wait. I am waiting to get really aggressive in the fall of 2010 or later.

It doesn't really matter when you get started as 2010 will be at best the beginning of an upward cycle. At worst I'm wrong and we continue on a flat market for a few more years, which won't hurt me in any way. If you begin in late 2010 and start accumulating properties until the top of the cycle, you could be looking at a fifteen-year commitment to your real estate portfolio. As your portfolio gets larger and larger, it won't be easy to manage so many buildings. Especially if you have a full-time job that you want to continue doing, you're going to find it to be quite a hassle. It's been my experience that a dozen properties is not that difficult to manage in your spare time, but once you start going north of that number, it gets very difficult. If you make it to two dozen properties, you're going to notice a distinct difference from a dozen and an enormous amount of your time is going to be needed to be spent taking care of your new business.

People always tell me that when they get to that level they're going to hire a property manager who is going to handle all the problems that this business presents. That's the standard line that gurus tell you when they're trying to get you excited about the package they're selling that's going to make you millions of dollars by sometime next year. It also sounds like such a wonderful strategy, but the reality of it is it's bull. I am not saying it's impossible, but if you think your business is going to run smoothly while you ignore it and sip cocktails by the pool, you are only kidding yourself.

What is possible is that you would manage the portfolio with as little involvement as possible if you build a good team of people around you. For years I have relied on my younger brother Matthew to do a great deal of maintenance on my buildings. Sometimes when we do flips, Matt and I work side by side together to renovate the properties, but mostly he works independently running around on a part-time basis taking care of the issues at hand. Over the years with my help as well as independent real estate projects that he's done, he has become a well-rounded handyman. He's certainly not an expert in every aspect of real estate construction, but he is the kind of a guy who can do a little bit of everything. That's what you need in this business.

Another thing about my brother Matthew that makes the strategies that I have work beautifully is that he's very trustworthy. He has a company credit card that he can use as he sees fit to make purchases for whatever project he's working on. I don't have time to be keeping track of every dollar he spends and every minute he works on my buildings, so if you can't trust your part-time handyman, you've got a big problem. If Matt can't handle the issues at hand, I either do it myself or I hire a contractor. When doing too many flips at the same time or too many apartment renovations, I always have the option to hire additional people. But I never make any of the people I hire permanent employees. Everything I do is on the job by job basis with no guarantee of work coming next week. That way if somebody disappoints me or doesn't do what I think he should be doing, I simply stop using him as opposed to actually having to fire him. This is a strategy I've used to manage a large portfolio of real estate while I'm busy doing other things.

I never said this was an easy business; in fact, I have to tell you it's a pretty tough business when you get to a couple dozen properties while you're still trying to hold a full-time job. If you don't have a full-time job, your ability to manage many more than a couple dozen is certainly possible. To become a full-time investor is hard to do strictly off of your real estate holdings, as most real estate investors find themselves equity rich and cash poor. I think if you got an honest answer from almost every landlord you'll ever meet, they will tell you that most likely is the problem. Being equity rich and cash poor is the nature of this business, and there is not an easy way to avoid it. I was cash poor for the first seventeen years of my real estate career until I bought Executec Suites.

Executec Suites made more cash flow than my entire residential real estate portfolio combined at that time of my career. That's why I strongly recommend that you build a real estate portfolio of residential properties with the ultimate plan of converting them using the 1031 exchange program into a large commercial building. Before you ever get to that level, you're going to have to learn how to accumulate a mass quantity of properties in a rising market so that you can be positioned at the top of the market in the estimated year of 2022. If I'm right and the market is near the top at that time, the size of your portfolio will be the only factor in determining how much money you're going to make. The cash flow that you have coming in from your properties at that time really is insignificant as long as it allows you to continue living the lifestyle you choose and paying for everything the properties need. I believe that it's extremely difficult to make any real money from residential real estate through cash flow.

The big bucks will come when you've reached the top of the market and you have accurately determined that we are at the top of the market. If you're lucky enough to get to that point, I think you'll learn that one of the hardest decisions you have to make is to start selling your buildings and look for a large commercial piece to roll the money into. Then you will be left with the problem of finding a commercial piece you can actually do something with and make some real money.

CHAPTER 32

Commercial if I Can Do Something with It

As I write this book in early 2010, one of the biggest problems I have with the commercial real estate business these days is after I find the right building, what will I do with it? I have more than one building that I'm keeping my eye on, but I just don't have a lot of faith that even if I was able to put the deal together that I would be able to do anything productive with it after settlement. The 1600 Building is still sitting there empty in the same condition it was when I first found it early 2007. As far as I know, the owners had been losing money before I ever looked at the building.

In the areas close to where I live, there is a need for an executive suite center, but with hundreds of thousands of empty square feet of office space, it doesn't seem likely that it will happen any time soon. I keep thinking that the medical office business is a good area to be in, but you really have to have a perfect building to fit the doctors' needs and I haven't found a building like that.

With everyone losing their homes to foreclosure, you would think that apartment buildings would be a terrific way to make money in commercial real estate today, but that's far from the case. The people are doubling up with their friends or going back home to live with their family. Landlords who strictly do buy-and-hold real estate deals are constantly looking for good tenants. The quality of the people who come around to look at your property are often completely unqualified to rent it. The quantity of people who come around to look at your property has diminished dramatically. Therefore, your only option is to drop the level of quality person you're looking for, which ultimately ends up getting you a questionable tenant. Every indicator would lead you to believe that the residential rental business would be strong right now if people are losing their homes, but it is not the case.

I'm beginning to look at retail operations again because despite all the bad press that arena has gotten, they're still very strong where I live. We lost a few big-box stores around here like Circuit City, but the rest of the stores seem to be going strong. I really like self-storage as well. I've talked about it in this book how we have a massive amount of competition around here in self-storage so that's not a likely option. As hard as I tried to deviate from what I'm doing, it's pretty clear that the office space arena is where I'm going to hang my hat for the future.

As much as I want to be a commercial real estate investor right now, I don't want to force a deal to get done that I maybe shouldn't have done at all. So I continue to scour the earth looking for that perfect office building deal with the idea that if I can't find it I'm going to buy foreclosures at sheriff sales and do flips to keep myself busy. I'm also planning on keeping a few of the flips while I'm at it if they look like properties I wouldn't mind holding for the next fifteen years.

One idea I have been putting a lot of energy into is using the lease option for commercial buildings. A lot of people right now would like to sell their commercial buildings, but they don't have a chance in hell of getting it done. If they found someone who actually wanted to buy it, they certainly wouldn't be buying it for a good price today, and even if they were able to buy it at a good price, they'd never get a mortgage. Just the word commercial for real estate right now is like a dirty word to banks, and they are very worried about the next shoe dropping. The lease option gives the owner a way to get out of this real estate deal now and break even for the next so many years. For example, as I did with Bucks County Suites, I get the owner out of this building for the next five years, and I'll either buy the building or sell it to somebody else in a much better financial economy. Of course, I'm assuming that the economy will get much better in the next five years. I also retain the right to walk from these deals, so if things don't shake out the way I expect them to, I can leave the arrangement, and I don't put any money down. I basically gain control of a piece of real estate I don't need to own and profit off of it if I'm able to rent it out. I also have to cover the losses if the building loses money that I promised him he would break even every month. I think it's a creative way to get a deal done in an otherwise difficult time.

If this idea doesn't float your boat, I suggest you come up with one that does. You're dealing in an amazing time in real estate right now where sellers are willing to give you anything to make the deal work. If you could do a lease option with no money down and the right to walk, I don't see how there's any risk it all for you to try. As I always say call the signs and sit down with the owners because you don't know what's going to happen. Keep thinking outside the box and keep calling the signs.

CHAPTER 33

Commercial Cash Cows

I often complain that in the residential real estate business does not really make enough cash flow. I know people claim to make all kinds of cash flow, but that has not been my experience over the years. As I said many times, I worked my tail off for a small salary with the hopes of one day cashing in on the huge equity from my portfolio. But in commercial real estate, that cash is really there to be made. Every multimillion-dollar commercial deal I ever seriously considered buying paid enough cash flow to equal the full-time job of an intelligent individual. When buying a multimillion-dollar property, many times it may have a manager who's already making $40,000 a year plus it's making the owner another $75,000 a year. In addition to these numbers, you may find $25,000 in miscellaneous fluff in the QuickBooks files that were used to renovate the kitchen at the owner's home and God knows what else. When you add all these numbers up, you have $140,000 a year income, and you might be collecting $50,000 in security deposit upon settlement. Now these are the kind of numbers that I feel my time is worth.

I don't feel as if I have to get rich off of every deal I do, but if I'm going to roll the dice and take a significant portion of my net worth, I expect to be compensated well for my risk. Generally speaking, commercial real estate is a huge cash cow if you can find a great deal. I have found many deals over the years that had the potential to feed my family, but if it's not the perfect deal, then I am not going to go for it. I've made all the mistakes I want to make when it comes to real estate, so at this point, I'm being extremely cautious. As I describe in transforming a portfolio, I tripled my cash flow after converting my portfolio to commercial.

I don't think it would be uncommon if you had a portfolio of fifteen to twenty residential real estate buildings, and you sold them all to buy one multimillion-dollar commercial piece of property. You could triple the amount of cash flow your entire portfolio made. I think those ratios are available in your market. You just have to find them. So start calling those signs and find your cash cow.

CHAPTER 34

Leveraged to the Hilt

There are many different philosophies of how to get rich in real estate. Mine is to start by leveraging to the hilt. The goal in my philosophy is to have the largest possible portfolio to ride its up surging direction and benefit from it. Therefore, you have to buy as much real estate as possible with the money that you have. You achieve that by using banks and leveraging yourself to the hilt as many times as possible over and over again throughout the process. I have never put down one more dollar than I had to in a piece of real estate in my career. Using other people's money to buy investments with the minimum money down and continuing the process to increase the portfolio size is worth repeating one thousand times until you get it. That's the game, as I like to say when talking about the real estate business. My wife always corrects me that it's not a game, it's a business, but everything is a game to me if I'm having fun while doing it.

So now that we're clear on how we're going to buy this real estate at settlement, let's talk a little bit more about leveraging it throughout the process of owning the real estate. I do not recommend using an amortization table to pay down your mortgage although I admit the benefits are huge in the first couple years if it's a thirty-year mortgage. Even I am willing to admit that it still doesn't excite me one bit since I don't plan on keeping any of these pieces for thirty years anyway. If you are going to participate in amortization, I wouldn't do it past the first couple years.

I also would choose a mortgage that has the longest possible payment terms of thirty years or more. You can always turn a thirty-year mortgage into a fifteen, but you can never do it the other way around without refinancing. That's the critical point of understanding how mortgages work. If this recent downturn taught us anything, it is that you never know what's around the corner, so you have to be careful with your real estate investments. Keep your payments as low as possible to maximize your cash flow and free you up to buy more buildings. Many new investors start focusing on paying down one particular property's mortgage instead of building their real estate portfolio.

I would also suggest that you do not participate in any biweekly payment plan, which has popped up throughout the years in the mortgage business. These strategies prey on first-time home buyers and tell them that if they pay their mortgage every two weeks, they would actually pick up extra payments every year. The banks and mortgage companies will also charge you a fee for these programs that you could've done yourself for free anytime you wanted simply by paying extra on each month's payment. Some owners may have prepayment penalties, but that usually is for loans that are paid off completely and does not include a minor prepayment such as what we are discussing now.

In summary, I am suggesting that you put the minimum money down as possible on any deal you do and keep it that way throughout the life of the loan. Once you've made a deal that is sustaining itself and providing cash flow, take your money and start focusing on the next building. That deal is done, and it's time to move on to the next one, building your ever-growing portfolio. It takes a tenacious person to build a massive real estate portfolio. Don't waste time screwing around with little details that will have a minor if any impact on your future net worth.

CHAPTER 35

Partnership Only When

When it comes to discussing partnership, you should only do it when there is no other way you could make this move that you have to make, without getting a partner. Partnership only when you absolutely have to. The only partner I have ever had in a real estate deal is my wife although I have entertained having partners on many big deals. It just hasn't worked out that any of my partnerships ever came to fruition, and I think I'm damn glad they didn't.

When you get to the point in your real estate career where your portfolio is large enough that you can go out and look at multi-million-dollar buildings you may spend years doing exactly that. So try to imagine that you're spending years looking for that perfect building, and when it finally comes around, you need to dump what you have as quickly as possible to make the deal happen. If you have a bunch of partners who own different pieces of your portfolio, it's going to make that difficult. Having a partner might make a particular deal get done that you could not have done otherwise, but it may also stop you from buying the one you need to buy down the road.

In summary, I have to think about a partner as a last resort. My mother is a smart businesswoman and always used to say that partnership is a dirty word. I don't think it's a dirty word, but I think you should be careful going down the road of a partnership.

CHAPTER 36
Know Your Market

Knowing the market that you intend to invest in is probably one of the single most important things I could ever say to a new investor. I live in Warminster, Pennsylvania. Make no bones about it that in Warminster I know my market. Some people in this town may own more Warminster real estate than I do, and there are probably investors who own the bigger pieces of real estate in Warminster than I do, but I doubt that anyone knows this town's real estate market better than I do. I don't have to own everything to understand what's going on here. I gained my knowledge on Warminster by scouring every piece of real estate that's come up for sale for years on the MLS. The multiple listing service will provide for you 95 percent of all of the real estate for sale in any town anywhere in the United States. I don't need to physically go out and look at each piece of real estate to understand what it is, but I do have to be on the look out of each development over the years to the point where I've seen this type of property numerous times before, so now the photographs and the information provided by the MLS is sufficient for me to know what it is. Being a realtor and having access to the MLS is one of the greatest tools you can add if you want to become an expert and know the market of a particular area.

I own or have owned many homes in Warminster, and as an experienced landlord, I'm familiar with what things can rent for as well as what I can buy them and sell them for. When you own a piece of real estate in Warminster, you're going to find you'll become intimately familiar with the local government and their involvement in your ownership of that piece of real estate. Warminster is no different than a lot of townships in the United States today where you could describe their involvement as overreaching. For starters in Warminster, you need a $75 landlord license for every piece of real estate that you intend to rent. You also need to get a use and occupancy permit for that building, which requires an inspection by the township that will cost you $100. If anything is found wrong during that inspection, after repair you will have to have another inspection that will cost you an additional $50. In Warminster even if you don't do any electrical work to the property, you are required to have the electrical circuit panel inspected each year by an approved inspection company for Warminster. Same thing goes for the flue pipe of your heater as well as any exhaust venting for a gas or standard fireplace.

The township's argument for having so many inspections of each particular piece is because that is where all the fires start, and since Warminster has a volunteer fire department, they have the right to make sure that we incompetent landlords follow the rules. While I will agree that they have a point on that issue, I think that funds generated from these inspections is the real reason for having any of them, but that's an argument for another day or should I say another chapter.

Another great way to know your market is to attend the open houses that other realtors hold in your area. Since I'm an atheist and don't go to church, I find myself with a lot of extra time on Sunday morning that I use to go to open houses. A quick and easy thing to do even if you're not a realtor is to look in the paper and make a couple of stops on Sundays to see the properties in your area. You don't need to make any phone calls prior to going or book any appointments with each showing. Grab yourself a cup of coffee and hit the road for forty-five minutes. You do this for a few years and I have no doubt there will be anything in town you're not familiar with.

Another great way to know your market is through for sale by owner properties or as some people like to call them FSBOs. I actually like to call them "fizzbose." Usually the information you obtain from a sale by owner property will be the least useful information you'll obtain anywhere, but it's still good to check them out. I also attend sheriff sales for the county that Warminster is located so that I can find out what the banks and the attorneys think the bottom-line prices are in this area. The upset price is the price that the foreclosing entity such as a bank would put on a piece of real estate at the sheriff sale. At the sheriff sale in Bucks County, Pennsylvania, where Warminster is located, the upset price would require the buyer to buy that piece of real estate for 100 percent cash payment within ten days of the sale and 10 percent down at the sale. The banks know that the sheriff sales are filled with real investors who have money and the skills to buy a piece of real estate. So coming up with the perfect upset price is not an easy thing to do for these banks. They definitely want the piece of real estate to move at the sheriff sale, as it's the quickest and easiest way for them to get rid of it. So the trick is to come up with an attractive price without taking too much of a loss. I think you'll find if you do your home work as I have that the lowest price for a particular development that you will hear will most likely be at the sheriff sale.

If that statement is true, you're probably wondering, why don't I buy every piece of real estate at the sheriff sale? Like a lot of things in real estate, it's not that simple. While it's true that I can buy real estate cheap at a sheriff sale, I also take a lot of risk because I have not had an opportunity to look at the property from inside. So let's say for argument that a house comes up for sale at a sheriff sale for $95,000 as the upset price and I pass on it. The next move is this property becomes what's called an REO or real estate offering. My guess is that the realtor who gets the real estate offering will put the house up on the MLS for $107,000 as an example. Maybe I make a deal with that realtor after thorough inspection for $97,500 making my cost $2500 higher than I could've bought it at the sheriff sale.

So what do I get for my $2500? The answer is I get plenty. First of all, I only had to use a small amount of my own money because I have plenty of time now to get a mortgage, and since I am a leverage guy, that works great for me. Another advantage is that I had multiple opportunities to inspect the property with as many inspectors I wish because access is now completely open to me to make sure that there are no secret surprises. I have found more than my share of secret surprises in properties that came from sheriff sales and ones that didn't. So let the buyer beware as the old Roman saying, caveat emptor, tells us.

Another great way to know your market is to deal with all of the realtors who make the moves in your town. How do you know who these movers and shakers are? You'll meet them as you go to open houses and you see the names repetitively in the multiple listing service as you look for properties. Start making phone calls to them letting them know you're an investor in town and that if they were to give you a heads up you would be happy to make it worth their while. I do the same thing with all the short sale experts in my town. People who negotiate short sales with mortgage companies can often be found at the sheriff sales.

Technically speaking, a short sale process begins when the home goes into foreclosure and doesn't end until the gavel hits the table at the sheriff sale. Anyone who tries to negotiate with the mortgage company prior to the sheriff sale can be described as a short sale negotiator. I bought many properties from short sale negotiators that they did not even own by having them get a contract with the owner of the home whose home is being foreclosed on and assigning that contract to me. Connections with these people can be valuable. If you're an honorable person with integrity and they also have those same qualities, it can be a real win-win for the both of you.

I'm at the point now when I review the multiple listing service each day for the new pieces of real estate that may have come up for sale in the Warminster area, it takes all of about ten seconds to determine if the piece is the real deal. I know by memory almost every street name in this town, and by photograph I can tell you the developments fairly easily. One quick look at the price and I have a pretty good idea where the bargains are.

The point to all of this is that I can sit in my office now with my feet up on my desk and with one hand thumbing through the multiple listing service I can immediately determine if there is a piece of real estate I want to buy. If I do find the right piece, I can spring into action faster than anyone because I am a realtor and drafting up the contracts won't take me longer than an hour. I usually run to see the property before I submit the contracts, but as I'm generally looking for destroyed properties that I can fix up and keep or fix and flip, I don't really care that much about the insides. The bulk of all the residential homes I've purchased over the years have been destroyed inside from one end to the other. It allows me to lowball the offer and gives me little competition, as most normal people don't want anything to do with the house that is destroyed.

So in my market I am king at finding good deals and moving on them quickly, but the greatest advantage to knowing your market is making sure you never screw up. Because I know my particular area so well, it is virtually impossible for me to make a mistake. That is the greatest advantage because after making many mistakes in my career I really don't wish to make any more. Knowing my market allows me to do one successful deal after another. So I hope I've explained to you properly the importance of knowing your market.

I can't tell you how often I meet new investors who tell me they are doing this deal downtown near the colleges and then doing another deal over here with this and that, and I always go right back to know your market. I'm not saying that you can't own properties in different places as I have done many times in my career, but you have to know those markets as well as you possibly can. So get out there and start learning your market as you have a lot of homework to do.

CHAPTER 37
Timing the Market

Timing the real estate market looks so easy when you use hindsight and so easy to determine what was going on, but when it's actually happening to you, trust me, it's not that easy.

"Timing and strategy are the red woods of real estate success. Everything else is a bonsai."

~ ROBERT CAMPBELL

Robert wrote a terrific book in 2002 called *Timing the Real Estate Market* that I read in 2005. I met Robert while he was on a national speaking tour and purchased his book that evening and read it a few days later. He has a semi sophisticated system of determining exactly when the real estate market is at the top of the peak. I don't know if I buy into all his scientific mathematical equations, but I did enjoy his book as well as the advice that he dishes out from it. Robert says the meek may or may not inherit the earth, but it is almost guaranteed that they won't make the most money in real estate. Timing and assertiveness pay the biggest dividends in the long term.

Today I simply use all of the information at my fingertips, such as the many articles on the Internet or the statistics of home sales from the multiple listing service. I read and store as much as I can about the real estate business while also paying great attention to the political arena. Politics plays an increasingly larger role in the real estate arena with each year and can no longer be a topic that's ignored by any businessman. I find a huge number of decisions that I make or don't make for that matter are because of my feelings toward the current politicians running this country. I think they have a great deal of involvement in causing this economic downturn and more importantly too much to do with keeping us here. If they would just get the hell out of the way and let the free market capitalism take over and let entrepreneurs do what they do best, we would already be out of this recession by now. I have a T-shirt that says a recession is when your neighbor loses his job and a depression is when you lose your job while the recovery will begin when Obama loses his job. I truly believe that a far left socialist like Obama is the worst thing that could have ever happened to this country in this economic downturn. His ass backward policies are the opposite of what this country needs to get out of this recession.

Every decision that I make about real estate is based on timing the market. In a flat market like we have now, I'm always looking for commercial deals with cash flow, hoping to find one that's an amazing deal and the owner is selling only because the rest of his portfolio is not performing properly, but the piece I am interested in is performing quite well. I know from my own experience that most real estate portfolios consist of some well-performing properties with some very bad ones. So I'm looking for a guy who has a $2 million building that makes a boatload of money while the construction of forty homes that he did totally tanked. The only way he can keep from going bankrupt is to sell the profitable $2 million building to buy his way out of the construction mess of the forty homes. I've been out looking for this kind of person for several years now, and I believe he's out there although I haven't found him yet.

From a residential side in a flat market, I simply don't believe in acquiring buy-and-hold properties, so I do flips to earn income. Although occasionally I will do a house that I purchased so much under current market values that I decide to keep it. After all, I consider myself a buy-and-hold investor, and I consider that to be the best overall strategy for anybody regardless of how much money you have or the size your portfolio.

In a declining market my advice is to sell any property that you have an equity position in and the cash flows are mediocre to poor. If your cash flows are good I still might sell the properties, but they're a little harder to decide. If I can get ten years of cash flow from the sale of a building, then I have no issues selling it. I would not call it a rule but more of a guide line when selling. One of the beautiful things about the real estate market when it comes to timing is that over the years you learn things move rather slowly in the real estate cycles. While the professional investors and some of the professional realtors will know prices have begun to shift, the general public won't know for quite some time. As a general rule the uneducated are not really paying attention, and the public usually takes a year to catch up with the professionals. It has always been my opinion that the top peak of the real estate market was reached on Labor Day in the summer of 2005, but some people were still buying properties like the market was still red hot for almost a year after that. Some people laugh when I tell them that the peak happened on Labor Day, but there is a lot of logic behind why Labor Day tends to be a key moment in real estate cycles.

Summertime is always slow in the real estate market, and people generally take a lot of vacations. So when prices drop and houses sit over the summer, it's really nothing more than commonplace. Even the professionals will say wait and see what happens when we return in the fall, but shortly after arriving back in their home offices, they quickly determine that this market won't be coming back anytime soon. So does the peak really happen on Labor Day or isn't it just fun to be able to pinpoint it right down to a particular weekend? I suppose the answer to that question is a little bit of both.

In the fall of 1990, there were clear signs that the real estate market was about to tumble, which was then followed up by the Persian Gulf War in the early 1991. I didn't know it at the time, but clearly looking back, it's safe to say the problems started after Labor Day in the summer of 1990. I settled on my second property in October of 1990, completely unaware of the real estate cycles. I was just in a mode to acquire as much property as I could as fast as possible.

" 'No tree grows to the sky' is a great warning that even the healthiest growth can't go on forever. Nor can it continue at the fast pace that marks a sapling's first few years. You'll hear people repeat the mantra location, location, location is the number one rule in real estate and for most of my career I have to say I agree with them. I find it equally as important tounderstand the timing of the real estate market and the strategy for which you plan to invest along with choosing good-quality locations to be all part of the grand master plan."

~ ROBERT CAMPBELL

CHAPTER 38

Get Your Real Estate License

If you're going to be a serious real estate investor, there really isn't anything to discuss about getting your real estate license. In my opinion, you absolutely have to. You take a two-week class where you study all about the real estate industry learning things that I carry with me to this day followed by a test that while difficult is far from impossible to receive your license. While your license will cost you approximately $1000 per year, the amount of commissions it saves you on just one deal will more than pay for itself. Therefore if you do one real estate deal per year even on a modest home, a license is a free tool in your toolbox. I once had equitable title in a deal for $1.5 million where my commissions were to be $75,000 and my end after paying my broker would have been $63,000. If that one deal had gone through, it alone would pay for sixty-three years of my real estate expenses.

I do flips today where the money I saved on the real estate commissions and the money I saved from doing my own construction alone was the profit. What I'm saying is by buying the house to be flipped and selling the house at the end of the construction may have saved me $12,000, and by being able to do the construction myself, I saved another $10,000. Those numbers represent almost all of the profit that I received from doing the flip in the first place. This enables me to make money off of the deal where other investors who can't do construction and don't have a real estate license must pass on. In a way, it gives me many more homes to choose from when I'm looking for a flip, so it's easier for me to find them when I'm ready to flip one.

The multiple listing service also gives you the ability to run your own comps so you can determine what a comparable value for the house you're about to buy or sell is going to be. I also can do searches of public records on the multiple listing service and determine what the buyer might have paid for the house five years ago when he bought it as well as tell me what the mortgage was at the time of purchase. This information is invaluable to me, as it not only makes it easier for me to determine if I want to flip a home but it also makes me move faster than the competition. Quite frankly, I can't imagine doing what I do for a living without having a real estate license.

The only negative I've ever heard about having a real estate license is the fact that you have to disclose to everyone that you're an agent. While I don't deny that I could make one deal a little more confusing than the other, I have never come across a single deal that was ruined because I had a real estate license. It sounds to me like a minor hurdle that I would simply jump over as I do all other hurdles to accomplish the final objective. All the real estate deals have bumps in the road that you have to overcome, and this one certainly doesn't sound like anything I'd lose a moment's sleep over.

CHAPTER 39
Learn Construction

I realize that it's not for everybody, but definitely for me learning construction was a huge part of the success I've had in real estate. When I bought my first duplex in 1989 at the age of twenty-three, I'd never even painted a wall before. My father was not one to fix things around the house, so I really didn't have anyone to show me how to repair anything. I also remember my mother complaining all the time that she married a man who did not repair things and how much it cost to hire somebody every time something needed to be done. I thought a man should know how to fix things.

During the first five years that I was a landlord, I insisted on fixing everything myself mostly because I didn't have any money, making my choices limited. I remember once fixing the water heater by replacing the tank and soldering together my first line of copper fittings. I got in my car and drove home only to hear the phone ring and be told by the tenants that the fittings blew and there was water all over the basement. I had a hundred stories like that of things that I did and it didn't work out so great. But that's how I learned how to fix things. As my confidence grew year after year, I began to tackle larger projects. I remember the first construction project I took on was to build a bar in the apartment I was living in. Now you know where my priorities were. Little did I know I'd spend the next three years leaning up against that bar.

The next project I took on was to turn an attic into a third bedroom with a staircase dropping down. That was quite a project of a twenty foot wide by twenty foot long additional room above my apartment. I did this in the second building that I owned when I lived on the second floor of a two-bedroom, one-bathroom apartment that was already pretty big. It was a huge attic, large enough to stand in above the apartment, and that's the room I converted. I didn't need the extra space and didn't have the money to invest in doing it, but I completed the project anyway. It was an interesting construction project, and I learned a lot, but I don't think it added any value to the building. It was impossible to keep the room cool in the summer, so most people just used it for storage or an office.

Feeling confident, I decided to move out of the second floor of that duplex and move into the basement, which I then converted into an apartment, making my building now a triplex with living space on all four floors. When I first moved into the basement, I had to build a wall that separated the space I was going to use as my apartment from a very small area where the washer and dryer was. For the first two months, I had to take showers at the gym while I built the bathroom that I would use for the next five years. I had an electric radiator heater that I moved from room to room as I lived in the basement. I had a water bed that was heated, so that's how I kept warm at night. I had to build a bathroom to be a step up like a platform so that I could plumb in the toilet without busting up the floor. There was already a backdoor and a one-car garage door, which I left on the outside so that I wouldn't alarm anybody I had moved into the basement. On the inside of the garage door, I just framed a wall and sheet rocked it closed. Of course I'd build an even bigger bar than the one upstairs and ended up living in this apartment for five years.

I was now living in my triplex for free while the other two apartments paid the mortgage with all the expenses and some extra profit. While the basement apartment was a little crude, it turned out to be one of the most intelligent decisions I ever made. It was more than a suitable place to live for a person in his twenties, and I began to really get a handle on my financial situation. While the apartment was, technically speaking, illegal, nobody really noticed or cared what I was doing. The money I saved living in the basement was used to buy other investment properties, including the primary residence that I still live in today some twelve years later.

Even more important than all of the financial advantages I gained were the construction skills that I learned during the time I built this basement. In the basement, I framed my first wall and did sheet rock, built my first bathroom and kitchen, and my first ceiling. I also did electrical wiring, HVAC ductwork, and ran plumbing for rather large studio apartment that I enjoyed living in for five years. I began to have confidence in my abilities to perform construction.

These construction skills were used so many times I can't possibly mention throughout my career, enabling me to renovate vacant apartments quickly and inexpensively by doing it myself. I believe that the skills are priceless if you're going to be an individual who does nothing but real estate investment for a living. After twenty years in the business, I feel as if I have the capability to build a house from scratch although I never have. I have always bought existing buildings and then renovated them, and God knows that's plenty of work in itself. So don't be afraid to acquire tools and learn construction skills. I consider it to be as important as any other skill a real estate landlord will need to use throughout his career.

CHAPTER 40

Tools in the Toolbox

When I say tools in the toolbox, I'm referring to all the skills that a real estate investor needs to develop over his or her career. Everything that you learn about this business essentially becomes a tool in the toolbox that you can pull out and use whenever you need it. Some of the things that I consider a tool would be a buy-and-hold strategy to purchase properties. The knowledge about how to acquire a mortgage using lending institutions is an essential tool to finance your next moves. Access to the multiple listing service and skills a realtor has are also important to getting things done in this business. Other tools are construction skills, negotiation skills, communication abilities, management capabilities, and QuickBooks experience. Speaking of experience, knowing how a short sale works, a sheriff sale functions, an REO works, a "subject to" gets put together, and wholesaling can be accomplished are all important tools. The point to all of this is don't let a sector of real estate worth knowing be ignored. Make an effort to learn everything that you can about each one of these sections of doing business. Every time I go to a real estate meeting and I hear somebody talking about something I don't understand, I always go over and introduce myself. I really don't like anyone knowing anything I don't know, and that brings us to our next topic.

CHAPTER 41

I Don't Like Anyone Knowing Anything I Don't Know

I love the real estate meetings with the local group called DIG, which stands for Diversified Investors Group. They meet once a month in Fort Washington, Pennsylvania, at a Holiday Inn where approximately four hundred people show up for every meeting. I believe there are approximately eight hundred members of this organization in the Delaware Valley of Pennsylvania. In addition to the main meeting, there is what they call subgroups. We have commercial subgroups, New Jersey shore investors subgroups, a group called the masterminds, and a movers and shakers group as well as many others broken down on basic investment geographic areas. This group has been beneficial to me obtaining all the tools in the toolbox that I needed to have. At these meetings, I network my way through the organization trying to find somebody who's doing something different than I know or have ever had to do.

Some people there do nothing but lease options, and others do nothing but "subject to" deals. It's great to figure out who are the experts in each category and make friends with these individuals, so you can pick up the phone and call them should the opportunity arise for you to do such a deal. Many of these so-called experts take time to be a speaker at the monthly subgroup meetings or even the main meeting.

The answer line is an amazing tool that DIG offers to its members free of charge. I can e-mail a question I have about a certain type of real estate problem, and it automatically goes out to hundreds of my fellow real estate investors. They can in turn respond to my e-mail and try to help me solve this problem I'm having. This is one of the coolest tools I've ever had in the real estate business and well worth the cost of the membership alone, which happens to be only $125 a year. It is used often for recommending contractors, so I can help my fellow real estate investors who need a roofer and also support the roofer who rents office space from me.

I also speak on many of the things I consider myself an expert on in the real estate business. I have spoken at many of the subgroup meetings and am scheduled in October of 2010 to speak at the main meeting, which I have not done before. My areas of expertise are having twenty years experience in the business and owning some of the largest buildings in the commercial arena by a DIG member. I get a great deal of pleasure out of sharing what I know with others and also because I love to hear the sound of my own voice. I can talk real estate all night long if I could simply find somebody interested in listening. My wife gave up listening a longtime ago, and my friends don't mind listening but I don't see them very often. My three best buddies are all in the business as a mortgage banker, a realtor, and in real estate franchise sales.

I really do love the real estate business, so for me it's a lot of fun to hang out with people who have a similar interest. I also get a great opportunity to market my business as I network around the group. Landlords don't want tenants knowing where they live, so a guy who rents mailboxes can do well with such a group. Landlords are busy during the day with their regular jobs, so they like to have an answering service pick up the phone calls for them during the day. Any chance I get to talk about renting offices is an opportunity I won't miss. If you're dumb enough to start a real estate conversation with me, you'd better get your pillow out before it's over.

CHAPTER 42

Get Started Young

Because I preach to people that the best way to get rich in real estate is to do it slowly, then it certainly helps to get started young. I started at the age of twenty-three and was doing nothing but real estate investing sixteen years later. Unfortunately, the problem with this strategy is when you're young you're usually not paying attention to what kind of investment strategy you are going to be involved with your whole life. By the time you get smart enough to figure that out, you're usually at least in your thirties. If you are still in your twenties and reading this book, then my hat's off to you. As I've mentioned in sections of this book, I am not so impressed with the twenty-something-year-olds that I have met. If you're not that young anymore, I don't think it makes that much difference as you always have time to ride the cycle from bottom to top to make this strategy work. By the time we get to the peak of this cycle, you may not be interested in going on to do the second one, which is generally where you get to the point where you can afford a building worth say $4 million. But maybe your life goals require you to earn seven figures in real estate equity and retire, and that can certainly be accomplished in one real estate cycle.

I recently became friendly with two people from my real estate investment club who are in their early fifties and just getting started. While they may be new to the real estate business, they certainly have the intelligence, the enthusiasm, and the desire to succeed. From what I learned about them from the time we spent together, I would give them a high probability of succeeding in real estate investing.

Get started young is something I keep preaching to my son at the age of twelve. I don't think he really wants to hear it. I constantly try to get him excited about buying a condominium for

$55,000 with one bedroom and one bath in our local area. He seems semi-interested, but with $5000 I don't know that I can pull it off with him being twelve and today's financial lending policies. But imagine if he could acquire a property at twelve years old with a thirty-year mortgage—how amazing would that be. This first property would be paid off by the age of forty-two.

Every time the property needs to be renovated or rented, I obviously would be the one in charge, but I see him assisting with the renovations and being present to approve potential tenants. Can you imagine that by age eighteen he's an experienced landlord, and when he's shooting his mouth off to me, I can only say the following: "If you don't like living here, why don't you live in your own stinking condominium?" I think the plan is genius. Never before has it been easier to kick a kid out of the house, and you know I'll be thinking about that every time this property is vacant and he doesn't show up to help me fix it.

I often think about my own mortality and how writing this book puts all my real estate ideas down on paper for my son to see should I not be around to explain them later. People sometimes laugh when I say that, but I assure you I am not kidding. Imagine I fall off the face of the earth. Before I wrote this book, he would have heard a few things about my love for real estate, but that's where it ends. Now because of *Addicted to Real Estate*, I can make him read it twenty times for homework. When and if the day comes in his twenties that he decides to really learn what a great investment vehicle real estate can be, even if I am gone, this book will always be important to him. I can tell him exactly how to proceed without actually being there to do it, as well as help other people in the process and maybe even make a few bucks for the people I love.

CHAPTER 43

Manage Your Own Properties

Gurus preach to the real estate investor world that the way to get rich in this business is to buy buildings and have other people manage them for you. I have managed my own properties from day one in this business and continue to do so today even though my portfolio is rather large. If you're just getting started in this business, don't even think about hiring someone else to manage your buildings. All the lessons learned in this business and all the skills obtained come from managing your real estate. Even if you could find an affordable and talented property manager, he would be in such high demand that before you know it he would be too busy to take care of your properties in the way they need to be taken care of. Many of my fellow investors constantly say that they're in need of a good property manager, but I suspect it's mostly for properties that are out of the way from where they currently live, making it difficult for them to manage those particular pieces. I don't think most investors would hand over their entire portfolio to a property manager, but I could be wrong. The way I've dealt with handling a portfolio my whole career has been to manage it myself and do as much of the work as I could. The only thing that I've changed over the years is the level of involvement that I have and the number of contractors that I use to assist me in completing various projects.

Today the area of property management that I have partially delegated to others is the handling of all the perspective office tenant approvals and lease signings. Basically, all of the sales work starting with the marketing and showing of all the office rental units as well as approving and closing the deal is the area I'm referring to. I have the assistance of my wife who does a great deal of our office renting for me, and we have an operations manager at Executec Suites who has also done some of the sales-related work when my wife or I are not available. Since

I consider sales to be the essence of business, this would probably be a difficult sector to completely delegate to someone else. I give it a very high priority in the property management list of duties.

When you get to this stage in your career when your buildings are large enough to house seventy-seven tenants, such as Executec Suites that has forty-seven offices and another thirty virtual tenants, you can afford to have a full-time property manager on site. My wife and I still continue to manage this building ourselves as I had done for the first two years we owned the building and she has done since.

With my wife, Terry, managing our largest property, I have free time to look for new acquisitions into commercial and residential areas. I do all this searching for new properties to buy and act as the realtor involved in each agreement of sale. I also manage all the sales for the remainder of my portfolio, and I oversee or get personally involved in the construction of all of our flips. When the workload gets heavy from doing three flips at the same time as well as managing the existing portfolio, it's easy enough to hand off construction projects on flips to others. Several areas of construction that I have found just easier to delegate would be all roofing projects, electrical and plumbing work, as well as all the flooring. We use several contractors for our flooring, which consist of all the ceramic tile work, hardwood, and carpet work. I still like to do all my own kitchens and bathrooms if I have the time with the exception of the ceramic tile work that will go on the wall in both cases. I am capable of doing my own ceramic tile work, but one person can't do everything. I put a lot of effort into being my own plumber but ultimately decided it made no sense. I can do some basic wiring, but I don't really know the codes, hate being shocked, and am afraid of burning down my own building, so all that work gets subbed out as well. When it comes to roofing, I have been involved in many preventative maintenance projects such as going on roofs and trying to determine where the problem is, as well as caulking and sealing various areas when the problem is obvious. Many roofing projects are obvious in the beginning, but if the leak continues to occur, I usually give up and hand it off to the professionals.

Because I'm the realtor in the family, I also handle all the sales work related to selling our properties as well as any mortgage or refinancing negotiations that need to take place. Depending on the workload I have at the current time, I can sub out all of the contracting work or very little of it to fill or loosen up my schedule. As I look into the future, no matter how large my portfolio gets, I can't imagine a scenario where I would not be involved in the property management at the highest levels. Since I truly love this business and enjoy what I do, it's hard for me to believe I'd be sitting around playing golf all day.

Another area of property management that I do not recommend letting anyone else handle is managing the finances. I do all the invoicing using QuickBooks and tracking of the tenants' payments as well as collecting on bad or old debt. I also get involved in handling all the evictions whenever they arise, which unfortunately is more often than I prefer. I find it hard to imagine a time when I'm not involved in it at the very least signing the checks that go out from a company and regularly reviewing the QuickBooks files. I know too many businessmen who have had fortunes stolen from them by their partners, bookkeepers, or someone else managing their businesses. Also, by reviewing your financial situation as often as possible, you can easily decipher what areas of your portfolio need improvement. For the last five years, it always seems to be the same answer to the question where my portfolio needs improvement. I guess my style of investing creates an equity rich and cash flow poor scenario. I've been working hard to improve cash flow without giving up the equity for many years now, and I continue to believe that I am only one large commercial move away from solving that problem forever.

CHAPTER 44

Don't Fall in Love

Falling in love with a real estate deal can be the kiss of death. When you work on some of these long hard commercial properties and the deal seems to take forever, you tend to get attached to the building. You work on something so long it tends to become somewhat of an obsession, and the longer you're involved in it, the harder it is to walk away. I found myself in this situation more than once where I wanted the deal so bad I was thinking of making concessions I maybe should not think of offering. That's why I suggest you be aware not to fall in love with the real estate deals you are working on.

When I chase residential buildings to purchase, the success rate of closing these deals is very good, but the commercial arena is completely different. I don't know if it's me or the deals I am chasing or if its commercial real estate in general, but I have had four deals fall through for every one that went through. It can weigh on you over the years as you write contracts and incur lawyer fees and spend tons of time working on deals that don't come to fruition.

If you find yourself in a situation where the smartest thing for you to do is walk away from the deal, you can feel good about the fact that at least you gained some knowledge while working on the one that didn't go through. Sometimes you win and sometimes you learn is a good way to look at a deal that doesn't make it to settlement.

CHAPTER 45

Buyer's Anxiety

Whenever I buy a piece of real estate, I find myself going through a period of buyer's remorse. I see many things that can come up with a piece of real estate that could make me regret buying it later, but I just can't resist going through a least a short period of buyer's anxiety. In the early stages of my career, I used to try to talk myself out of feeling this way, but now I kind of view it as a positive thing. The buyer's anxiety that I experienced with each purchase helps me to make sure I've done my homework carefully before buying anything else. At least if I did all the proper homework, I can deal with the fact that that one sneaky problem out of one hundred got past me. If the mistake I made was something obvious that I shouldn't have missed, then torturing myself is the next level. The point to all this is that in order to be a successful investor you have to constantly be putting pressure on yourself to do the homework and make smart decisions. You are accountable to yourself as well as all the other people who count on you to run this business in a professional manner and to make each and every property a successful business of its own on its own.

CHAPTER 46
Torture Yourself

When I make a mistake, I come down on myself like a ton of bricks. Depending on how serious the mistake, I would determine how much I will torture myself. I've made more than my share of screw-ups in this business, so much so that I thought about naming this book *How to Make Every Mistake in the Book Twice and Still Be Here*.

I don't think I invented the torture-yourself program, as I have met several successful friends who claim to do the same thing. Maybe it's a trait of successful people or maybe it's a sign that you're a little crazy. I'm sure a therapist would tell you that your father yelled at you a lot when you were young when you made mistakes and now that he's not available you fulfill that need by torturing yourself. I guess I don't really care why exactly I do it, but I definitely think it's worth discussing as it forces me to always be improving myself and taking my game to the next level. This is a tough business we're in, and you have to be tough on yourself to make sure you're doing things to guarantee the greatest possible chance of success. Many of us spend our lives working for companies where our boss does that for us, but in the real estate business where you are the entrepreneur and the highest person on the food chain, you need to sometimes kick your own ass.

CHAPTER 47

What Makes an Investor?

Real estate business is a tough way to earn a living, and as you're going through the growing pains, you're going to second-guess yourself more than once. But at some point you have to trust me that there is real gold at the end of the rainbow and it only takes one real estate cycle to get there. Some of the characteristics that I think make up a great real estate investor is having a high level of intelligence. You don't need to be a brain surgeon, but you'd better have a higher level than that of a ditch digger.

Sales skills are something I've put a great level of importance on as I mentioned many times in this book. You'll learn as you go through the business world that a lot of people don't have respect for sales skills, but I consider it to be of the most importance. Now that you sold your new clients and they are already in your building, they have to be serviced, meaning taking care of them every way possible. I constantly tell the people who work for me to put sales and service at the top of their minds every day. Always be thinking sales and service. We want to constantly find new tenants, and we want to keep everyone who is currently in our building happy. When you have one hundred tenants, you could be losing two or three people a month, and a rotating cycle never seems to end. Doing everything you can to keep your current base happy while you're out selling is the key to success.

You have to spend some time developing communication skills so that the people in your office building genuinely feel that you are not just their landlord but their friend. Take an interest in the businesses that they have and the situations that life is dealing to them. The key is to be honest and be genuine as everyone can usually smell a fake.

Construction skills are something that I think is essential to being in the real estate business although I have quite a few colleagues who disagree. That being said, I can tell you without a question in my mind that the skills I've acquired in construction have been a huge part of my real estate success.

It takes a lot of guts to be a real estate investor. You can call it guts, chutzpah, balls, audacity, bravado, cunning, daring, or tenacity. It doesn't matter to me what you really call it as long as you have it. This is a tough business and you will run across some very difficult characters to deal with. Tenants who know how to work the system will rob you blind if you're not careful. Owners of commercial buildings I purchased after settlement bought a building down the street and tried to steal half of my clients even though there was a non-compete clause in the deal.

Here's the real thing to remember about commercial real estate. The bigger the deal, the smarter the owner usually will be, and the more money he will have to fight you in court if there is ever an issue. There are some real slick fish out there that can make your life a living hell, so you have to be extremely careful when you get into the larger deals. I once did a deal with a guy who owed me a lot of money, and even though he knew he was wrong, he simply said, "I can outspend you in court."

No matter how tough this business is, this is the greatest country in the world in which to be an entrepreneur. I love America and I love the real estate business. Remember that American ends in "I can" so go out and make it happen.

CHAPTER 48

Internet Marketing

The world of marketing a rental property has changed dramatically over the last few years. Web sites like Craigslist, Facebook, Twitter, Myspace, Linkedin, and many others have really changed the options for landlords. I currently have two marketing experts to assist me in advertising my business. One is a traditional marketing guru who can develop professional brochures for me that we mail out to the surrounding homes and businesses after we purchased a specific address and e-mail lists. This style of marketing can be expensive, as you have to pay for the development of the brochures, the printing, e-mail lists, the address lists, stamps, and someone to send them all out for you. Lately, I've been using more of the Internet marketing, which can reach a large audience quickly for a much cheaper price, and the only thing I give up is I don't get specific targeting. I have a Facebook page for Executec Suites that you can become a fan as well as a Twitter page and connections on Linkedin. I have created commercials that you can find on www.executecsuites.com or any of the other sites I listed above, including YouTube.com.

www.facebook.com/executecsuites
www.youtube.com/executecsuites
www.twitter.com/executecsuites
www.addicted2realestate.com

Getting the word out constantly about what you do for a living to the people you know cannot hurt your business anyway I can see. I'll try to turn many of my friends on Facebook, for example, into salesmen for me simply by planting a seed that I do all of these things and they might one day think of me when the opportunity arises. The other day I was on the phone with a client interested in renting office space, and I told him about my videos on my Web site. As I was on the phone with him, I could hear him playing my video with the introduction music in the background. This can be done with rental apartments or anything that you're trying to sell or rent. When someone calls me about an apartment today, I say go to this Web site and check out the video of the building for a virtual tour. Using technology to help sell is all I'm trying to do. Below is an example of an e-mail that I send out to all perspective clients who talk to me about office space.

I have space for you now at Executec Suites, 67 Buck Road, Huntingdon Valley, PA 19006. We have office space now starting at only $495.00 per month per office with multiple offices as you need and that price includes the following:

Receptionists who answer the phone in the name of your company and greet clients in a friendly manner
Fully furnished office any way you prefer
High-speed internet access for as many users as needed
Telephone handsets and all line charges except outgoing calls
Voice mail for each extension with remote message checking capability
Phone numbers and fax numbers if needed
Conference rooms and convenient free parking
Twenty-four-hour secured access to your office
All utilities, janitorial, and maintenance costs included
Mailboxes and package receipts in your absence
And many other additional services

Please visit our Web site for photos of our building or view this video link below.

http://www.executecsuites.com

Sincerely,
Phil Falcone

If you happen to check out the videos and think that you might be interested in producing some for your business, you can call my friend Dennis Sinelnikov at 267-784-0508 or check out his Web site at http://www.mediacomponents.com. Dennis is a talented guy who will create the videos for you and do all the editing as well as spread them throughout the many vehicles on the Internet so that you can take advantage of today's inexpensive marketing techniques.

Since you're going to be placing ads out there on all these different Web sites and information about your business, try this one on for size. Offer to pay a commission to everyone that you talk to just like you would for a realtor or an Internet Web site. I spread the word around all the time—how would you like to make a month and a half commission for just giving me a name? That's right. Just send me a name and I'll run with it, and if I close the deal, you get a month and a half commission simply for sending an e-mail. Some of my offices run for $1000 a month, so I assume that a $1500 payment for sending an e-mail would be well worth the effort. I'm not just telling you about this deal I'm also offering it to anybody reading this book who knows someone looking for office space or any of the other services I provide. My email is falcone@comcast.net.

CHAPTER 49
Get Rich Slow

When you are first getting started in real estate, you need to have a plan and a realistic goal of what you can accomplish. I think one day you'll find that if you own dozens of buildings you will work hard for very little money. You'll be able to show a cash flow of several hundred dollars a month for every property you own, and put together, it may work out to be a substantial amount of money. For the sake of argument, let's say its $75,000 on paper a year. By the time you have vacancies and add repair costs on a bad year combined with taxes, the reality is you may only bring home half of that and work hard to earn it. So how does a real estate investor make money, if I'm correct? You make it in the equity that you have accrued in your buildings over many years of riding the cycle of real estate from the bottom to the top. You buy wisely and pay down your mortgages over the years as you increase your rents so that the values of your buildings increase. After riding the cycle for fifteen to twenty years, if you bought at least one property a year, I don't think it's unreasonable to expect $1 million in equity could be accrued.

When I started buying in 1989, I mentioned it was the top of the market as it began to crash in the fall of 1990. The real estate cycle continued until Labor Day in the summer of 2005. Historically speaking, the first cycle I experienced was a short cycle only lasting fourteen years. We have been in a flat or declining market since 2005 making real estate prices very attractive right now. But nobody really knows how long it will take to get back to the top of the market. My faith in people's short memory leads me to predict that this cycle will last twenty years, and I'm already counting the cycle starting in the summer of 2005 so we are already one quarter of the way through it. I don't like to make projections because they're only guesses at the end of the day, but if I have to take my guess, I'd say we're going to continue to decline or flat line for several more years before things return to normal cycle. A normal cycle may or may not run for fifteen to twenty years, and hopefully we will experience some kind of aggressive run up in the last five years. So assuming I could be right if you get started now buying at least one house a year, you can get rich slow and be almost guaranteed to be a millionaire by the year 2022.

Of course, I have no idea if any of this will pan out, but its fun to project what may happen in the future. I hear people say sometimes that this will never happen again because of this reason or that reason, but I don't believe any of it. People have short memories, and ten years from now no one's going to care about what happened in the last cycle. The people who do pay attention to the last cycle will find all the lessons they need to learn if they just pay attention. We all probably know people who were aggressively day trading in the late 90s and even people who were quitting their jobs to become day traders. I can guarantee you that one out of one thousand day traders survive today to continue to do that business. How many of us know individuals who were buying investment real estate in 2004 thru 2006 who got creamed? You never want to go to a party late when it comes to investing. I would predict investing in real estate between 2010 and 2015 would probably prove to be a profitable investment.

To get rich slow, all you have to do is buy one property a year, so if you have an income stream from a job, it should provide you some extra cash, and then it's a very possible goal for a regular Joe to accomplish. After buying one or two properties, you can always change your mind if you determine this business is not for you.

CHAPTER 50
Transforming a Portfolio

Have you ever given thought to what might happen to your business of residential real estate after transforming it into a commercial one? Let me tell you what happened to mine. During the three-year period as I transformed the bulk of my portfolio from residential buildings to commercial buildings, a lot of changes were happening to my real estate business. The most amazing change was that the cash flow my business produced tripled. That's correct—I said that it tripled. I've always felt that you work your tail off in the residential real estate business with very little payment. People will always tell you how much profit they make on real estate investments, but I think a lot of it is not really true. I certainly was paid profit and cash flow for my real estate investments, but I never thought the payment was adequate. The real payoff for me was the equity that I accrued after riding this cycle from the bottom to the top. The trick to making the system work is to know when you're at the top and sell your buildings accordingly. But if you're lucky enough to time the market properly and smart enough to get out while the getting is good, you may see your cash flow tripled as well.

The funny thing is that the portfolio size really stayed about the same. What I mean by that is that the purchase of a $2 million commercial building required the sale of $2 million worth of residential buildings to raise the money to buy the commercial building. I'm a minimum wage kid from Northeast Philadelphia, so I don't have anything other than my real estate investments to fund my future real estate purchases. I have to sell my buildings and take the equity and roll it into larger commercial buildings utilizing the 1031 exchange program. I have no other way to raise the money. It would have been nice if the portfolio size increased as well, but it didn't work out that way for me.

Another interesting change that happened was that the quantity of my properties went down to one-third of what I used to have. I suppose I find this number interesting, but other than that, I really don't care. When residential landlords measure themselves against other residential landlords, they often do it by saying how many homes do you own, and to me I always thought that was silly. Who cares how many homes you own as we should be measured by how much money we are making and how much equity we are accruing. When people ask me today how much real estate I own I could say my portfolio size is X or the amount of tenants I manage is Y. At the end of the day I suppose it just matters how much money you make is Z.

As far as the quantity of my tenants, that number more than doubled. I suppose it's good to have as many tenants as possible because as that quantity increases the landlord's reliance on any one tenant becomes less and less important. The stability of the landlord's rent roll becomes more solid as well.

Another great thing that happened during the transformation of my portfolio was that I consolidated my tenant base into fewer locations, and that is a no-brainer to be a great improvement. I spend less time traveling and more time addressing the direct issues that need to be resolved in my portfolio. When you own one hundred houses, you could spend half your life just driving around between them; when you own a building with one hundred tenants in it, your efficiency level goes way up.

The last thing I would say about the transformation of my portfolio is I always thought before I did it that I'd end up with less to repair, but I don't think that turned out to be the case. I have to say in hindsight the amount I have to repair seems to be the same. The largest building I own in my portfolio today has a never ending list of things to be fixed. No matter how hard I work and how hard I focus on that list and how much money I throw at it, there are new items added to it constantly.

CHAPTER 51
Pick a Sector

Once you have decided to become a commercial real estate investor, you have to decide what sector you are going to try to enter. My favorite if you haven't guessed by now is the office arena. I also owned several apartment buildings and happen to like that business very much as well. But if it came down to investing in offices versus apartment buildings, I use the following saying to help me decide.

"The one thing I like about the office business is that everyone goes home at five o'clock. The one thing I hate about the apartment building business is everyone goes home at five o'clock."

~ PHIL FALCONE

That is an original Phil Falcone quote, so don't let anybody tell you otherwise. When five o'clock rolls around, I want to be home with my family having dinner and making plans to go out or go to the gym. I don't want to be receiving calls from tenants at that time of the day with issues that need to be addressed immediately. In the office business, everybody goes home at five o'clock, so usually you will get most of your phone calls early in the morning with surprises, but you won't get them around five o'clock. In the apartment building business, everyone goes home at five o'clock, so that's when all the trouble starts. People in apartment buildings start arguing about everything from a parking space to cooking smells and trash removal around five o'clock. It's just human nature that the phone is going to ring at that time of day when everyone goes home.

Another thing that I've noticed about the apartment building business is that one rotten apple can really destroy the place. It takes a while to evict a tenant from a residential apartment, so if you end up with a bad one that causes a lot of disruption in your building, it's going to take a while to get rid of him or her. Especially now in this economy as I write this book in early 2010, the residential business has not been the greatest in the Philadelphia area. With all these people losing their homes to foreclosures, it would only make sense that they would rent more properties, so every trend leads you to believe that the apartment building business should be strong. That being said, I have not seen a strong apartment building industry in the Philadelphia area.

There are also a lot of unqualified people out there to rent apartments, which is fine if you have low-grade properties where you can accept section 8 tenants or some other kind of government assistance. If your property is a high-end property like most of mine, then I think it's a little harder. So if these people are not going into apartment buildings, where are they going? I think they're going home and doubling up with mom and dad or they are doubling up with their friends somewhere. If I took my guess, I'd say that doubling up somewhere and reducing the amount of rental properties needed puts downward pressure on rents and occupancy rates. The people who are doubling up may be making smart decisions because they're responsible and leaving the people who are out there to have a higher percentage of less qualified tenants.

Industrial buildings are a category in the commercial real estate business that I have little exposure to. I am indeed about to acquire a building that has industrial space, but I plan to convert it to office space as soon as possible. In the meantime, I'll rent it to somebody for industrial purposes if the possibility is presented to me, but my long-term goal is office space. I wouldn't kick out a paying tenant from an industrial space to convert something to office, but you can bet your life that every time it's vacant I am going to explore that avenue.

Warehouse space is generally large buildings with considerable ceiling heights to work with. They also have large parking lots with many loading docks and other characteristics unique to this type of building. I have never purchased a building like this, and I don't know anything other than the basics about warehouse buildings. I would say that they are required to be geographically located near a large customs receiving area such as Elizabeth, New Jersey. In Elizabeth, New Jersey, located just outside of New York City, many large ships bring imported goods to the United States. These goods come off of ships and end up on eighteen-wheeler trucks headed for a warehouse nearby. If you have the connections in this business, I imagine you could become very wealthy. I would also imagine one has to be fairly wealthy to get started in this business in the first place. In closing, I would suggest this is not an area for a new investor to venture into.

The retail sector of the commercial real estate world has always been very interesting to me. I have worked on more than my share of retail projects but have never been able to bring one to fruition. Because I'm an entrepreneur with new business ideas all the time, owning a retail strip center would be a wonderful place to allow me to try out new ideas. I think it's safe to say that 2008 and 2009 were not very good years for the retail shopping industry although in my neck of the woods these investments still look strong. The down turn I expected to come never happened. I would say in the Bucks County section of Pennsylvania just outside of Philadelphia, the retail industry here is doing okay.

In the last twelve months, I went from having zero interest in retail and considering it to be the most dangerous commercial real estate sector out there to really being interested again in investing in retail shopping centers. I think you can make a lot of money in the retail shopping center, but it also comes with a great deal of risk. One way to reduce that risk is to stick with a small three-to-five-unit mom-and-pop type retail operation somewhere where real estate is still affordable. While I'm not exactly out there looking for this kind of investment right now, I believe in my future is a strong chance I could own such a place.

I'm currently looking at a mixed-use building that has a combination of retail, office, and industrial space all-in-one piece of real estate. It's an affordable piece in the low seven figures with some real upside potential. The owner listed it two years ago for $1.5 million, and now the price has dropped to $1.1 million. I know his note is $860k, and he will carry a second above that number. The problem with the deal is even at a sale price of $860,000, the banks require a debt to income ratio of 1.25. This means the building must have an income that exceeds the mortgage amount by 125%, and it currently does not. Maybe before I finish this book, I will come back and write more about it, but as for now it's just a pipe dream that I'm currently exploring.

Self-storage is a sector of commercial real estate that's unique and has some similarities to the executive suites that I invest in now. I have a great deal of interest in self-storage facilities, but I think at least in the area where I operate the overbuilding of this type of business has already been completed. If I didn't feel the sector was overbuilt, meaning there are too many of them in a small area, I would probably already own one. Since that is definitely the case here, my strategy has been to bid on them when they come up for sale with poor offers. I don't give that strategy a great deal of a chance to succeed, but at least it's a strategy. You never know when you're going get lucky.

In 2009 a self-storage building in business was for sale for $2.3 million close to where I live. The property was in excellent shape, and I very much wanted to own it, but of course right down the street was a competitor of equal quality and size. Both operations were running at about 40 percent occupied. They were both still making money, but nobody was getting rich in the process as overbuilding has killed both businesses. Nobody wins in that kind of scenario. I decided to bid $1,400,000 on the operation that should have made me about $150,000 a year in profit from day one. The listing agent never even responded to my offer. I called him after a few weeks, and he said it was not a serious offer. What a fool. In an economy like we have today, $1.4 million is still a lot of money. He should have reached out to me for possibilities of future deals. No sales skills whatsoever.

If I am going to sign a note for seven figures, I want some pay off and a cushion in case the business slips further down, and $150,000 per year sounded comfortable. I would have come up some, but I think they were looking for at least $2,000,000. With a competitor down the block, I did not see that as a possible purchase price.

Sooner or later you have to figure out what you're good at and what you want to do with the rest of your life. I know all I plan to be doing and all I ever wanted to do is commercial real estate investing. The office arena fits my skill set very well, and I've been extremely happy ever since I took a huge portion of my net worth and rolled the dice into the office sector arena. The decisions I made to enter the office sector clearly sit high above the list of the greatest decisions I've ever made. So that's the arena I'll be investing in; however, everyone has to have a plan B.

My plan B would consist of buying residential real estate in a rising market using the all-money-down technique or something similar. That's how I made all of the money I used to buy commercial real estate as I went through my first cycle, from bottom to top in the real estate business. I can imagine that I wouldn't have made at least $1 million for myself rather easily by buying several dozen residential homes in a rising market and riding the cycle from bottom to top. Right now where I live, the residential real estate market is flat, but I would think that by 2013 to 2015, the market is going to start to come back at maybe 5 percent a year. If I acquired just a dozen properties in 2013 and another dozen in 2014 followed by another dozen in 2015, I would expect to make several million dollars by the year 2022. Plan B doesn't sound so bad, does it? It isn't a bad plan, but it's the second best plan that I have because the office building business will make me even more money. Maybe I'll end up exercising plan A as well as plan B. As long as I make millions and I'm happy doing it, what more can I ask?

I am forty-four years old now, and I have experienced one real estate cycle. I believe the top or the peak of the market was on Labor Day of 2005. When the real estate market began to drop, I called it the end of this cycle, so we are now in my second cycle.

Since 2005 we have dropped dramatically and now flattened out. I think we've been flat lining for at least a year and a half and will continue to do so for at least another year or so. If I'm right, 2012 will be the first year to see some very minor real estate price increases under 3 percent. If that happens, I will begin buying in the year 2012 with aggressive buying patterns for three or four more years. I may continue to buy for a decade as long as the trends return to a more normal scenario where real estate prices go up between 5 and 7 percent per year.

The reason I feel confident with these predictions is because I spend an enormous amount of time thinking and studying the cycles. I happen to be a workaholic who also is an insomniac. That's an amazing combination when your goal is to get a lot of work done. While the rest of the world is sleeping, I am up in the middle of the night looking at real estate on the multiple listing service and reading real estate blogs from my fellow gurus. I also think that the political arena will have a huge impact on the real estate cycle. I'm not a fan of the Obama administration and Democratic leaders who are in power today in Washington, DC. The pendulum clearly looks like it's swinging toward the Republicans in the elections coming in the fourth quarter of 2010. While I certainly don't think the Republicans are perfect and I have had more than my share of liberal views on social issues, I am a fiscal conservative and support the Republicans on most fiscal decisions. I also think a lot of money is sitting on the sidelines waiting to enter the real estate market. But because these entrepreneurs do not have a lot of faith in the current administration, it will remain on the sidelines until the ice begins to break. If the Republicans gain seats in the Senate and House in late 2010, then gridlock will most likely follow, and although I don't think that gridlock is a great road to success, it's much better than the far left liberal policies of the Obama administration.

Furthermore I think that the real estate market could truly gain momentum if Obama is removed from office in 2012. If that happens, the gains in real estate in the following years of 2013 to 2015 could be even greater. Of course, in the end, these predictions are not much more than educated guesses. While I feel strongly that I am correct in my assumptions, I caution all readers to make their own decisions about how they invest their money. I will gladly roll the dice with my own money, and you will have to feel equally as strong before you roll the dice with yours.

CHAPTER 52

Protect the Downside

Protect the downside and the upside will take care of itself has always been one of my favorite sayings. I've heard several interpretations of what that saying means, but I'd like to give you my understanding of its meaning. I thought about this saying a lot as I looked at real estate deals and I tried to imagine if things went bad would this deal be protecting the downside. Many deals I've looked at did not protect the downside at all, meaning that when things go bad they're going to go really bad. As I described in my section on the 1600 Building, the downside for me could've been a real disaster including losing my primary residence and twenty years of investment assets—in short, losing everything I accrued in the real estate business because of one deal. I don't know if I can take a chance like that again. My window of rolling the dice is closing as I get older.

"I hear and I forget. I see and I remember. I do and I understand."

~ CONFUCIUS

It's hard to make a large commercial real estate investment and protect the downside at the same time. Unless you have big money behind you, you're going to have to as I say roll the dice. Rolling the dice means risking the downside where you're putting things like your primary residence at risk. At forty-four, I try to be much more careful about my rolling of the dice, but the truth is my largest home equity line of credit is secured against my primary residence. So in effect, that line of credit funds every deal I do, and therefore I am risking my primary residence if the deal turned out to be a disaster. Of course I have other real estate that I could sell to pay off such debts, so the only time I could've truly been in danger of losing everything was the 1600

Building project. My point is that even today I'm using the equity in my primary residence as the main source of income for making new real estate deals.

That being said, protecting the downside means using what you have to make smart real estate investments without getting too crazy is probably the right way to go. If you continue to do that in life, the upside will take care of itself. My interpretation of that saying means that the smart decisions you make in real estate investing will ultimately take care of themselves and prove to be profitable ventures. Decisions that you make through your real estate career are really what it all comes down to if you think about it. Your life and your career are a series of decisions as time goes on. You can make a bad one, but you have to make enough good ones to keep you moving in a positive direction. I once told a young man that his whole problem in life was he made too many bad decisions and not enough good ones. If every bad decision was a step backward and every good decision was a step forward, then your bad decisions are the reason you're not getting anywhere in life; your bad decisions are the reason you're not advancing your life forward. It's a simple but interesting way to break things down in life as a series of decisions.

The moves you make in the real estate business or the decisions you make are clear with each purchase you make. When you buy a property, it's a decision that I would classify as a major one. It's also one you may have to live with for a very long time. Unfortunately in the real estate business, the bad decisions you make tend to be the ones you have to keep the longest. When you make the right decisions and purchase a terrific piece of property, your options usually are abundant. You can refinance the building, and you can sell the building because it was such a good decision there's still plenty of people who would like to purchase it from you. So get out there and make good decisions because if you don't you're going to have to live with it for a long time.

CHAPTER 53
Seven Figures Easily

I often tell people that becoming a millionaire in the real estate business is an easy thing to accomplish. They usually give me a look of bewilderment. I say that you don't have to understand every aspect of real estate in order to begin investing. The best thing to do is start with a basic buy-and-hold strategy purchasing whatever type of property you are capable of buying with as little money down as possible. How you buy something with as little money down as possible depends on your financial situation and what types of mortgages you're capable of qualifying for. Since guidelines for mortgages and government intervention changes daily, it's impossible for me to tell you the best way to do that. I can tell you how I did it for years using the all-money-down technique I described earlier in the book. But I'll give you a quick refresher course below.

If you bought $100,000 house through conventional means, you may have to put 20 percent down is $20,000 plus closing costs that will cost you approximately $3000. In this example, you put $23,000 down to buy $100,000 investment property. Using the all-money-down technique, you would buy a $100,000 property for cash putting all $100,000 down plus the closing costs of $3000. At this point, you have $103,000 down on the property and you begin to invest an additional $5000 to fix the property up. You now have a total of $108,000 of your money into the property. You put the property up for rent and you find a good tenant, so now you're empty investment property is a business making money and shows a profit. Now you go to the bank and you get the property appraised with the intention of doing a cash-out refinance. Because you fixed up the property and it's a money-making business, the property appraises for $114,000. The bank is willing to lend you an 80 percent mortgage on the $114,000 appraisal giving you a mortgage of $91,200. You originally put down $103,000 and received back a mortgage for $91,200 making your out-of-pocket costs $11,800.

When using the all-money-down technique as compared to buying a property through conventional methods, you save $11,200. Now of course, you're going to have a higher mortgage and less cash flow coming from the property, but you're also going to have $11,200 to buy the next property with.

Sometimes the homes you buy are going to cost you $10,000 to buy; other times you're going to break even on the deal. You might even be lucky enough to actually get paid to buy a house, which has happened to me once or twice. The goal was simply to just keep buying as many properties as possible until you build up a portfolio worth millions of dollars. You will make a profit from the cash flow, but most likely that's going to go back and do things like repairs and vacancies in all the other issues that come up with real estate. If you do end up banking $10,000 during the year from the cash flow of your buildings, there is your down money to buy an additional property and expand your portfolio further.

I have constantly repeated that you're not going to find the cash flow to be something of tremendous value to you. The cash flow will help pay for the necessary things and give you down money for future deals, but in the end you will work hard for very little money. The real surprise will come when you've ridden the cycle from bottom to top and created a gap between your portfolio's value and the amount of mortgages that you owe for the building. Accruing equity in your buildings, you will slowly begin to see your net worth increasing as the years go on.

For example let's just say you bought one property a year for five years valued at $100,000 a property. Since the five years that you bought the properties, values have gone up somewhat and the mortgages have gone down, and your net worth is the equity in between. As you begin to see this throughout your investing career, especially when the market is on the rise, it can be an exciting time.

I even track all the principle that's paid off on each mortgage every month, and that goes into the net worth calculations I use on my equity-tracking chart. I will make my equity-tracking chart available to interested parties at www.addicted2realestate.com. Over time you continue the process utilizing the same money over and over again putting as little money down as possible to purchase buildings. As your portfolio grows, your free time will shrink because this is not an easy business to operate.

Your expectations should be to live off of the income from your job while the profit from the rental property business is used to fuel its needs. You'll usually get to a point somewhere when a real conflict will develop between your current career and your real estate investments. It's hard to be in two places at once, and ultimately it will begin to catch up with you. For me this conflict was easily resolved since I only wanted to be doing real estate anyway, but if you love your day job and you plan to continue it through your life, you're going to have to make some tough decisions. You could keep your day job, but someone is going to have to run your portfolio.

I maintain that getting a seven-figure net worth in equity strictly in your real estate holdings is not that difficult to do. I recommend you join real estate investment clubs and read as many books as you possibly can. As you begin to make investments, you'll find friends in the businesses that relate to your industry such as people in the mortgage business. I recommend that you associate with as many of these people as possible so that your knowledge of the industry expands tremendously.

A friend of mine who's an intelligent guy took some of this advice and began moving quickly. In his first year, I think he bought two properties, but by his second year he was already doing $300,000 flips and buying multiunit investment properties with a partner that he has. First of all, I'm not a big fan of partnership for the deal size he was doing, and second, I think he was growing a little too fast. If he didn't have a job, I wouldn't have a problem with the speed of his growth, but because he had a well-paying job, I cautioned him not to move too fast. The second half of 2009 was a rough year for him as his $300,000 flip was not selling, and he's already had to do two evictions. Carrying the mortgage and his $300,000 flip was expensive and was already causing some tension in his partnership. It's not going to be all fun and games; as your portfolio grows, your problems grow with it and the workload grows.

Another thing I can say about the issues in the real estate business is that they seem to come in waves. Even when I owned dozens of homes, I would go six months where I wouldn't need to change a doorknob and then all of a sudden all hell would break loose. I'd be dealing with an eviction, two vacancies, and apartments that were destroyed. When it rains it pours in the real estate business; at least that's the way it worked out for me. I remember on two separate occasions during the summertime one year followed by the next summer a year later I was bombarded with all kinds of issues. In this business, you can't let a vacant property sit and wait because you're losing money every day it's not rented. The process of getting it renovated and re-rented is the highest importance.

As bad as I make it sound, I think you'll find it all to be worth it in the end. It seems that no matter how much money I made, I have learned in my career I never really save. As you earn more money, your lifestyle increases and you begin to upgrade your homes and cars to the point where your bills go right along with your salary. The real estate business is almost like a bank account you really can't touch easily without selling a building, so it continues to grow and feed off of itself. It's a terrific feeling when you realize that your $550,000 portfolio experienced a 10 percent increase in values in the last year and you're up an additional $55,000.

I'm using the same principles today in the commercial arena buying larger buildings with similar strategies. I can't buy a $3 million building with the technique, but there are many other things that can be worked out in the commercial world. Nowadays I use strategies that involve complex negotiations with the sellers where I convince them to carry paper or lease option the building. I can also borrow money from banks for commercial investments giving the bank that piece of real estate I am buying as collateral as well as existing pieces of real estate as collateral. I call it redundant collateralization and am seeing more and more of it every day from banks.

If you can go from broke to seven figures in one real estate cycle as I've suggested easily making yourself $1 million during your first real estate cycle, then just imagine what you can do in your second real estate cycle. I plan to be carrying a real estate portfolio with the value north of $10 million and have that portfolio under my control before the real estate market begins to show any gains. I expect the gains will begin to show sometime around 2013 or later. Can you imagine if you're holding a $10 million portfolio and the real estate market goes up a meager five percentage points? It doesn't matter how much money I made that year in income because as long as I can keep my business afloat I am up half a million dollars in equity in one year. If I'm ever lucky enough to see the crazy increases that we saw in 2005, can you imagine what it will feel like to see a 20 percent increase in values in one year when you're holding a portfolio worth eight figures?

"Far better it is to dare mighty things, to win glorious triumphs even though checkered by failure, than to rank with those poor spirits who neither enjoy nor suffer much because they live in the gray twilight that knows neither victory nor defeat."

~ THEODORE ROOSEVELT

Let's dream about holding a portfolio worth $12 million when the market goes up 20 percent giving me a one-year tax free gain of $2,400,000. I believe that this is a realistic expectation for my second cycle of the real estate business. In the year 2025, I will be sixty years old. I feel certain that if I continue to just do what I've been doing my whole life, I surely should have a net worth of many millions of dollars strictly for my real estate holdings. I know of no other way to make money in these types of numbers as easily as I do in the real estate business. I don't deny that other people have the means to make this kind of money or even more, but I am not familiar with those methods. I consider myself an expert on real estate, and I certainly feel as some of the things I'm talking about here will happen to me as long as I'm lucky enough to still be breathing when 2025 rolls around.

This is why I love the real estate business, and this is why I'm pumped every day to get out and keep it going because I can see my future is filled with bright and sunny days. I feel terrific about getting up in the morning and going to work, and when you have that kind of attitude, there's no way you can fail. This morning I woke up at 5:30 a.m. and went to my office building to reorganize some equipment in our communication room. I'm spending some afternoon hours on a Sunday working on my book and feeling great about my possibilities. If you love what you do, you will be much happier and much more successful at whatever you try.

I don't even consider the things that I did this morning or writing this book as work in the regular way people think of it. Obviously, it is work that I'm doing, but I don't have a negative feeling about the word *work* or what it entails. I get a terrific sense of accomplishment from getting up in the morning and making things that happen furthering along my career each day in baby steps toward the ultimate goal of massive wealth accumulation. I hope that some of you reading this book will really grasp the things I'm talking about above. I feel that may be the most important message in the entire book.

Here's an idea you should think about after you buy your first property. Make sure that you take some time after you bought it to really analyze what's going to be involved in being a real estate landlord. If you like it or even love it, let's get the party started, and if you don't get out right now. If you're going to proceed in the business just for the money but despise dealing with tenants and working on buildings, you really have to be careful and reconsider what you're about to do. This business is not for wimps, and it takes a heck of a lot of guts to be a real estate investor. To get to the level that I have achieved, you may have to take half of your net worth and roll the dice on some large commercial building risking the twenty years of hard work on one deal. Until you go through that process, I can never truly explain to you what that will feel like. My name is Phil, and I'm addicted to real estate.

CHAPTER 54

Enhance the Location

Whenever I walk down the hallways of an office building I own, I am constantly noticing every little thing that could be improved, such as a mark on the wall. I take great pride in the appearance of my building. I constantly make notes of every little thing that I might notice such as a stain on a drop ceiling or a dirty carpet. I'm an anal guy, and I usually keep a detailed list of all the items that need to be repaired at each building I own. Sometimes I'm the guy who goes down and fixes the problem, or I might sub it out to somebody else. Either way it requires a certain amount of diligence to see that the project is done to my satisfaction and in a timely manner.

When it comes to residential properties, every time there's a vacant apartment, I usually renovate a kitchen or a bathroom along with other items. In residential rental apartments, the kitchens are always done with off-the-shelf cabinets from Lowe's. I use a laminate countertop with a stainless steel sink or a white plastic sink. I also change the configuration of the kitchens to make them a straight section as opposed to an L-shape or U-shaped. The reason I make a kitchen straight is because there's less cuts on the countertop and it's easier to replace it eight years later, which is all you're going to get out of this kind of kitchen. The point is to make it look good so you rent the apartment. Imagine if the kitchen was ten feet long in one straight section. I could replace that whole section for about $2000 in a matter of two or three days, and the apartment looks beautiful. My flooring guy comes in and puts down some carpet along with a one-piece vinyl floor, and I'm done. This is the strategy I use for my residential apartments, but if I was doing the flip, it's a whole different story. For my flips, I still use right off-the-shelf at Lowe's cabinets, but I put granite countertops on with ceramic tile floors and also add beautiful appliances. Below you can see a picture of what I call one of my signature kitchens.

"One of my signature kitchens"

I did all this work myself, and as you can see I'm very proud of it. On this job, the appliances cost approximately $2000 and the countertop was about $1600. I probably spent another $3000 on all the cabinets, hardware, sink, and faucet. I usually buy everything from Home Depot or Lowe's. People always tell me you can get this cheaper here and that cheaper there, but when you're doing a flip you're probably at Home Depot or Lowe's every morning. It's just easier to get everything you need right there and have it all delivered. At Lowe's if you order more than $2500 worth of supplies, you get a free delivery. They never have everything that you need for the first truck, so they may end up coming back to the job site four times bringing you all the supplies you ordered with free delivery.

When it comes to bathrooms, I do the same thing. All my components come from Lowe's as I have all the serial numbers written down of the components I like to use. I leave out the tub and toilet as well as all the faucets unless I specifically want a certain kind. First I put in the flooring, and I can drop in the vanity, mirror, and medicine cabinet. My plumber would bring the tub and toilet and faucets. He simply hauls them in, mounts everything, and plumbs them right up.

The other items I almost always include on a residential rental are a complete paint job along with cleaning and whatever projects require improvement. I used the same color to paint everything in the apartment from the walls to the windowsills, from the doors to the molding, the bathrooms to the bedrooms, and everything else you can imagine. If you use the same color all the time, then you don't have to waste any time cutting in the corners. I just pull out the same paint color I used two years ago and roll the walls. It enables you to paint an entire apartment in one day. I use an inexpensive paint from America's Finest Glidden called Antique white flat. It costs only $39 for five gallons, and you can buy at Home Depot. The Glidden serial number is #HM-1222.

When it comes to residential rentals, you have to always be enhancing the location. Every time there's a vacancy in the residential rental, a kitchen or bathroom usually gets done. I've heard some landlords tell me that they will make improvements right before they sell a building to get maximum dollar, but I think that is a flawed policy of a slumlord. You will never have the time, the resources, or the money to renovate all of your units when you get ready to sell them, especially if tenants are living in them.

When I found the commercial building that I wanted to purchase, I immediately put a few properties for sale that were already in excellent condition with tenants living in them paying high rent. In one case, a duplex I owned had vacancies twice on each floor in the last four years, and both times I renovated the bathrooms or the kitchens. Each apartment had a bathroom and kitchen that was less than four years old. When I put the property up for sale, it moved quickly because most buyers don't want to have to do renovations themselves unless you're giving the building away dirt cheap to a guy like me.

Now I do a lower grade of renovation in the residential rentals that I have as opposed to the flips, but that's because in this economy, the flips have to be drop dead gorgeous. I can't justify putting a $1600 countertop in a residential rental where guys pay me $795 a month. In flips I also provide the appliances, but in residential rentals, I never do unless an older owner or renter left them there. Every lease says that the appliances are there for your use; however, if they require repair or replacement, it is the tenant's responsibility. I am not discussing permanent appliances such as stoves or dishwashers, but I am referring to washers, dryers, and refrigerators.

Enhancing your locations no matter what kind of properties they are is the stepping-stone of a successful real estate business. When you improve your properties, you'll be proud of them, and other people will want to pay you top dollar to rent them. Your portfolio will increase in value faster, and your profit levels will make your business more successful. There's no way to get around enhancing your locations. I don't even consider enhancing the location to be an option. It's something you must do to be successful in the real estate industry.

PART 4

Outside the Box Ideas

CHAPTER 55

Sometimes the Move Is to Overpay

In a real estate market today where people are buying properties at $.60 on the dollar, it seems backward to say that sometimes the move is to overpay. This outside-the-box idea comes to you with a lot of experience winning bids for properties that cheap landlords lost. When you find a property that's really worth buying, you have to put in a solid offer. If your move is to be the cheapest bid on the block, every time you go out you're probably going to lose a whole lot more deals than you think. You have to use your head and recognize that the deal in front of you is a tremendous opportunity and you need to purchase it with a strong offer. Especially when dealing with commercial properties or you could be looking at a building that could provide an income for your family for the next twenty years, sometimes the move is to overpay.

When I bought Executec Suites, it was listed at $2,300,000, and I was only able to negotiate a mere $150,000 off the sales price. If you read the chapter about Executec Suites, you know that I do not regret paying $2,150,000 for that building. It has been feeding me $15–$20,000 a month in profit ever since and maintaining its value in a declining market.

The point is to use your head and your good business skills to know when there are certain times not to low-ball every offer. Many real estate authors talk about rules like the 100/10/1 rule. The idea behind this theory is that you would look at one hundred buildings, bid on ten, and buy one. I don't think there's anything wrong with a theory like that except to say that it's going to take an awful long time to look at one hundred buildings. I'd rather know my area inside and out, so the minute a street address pops up on the multiple listing service, I know it's a deal. I've already looked at so many of them over the years that I can move swiftly to purchase this one up. I'd rather have done my homework over the years passed so that today I can recognize the needle in the haystack from a block away and move quickly to acquire it.

Even as I write this paragraph, I just received a phone call from an REO agent who called to tell me that my offer was not accepted on a condo I was trying to buy. It was listed for $85,000.00, but I bid $65,000 as the place was pretty wasted. As I sit here today, I regret not bidding more because I could've made some decent money off the flip, but I didn't feel this was a move that warranted overpaying. As real estate investors, we constantly have to fight the demons inside of us, on one shoulder telling us to bid $65,000 and the other shoulder telling us that $80,000 is what it's going to take to get it done. I suppose I can take comfort in the fact that my instincts immediately told me $65,000, and I followed them through to the end.

CHAPTER 56

Create Multiple Profit Generators

When you are dealing with commercial real estate, there's usually a lot of ways to make money in addition to the rent. One obvious way would be to put a coin-operated washer and dryer in a duplex, triplex, or any multi unit apartment building. By doing this, you create a profit generator making that particular piece of real estate worth more money and more convenient to the people who rent from you hopefully making them stay longer.

A digital billboard is an idea that I came up with after waiting to get a table at a restaurant. In the waiting area was a television on the wall with a slideshow running various slides about the entertainment and meal specials at the restaurant. I spent about $1200 to develop the digital billboard in the lobby of my executive suite center. A Web site designer in the building named Dennis helped me put this together. We provide free slides to people in the building as long as they pay a one-time fee of $99 to get the slide created. We also sell advertising space to people from outside the building for $120 a year as well as a $99 one-time fee. It doesn't make me rich, but it does add to the profit at the end of the year.

Having a printer, copier, and scanner in our building is another profit generator as people use it and they get charged for making copies. People in an office building also use your phone system, and you can bill them for outgoing calls, which becomes another source of revenue. When you have a receptionist sitting in the lobby answering phones all day, they have time in between phone calls to type letters; we do various projects for the tenants. This is something you can bill accordingly for and charge additional monies above and beyond the rent to your tenants, who are in fact like a captured audience. I've also talked in other sections of this book about key fobs, mailboxes, answering services, and renting conference rooms. All of these things can produce additional income.

Having to Pitney Bowes automatic mail stamping machine is a great way to make a few bucks. Tenants drop off their outgoing mail that use standard $.44 and then mark up the price 20 percent. These extra items get billed along with the rent each month under the heading amenities. Tenants no longer need to buy rolls of stamps. They just drop off the outgoing mail, and we bill them monthly.

How about when a client wants to send a package out overnight? We ship it out the door on our UPS account number. When the bill comes in at the end of the month, we market up 20 percent and put it on their amenities bill—another added feature to being in our building.

When customers call in for our tenants when they are at home or on the road that day, we patch the calls to them taking an incoming call that was free and turning it into an outgoing call. We charge $.35 for each patched call we announce, whether they accept it or not, generating additional income. It also makes it sound as if the tenants are in the office hopefully improving their image.

We've even gone as far as to offer office supplies to our tenants meaning that we would stock up on things that people commonly use; when they need them, we provide it for them and bill them on the amenities bill.

Other things that you may not have thought of are services like taking your dry cleaning from the office and returning it later as a provided service. We also offer projectors for that important sales presentation that we would charge a small rental fee for. When you are having a big sales meeting at one of my buildings, my ladies offer a concierge service where we would take your lunch orders and provide a served lunch in a conference room. Of course, there's a charge for all these items in a convenience for our customers. If you really put your mind to it, you can find many different things that you can charge your tenants for that they would be willing to accept. In one of my buildings, I just recently finished doing a profit and loss statement for the year 2009. That building generated $36,000 a month in rent but averaged almost $42,000 a month in gross income. That's $6000 a month gross in amenities income generated from providing all the services.

Direct TV is yet another way to generate additional income. We have an account at our office building and run wires to any office that wants it. To us we are charged $4.99 more per month like an extra TV in a bedroom. The tenant pays us $49.99 per month for the luxury.

Now I know you're sitting there thinking that the only way I could do all these things as if I owned a big office building, but I say you're wrong. This kind of thinking can be applied to any type of real estate, such as for example a small duplex. Let's suppose for example that a young couple is coming to rent a one-bedroom apartment from you in a small duplex. Before you sign the rental agreement ask them if there are any additional items they might like you to provide along with the apartment. Maybe they would like to have ceiling fans, a refrigerator, a bed, and a lawnmower. Tell them that you will provide all of these items for an additional hundred dollars a month for as long as they stay in the apartment. You just created $1200 a year in additional income, and you can probably buy all of those items from around $1200. After one year, everything you collect from these people is gravy on top of your mashed potatoes.

So you need to think outside the box for additional ways to generate income off of real estate. How about offering them a television set or a security system for your property? If they have an issue with the storage space in your rental unit, why not offer to buy them a shed out back for an additional cost? The sky is the limit regarding how you utilize your creative thought processes to develop multiple profit generators in your real estate portfolio. This is one area of real estate that most landlords completely miss the boat; if all you're thinking about is collecting rent money, you are missing out on all the other things you could be doing. You need to take time to reevaluate your portfolio for multiple profit generators.

Below is a list of my favorite profit generators:

- Coin operated washers and dryers
- Vending machines
- Digital billboards
- Key fob systems
- Direct TV in office buildings
- Pitney Bowes mailer
- Printer, copier, scanner
- Telephone systems for outgoing call billing
- Call patching
- Secretarial skills billed out by the hour
- Mailbox rental
- Answering service
- Conference room rental
- UPS overnight delivery
- Projector rentals
- Office supplies
- Signage rental
- Furniture provided with rent

- Concierge service for lunch or dry cleaning
- Miscellaneous items added on like a ceiling fan or shed

CHAPTER 57

Hi, My Name Is Phil and I'm Addicted to Real Estate

The more you like something, the better you'll be at it, and the more you will succeed at it, the more you like it. Something clicked in my head over twenty-five years ago that made me fall in love with real estate, and I've never lost that love to this day. What keeps me going today is the fact that I can now see that kind of money I can make in this business if I stick in it long enough. I also enjoy and have enthusiasm about my success and love the opportunity to talk about it at every juncture. If you ask me a question about real estate, you'd better get your pillow out because I could be talking for a long time. Maybe I'm an egomaniac and I just enjoy hearing the sound of my own voice, or maybe I enjoy helping people a little. I could spend a fortune in therapy trying to figure out exactly what makes me tick, but in the end, who cares as long as it works?

I spent several hours this morning reviewing all the properties for sale in various counties and made plans to go out and see two of them. One I'm going to see on Friday is a particularly good deal, and I am excited about the opportunity to make some money there. You have to find ways to make what you do for a living exciting and interesting, otherwise you'll just become bored to death. And if you allow yourself to become bored, then the first sentence of this chapter will never happen. The first sentence I am referring to is "The more you like something, the better you'll be at it, and the more you succeed at it, the more you like it."

I like to say I'm addicted to real estate because I'm continually reminding myself that I have obsessive compulsive disorders about collecting things such as properties. I don't think I'll be able to find a support group to help me with this problem, so I have to keep reminding myself to be my own therapist. Where I live there are several condo developments that I really enjoy buying, and because they're so close to home and very affordable sometimes, I feel like I'm Gordon Gecko, the fictional character from the movie *Wall Street*, and if I could just buy up 25 percent of all the condos in these developments, I could take over the board and ultimately take over the entire development. The item I most want to communicate is you have to be aware of your own obsessions, as I think many landlords have obsessive-compulsive disorder or some kind of attraction to the accumulation of items. I bet most landlords collected baseball cards, stamps, or bugs when they were kids, and now they continue the same behavior collecting property.

CHAPTER 58

Honor among Investors

Depending on who you talk to, landlords have a pretty lousy reputation in the business world. I've heard people say the two worst things you can be in life is a politician or an attorney. After that usually comes car salesman followed by a landlord, or as people say slumlord. I can't tell you how many times people have asked what I do for a living and I told him I was a professional real estate investor. The next thing out of their mouths was "so you're a slumlord." Let's just come out and say that people really don't have a high opinion of landlords. I used to have the words "professional real estate investor" on my business card to combat being called a slumlord.

People certainly don't see a favorable view of us being portrayed in the courtroom as most judges I have met usually consider the tenants to be victims and the landlords to be evil rich capitalists. This is especially true if the courtroom happens to be located in Philadelphia, where getting screwed by the system is more like a reoccurring nightmare. So what can we as landlords do to improve the image that has been tarnished for so many years?

Well, we could petition Hollywood to create a movie with a landlord as the hero although I don't think the liberals in that part of the world will ever let that happen. The only people who are allowed to get rich off of their skills are the Hollywood stars. No way the hero of a movie could be a capitalist pig entrepreneur like a landlord.

The only way I know of to improve the image of a landlord is to conduct yourself in a manner of professionalism to the point where people can only think of you as a professional housing provider. When a prospective tenant comes to take a look at your apartment, instead of just questioning them make sure you take some time to tell them about yourself and the way you conduct your business in a professional manner. I usually say something like this.

"I just wanted to tell you a little bit about myself. I am a full-time professional real estate investor who earns his living solely on the profit from the investment properties I own and manage personally. I take what I do very seriously and I handle any concerns that my tenants may have in a professional manner as quickly as I possibly can. If you decide you want to rent this property and I decide that I want to sign the lease with you, I think you'll find the highest level of professionalism conducted by my company than you've ever seen before. This property has already been completely renovated. However, if any issues were to arise in the future, all you have to do is simply place a phone call as I have many people on the payroll in all different fields of real estate who will act swiftly to correct the problem."

That is usually the kind of thing that I say to prospective tenants when they're looking at a residential apartment. It seems to be an effective approach to residential tenants because they're generally not used to hearing anyone talk to them like that. Fifty percent of all landlords graduated in the bottom half of their class, so all you have to do is use your brain and think of things that separate you above and beyond the competition. I don't usually spend a lot of time calling signs in the neighborhood to find out what other landlords are charging for their apartments. I already pretty much know I'm charging more than most people because I always fix up my places and I have to charge more to justify that. Furthermore, I use my salesmanship and my personality to make the people feel comfortable renting from me so much so that they're willing to pay more to be with me.

If you don't believe me, just ask your tenants where they rented prior to coming to this place or why they're looking for a new place. I think you'll find that many times you will be told it was due to the landlord. It seems to me that almost every time I asked that question it always appears to be the landlord's fault. Maybe that's why landlords have such a lousy reputation. While I certainly don't believe that the landlords are the cause for most of the problems, every tenant needs a good excuse why they're moving out of their existing place. You'll have plenty of time to investigate that before you sign the lease. But strictly speaking from a sales point of view, many of the tenants tell you that they have had a problem with their existing landlord. I always ask what the problem was and then go right into my standard speech explaining to them the level of professionalism that they're going to experience with Falcone Real Estate Holding Corporation.

Another thing that I try to do when I conduct business is to have honor among investors. Especially when trying to buy a commercial building from an individual who is not unlike me, finding a win-win is incredibly important to getting that deal to settlement. You are not going to do that if you beat the guy up to death or if you're lying in order to get something done. You have to conduct yourself in a professional manner and tell the truth about what you're trying to do. If you're buying a guy's building at retail value and you have all the down money required and the financing in place, you don't need to concern yourself with all of this. But if your plan involves the existing owner to carry some paper, do a lease option, or even be a partner, there's no way you're going to get that done unless both parties gain something from the deal.

I know too many investors who go out and try to steal buildings from everybody they meet, and they may ultimately succeed with that strategy if they are buying cheap residential properties. However, in a large commercial deal where you're talking about many millions of dollars, I don't think that technique works. I might try a more traditional strategy if I was buying a commercial building I could straight up buy with 25 percent to 30 percent down. My appetite for commercial real estate generally tends to go much higher than the building I could afford with traditional financing; therefore, I have no option but to try to figure out a way where everybody wins.

Remember I'm not really looking for just another building to buy. I'm looking for a home run deal that's going to feed my family for the rest of my life. I view myself in a position where I don't need to buy a large quantity of buildings to make it. I'm more looking for quality of the building that fits the perfect mold for me to want to be there for the next however many years.

CHAPTER 59

My Pet Peeves

This section of the book has the potential to be the largest and most detailed portion of any book ever written. Let's start with the pet peeves I have about people in the real estate business.

I once went to real estate seminar where the speaker said that his number one rule for success in real estate was to never pick up a hammer. His reason for saying this was because if he wasn't working on his buildings, he would have more time to go find buildings. I doubt that theory works unless he has an unlimited amount of money to buy buildings and pay people to fix them. I would say the exact opposite about his theory is that one of the greatest keys to my success is my ability to fix things. I think real landlords and, for that matter, real men fix buildings that they own at least sometimes. I would agree when you have a $20 million portfolio that maybe it's time to stop working on your buildings, but most people never get to that pinnacle. So don't let me catch you going around saying that landlords don't work on buildings, especially if I have a hammer with me when you say it.

I have a problem with people who have no respect for sales. There are many people who are intellectuals and consider themselves to be above the level of a salesman. I think sales is the essence of good business, and I never met a great businessman who couldn't sell. The two go hand in hand, and I consider sales to be an art form that takes a lifetime to master. Sales is a lot more than getting people to sign on the dotted line. Sales to me is a much broader category that gets people to like you first so that you can then get them to do what you want them to do.

> "To get what you want you must communicate with others in a way that inspires them to want to give it to you."
>
> ~ MARSHALL SYLVER

How do you feel about people who apologize for making money, like there's something wrong with that? How many movies does the character always give back the money at the end like there is something wrong with making a few bucks for you? In the movie *Ghost*, why couldn't Whoopi Goldberg's character Oda Mae Brown keep the $5 million dollars? After all, the money came from the mob and they sure as hell didn't earn it honestly. So the writers make Oda Mae give it to a couple of nuns on the streets of New York City. The good guys never get to keep the money in a movie, and that's always been a problem for me. You probably don't think like that now, but now that I've got it to your attention, it's going to become a problem as you see it time and time again in the movies.

Other liberal philosophies in movies bother me with their backward message to our children. Let's take a recent movie like *Avatar*. After spending two hours and forty-five minutes watching this film, I'm supposed to believe that the humans are bad because they're trying to extract the raw materials from the ground of this planet. What's wrong with a little hard work and good excavation? Are we all supposed to live in the woods like the blue people shooting bows and arrows because we are incapable of advancing ourselves? Does the producer of this movie, James Cameron, expect me to buy into the notion that the blue people who live in the woods like a crazy ass tribe from four thousand years ago have a better way to live than the advancing intelligent human beings? Please, cut me a break.

Hollywood and the media are so full of dung that they clearly make the list of one of my pet peeves. The more you learn about politics, you will begin to understand that everything and I mean everything is political. I cannot casually read the paper, watch a movie, or listen to any news broadcast without hearing the political angle in everything. It takes a real dedication to politics to truly see this no matter what side you're on.

Spend some time during a good news day, meaning something important has happened. Watch some of FOX news and some of CNN. They both spin the story carefully to appear as if they are being fair when neither really is. As for the stations like MSNBC, they are so liberal I don't even consider them to be a news organization. The fact is that network TV is liberal as well as most cable news shows except for FOX. Radio is all conservative. Movies are liberal as hell.

Almost every movie made these days has an agenda. Here is just one example. *Sweet November,* during a street scene, a woman in the background is putting up a poster of Ernesto "Che" Guevara. He was an Argentine Marxist revolutionary, a murderer, and responsible for oppressing the Cuban people's freedom for what are now five decades. The director, producer, or financiers clearly are communist and wanted to plant this subliminal message. Once I noticed this I stopped on demand and rewound it five times. It is hard to enjoy a movie when you realize someone is trying to brainwash you or your children while you paid to be entertained.

Whenever I see somebody in a real estate meeting wearing a tie, I always make a comment about it. I'm half kidding around and half not kidding around when I tell landlords that they don't wear ties. They usually tell me some story like they just came from their regular day job, and I always say that if you really want to be a landlord, you can't wear a tie. Landlords have to be tough because this is a difficult business. Tough guys bring tools with them; they wear jeans, boots, and T-shirts and are ready to rock 'n roll. Real landlords don't wear ties, and they work on their own buildings, at least sometimes.

Clearly one of the greatest pet peeves I've ever had is the liberals running our government today. These clowns couldn't run a business like mine if they had one hundred years to try. They have no concept of what it means to be an entrepreneur or what it takes to run a business, and they never had to meet a payroll every week. They've created an attitude of entitlement throughout the United States that goes back and relates to many of the things I wrote about in this book. The overreaching of local governments and the lack of knowledge or ambition that the twenty-something generation seems to have about anything is enough to make your stomach turn.

I often think about Barack Obama and his decision to spend $787 billion of the stimulus money on political bribes and pet projects as one of the greatest missed opportunities in the history of the United States. If we had an honest and intelligent businessman in the White House with that kind of money, it represents $2200 of every American alive today including infants up to hundred-year-old seniors. What an amazing amount of money that could have been used to develop real business projects, rebuild infrastructure, and create jobs in addition to cutting taxes, but these liberals in office act like there's something wrong with cutting taxes. What cutting taxes will do is give us back our own damn money so we can spend it as we see fit. I've never kept any money in the bank, so I can guarantee you that whatever portion of my money I got back I would've immediately spent on a property in one way or another. I will create jobs for people who work on my buildings, and I would create income for individuals such as realtors and title companies that would be involved in my transaction in one way or another. I would've spent tens of thousands of dollars at the local Home Depot and Lowe's buying supplies to renovate the properties I had just purchased. This money goes directly back into my local economy; even though the stores are national chains, they employ dozens of individuals who live in my community. It sickens me to think that that money was wasted on all kinds of earmarked projects like a turtle tunnel we built for $6 million so turtles could get under a highway without getting run over. One of the worst things you can be in life is a politician.

I am a registered Republican with many social liberal views, but I am a fiscal conservative and consider being a fiscal conservative more important than any of the other political issues at hand. Because of all the stimulus money that Obama wasted, there's virtually no chance that they'll get another opportunity to spend that kind of money again, even if they have the right intentions the second time around. What a wasted opportunity for Barack Obama. I just think of the amazing things that he could have done if he was truly a great man worthy of the presidency. He is nothing but a cheap two-bit politician who couldn't give a hoot about helping the economy in this country, and we're all going to suffer because of it.

It bothers me greatly that many Jewish people are liberal. I too have some Jewish blood pumping through my veins. Please allow me to point out a few facts about the Democrats as it relates to the Jews.

FDR was an anti-Semite who developed a system of immigration so complicated no one could get through it during WW2. He had in his power the ability to save maybe a many as a million Jews but chose not to. He appointed an obvious anti-Semite to the State Department who created a whirlwind of paperwork so the Jews could not enter our country. Two hundred thousand Jews were trapped in southern unoccupied France during the first years of the war. He left them there including seventy thousand children. In my opinion FDR was a spineless, gutless excuse for a man. Any real man with an ounce of compassion would have tried to help these people. FDR is revered today as the great leader of the Democrats. I think of him as the man who helped kill two hundred thousand Jews.

When Jewish leaders in America pressed for the bombing of train tracks, crematoriums, and concentration camps, FDR refused. Bombers flew over Auschwitz almost daily hitting common targets nearby such as the oil refineries Hitler used for his gasoline. They could have easily put the death factories, killing 2500 people a day, out of commission permanently but never did. This is the party today's Jews voted for Obama at a rate of 78%.

In today's world, three leaders of the Democratic Party, who happen to be Jews, lead the way to abolish the Second Amendment. Chuck Shummer, Diane Finestein, and Barbara Boxer want to remove guns from American citizens. This was the first move Hitler made, removing weapons from the people after taking over Germany to ensure no opposition to his party from within his own borders. Do Jewish people today have no sense of history?

What about Obama's lack of a spine when dealing with Iran? He is going to use sanctions against them. Please? That will never work and Mao Obama knows it. Chairman Obama's treatment of Israel is another thing Jews don't seem to take notice of. Where are the Jewish leaders today and where is the anger from the Jewish community? The Jewish people were almost wiped from the face of the earth, and still today they support the same ideas that lead to their destruction. I hope the Jewish community reconsiders their allegiance to a party that has abandoned their heritage as well as my own.

Also I have a hard time liking anybody who refers to what I do for a living as a slumlord. I've only owned the few properties in ghetto areas in my career, and they were buildings I bought with section 8 tenants already in them. And even though I've decided early on in my career that this was not the direction I was going to go, I definitely appreciate it as a real estate strategy. In fact I'd even venture to say that there's more cash flow to be made investing in low-income properties than in virtually any other area of residential real estate. Of course, you have to deal with the fact that no matter how much money you make you won't be able to use it if you're dead.

I know of guy who used to buy properties in very bad neighborhoods. He told me stories of how he would send his plumber down to install a brand-new water heater, and he would leave the box out in the trash. The next day when they went to the house somebody had broken in and torn down all the copper water lines as well as the brand-new water heater. The house was in worse shape now than it was before he ever sent the plumber in there in the first place. Something sounds really counterproductive to me about working in low-income neighborhoods, but like I said before it's just not for me. I do think if you have experience coming from a low-income neighborhood and you have the stomach to invest there, you can do well for yourself.

Entitlement programs spread the wealth and create a generation of "sheeple" like the one I met today who wants to rent an apartment at Laclede. She has $590.00 of her $795.00 rent paid by welfare with first, last, and a full security deposit covered. Furthermore, her PSEG bill in NJ is also covered through some other political giveaway policy. She is scheduled to receive disability in August of 2010. The reason she is on disability? Stress-related problems. Apparently she has unusually high levels of stress. I can't imagine about what. She appeared to be young, healthy, and vibrant.

I think these government entitlement programs are well intentioned to help people but do exactly the opposite. This woman looked like she was completely fine and just working the system for everything it has to offer. I believe these entitlement programs forced on our country by liberals, progressives, and Democrats destroy the entrepreneurial spirit of millions of Americans just like this woman. She thinks she is getting over on the system, but I say she is screwing herself forever as the time to advance yourself in life generally happens when you are young. Her youth will be spent sleeping all day and waiting by the mailbox to receive her government block of cheese.

I apologize if I offended anyone as that was not my intention, however I must speak my mind as I see it. Venting is the only way to keep my sanity in this crazy world.

CHAPTER 60

Everything Is Always for Sale All the Time

When you practice what I preach about calling all the signs from the commercial buildings that you will find, you begin to learn a funny thing. Many people own these buildings won't talk to you but rather have you put an official bid in through the realtor. If you're really trying to sell a building, that makes absolutely no sense to me. Everything I have is always for sale all of the time. There is always a number that I would sell a building for; if you don't have that attitude, I don't understand where your head is. Don't fall in love with real estate, and don't fall in love with a business that you're running out of a piece of real estate. Everything should always be for sale because what you have could be worth a lot more money to somebody else who has another reason you're not interested in. I would never turn down a meeting with a prospective buyer as my door is always open to have a conversation with people like that. Talking to people and making contacts in this business is critical to being successful.

In 2007 I looked at a property that was for sale for $1.5 million that was a mixed-use property with thirty-something units. It was a little bit of retail, industrial, and office space all put together in one property. I offered the guy $1,350,000 and expected him to carry a $250,000 second mortgage making the sale price for the property $1.1 million. I would put the appropriate down money on a $1.1 million purchase and get a mortgage for as much as I could while asking him to carry a $250,000 second mortgage. He treated me like I was an undercapitalized buyer who had no right to even bid on his building, and I told him he was right but that didn't mean I couldn't get the deal done. He gave me one meeting and then told me he wasn't interested in carrying any paper or having any more meetings with me.

I recently noticed that the property was for sale for $1.1 million some two years after I looked at. I called him up to tell him I was still interested, and he said that the only change he had in his mind was the price of the property and now he was looking for cash offer. What kind of jackass would even say anything like that to a prospective buyer? Why did he care where the money came from, whether it's my own cash or some of my cash and an 80 percent mortgage? If the owner had just taken my deal that I originally offered him, he would be up $250,000 today in a second note with a full-price offer as it stands now. Knowing I was out there for the last two years, he could have easily called me up before he even lowered the price to try to open up the negotiations with me again, but no phone call ever came.

It amazes me that a person with no business skills could have ever acquired the property in the first place. Maybe he has a superiority complex or maybe he thinks I'm crazy. I frankly don't understand at all what he could've been thinking. I told the guy two years ago I owned buildings of larger value than this particular piece and that alone should have qualified me as a person capable of buying it, but he apparently wasn't impressed. This is why I always say everything is for sale all the time because you just never know what kind of deal you can make and what's going to happen.

How about selling your primary residence at the top of the market and renting a home for a few years? I have a friend whose home was worth $750,000 at the top of the market in 2005. Today it's worth approximately $500,000. His only child just went off to college a few years ago, so he and his wife are already thinking of downsizing. If he had done this in late 2005, he would be up $250,000 large. Just another outside-the-box idea I wanted to share. The rent he paid since 2005 is not an additional expense. He would have been paying his huge mortgage anyway. For most of us selling your primary residence and renting is hard too imagine but when I am closer to sixty at the height of the next real estate market it may make sense.

I write about these potential purchases a lot in this book because the way you think about business is more important than all the particulars about the real estate business in general. I know people in my real estate group who can talk more intelligently about "subject to" deals to a point where your head will spin. I know other people who know more about short sales than I'll ever know. While having that kind of information is a tremendous tool in your toolbox, one thing that these people commonly overlook is smart business skills and salesmanship. You have to consider yourself a salesman and always be willing to meet and talk to anybody who will give you fifteen minutes. The minute you start thinking you're better than everyone else is the beginning of your downfall. Remember that everything is always for sale all the time.

CHAPTER 61
Developing the Entrepreneurial Spirit in Children

I love the business that I'm in, and while there are a lot of ways to make money in this world, I happen to think this is one of the best. I very much want my son to follow my footsteps into this business. My son is currently twelve, but I already had countless discussions with him about the real estate business. Over the summer in between school, I was working on several flips, and I required him to work a minimum of four hours a week at my buildings. I paid him well for his time showing him what hard work paid. I had him painting doors and doing various projects. I've always believed that construction is an essential component to being a landlord. When you're coming up in the business, you need to learn how to fix things even if you intend to hire people to do it. The knowledge and skills have been priceless in my career, as I still to this day build a kitchen from time to time.

When my son gets to the age where he's thinking about college, things should get pretty interesting. I have some outside-the-box ideas when it comes to education. I work too hard for my money and have too much respect for my nest egg to see it go to waste if my son is not focused on going to college. I'd hate to spend $50,000 a year so he could smoke pot and chase girls and get mediocre grades. I would demand that he does much better than that for a return on my investment of $50,000 year. If he has no desire to attend college, then I would offer him a plan I call entrepreneur 101.

Entrepreneur 101 assumes that college costs $50,000 year for four years giving you a $200,000 investment in your son's education. Why not use that money to buy a $1 million apartment building with say fifteen units in it. I could buy an apartment building and have my son work there. As he learns about construction, communication with tenants, sales as he rents apartments and all the other various things that you learn when you manage a piece of commercial real estate. If he does well there, I could offer him a piece of the building, and if he doesn't do well there, he could take the low road and my money didn't go to waste.

I want my child to grow up to be an entrepreneur who steps up to be a man and make something of his life like the millions of Americans before him. To me American ends in "I can," and I believe that I can do anything if I set my mind to it. Working for yourself is one of the greatest experiences you can ever have, and being your own boss provides you with rewards you will experience every day for the rest of your life. No matter how much money you make if you're an entrepreneur who works for himself, I think you can guarantee you will be happier and healthier as your stress levels will drop off significantly.

Working for somebody else can be incredibly stressful, and when you throw in all the office politics, it's enough to make you nuts. I went to college for engineering and worked as an engineer for ten years as well as a salesman for ten years. So even though I worked in the corporate world for twenty years, my heart was always in being an entrepreneur. These ideas don't come without some effort. Your children need to be taught how to be entrepreneurs, and they need to be taught an entrepreneur's attitudes toward business. They certainly won't be taught this from some unionized teacher in a public school system that never made a payroll in their life. They need to be taught this by you and they need to see this lifestyle lived by you as an inspiration for them to enter into a business like the real estate business.

On the flip side, I don't want some liberal professor who spent his whole life going to college and then working in a college messing up the way my son's thoughts are processed. I've met more than my share of professors, and I think many of them have a liberal attitude in politics and an elitist attitude in general. I want my son to be inspired by business people who made their bones in this world by working hard and taking chances to become something. I don't want a liberal professor who never had to make a payroll in his life explaining to my son how the business world works because he has no idea how it really works. If he had any real business skills along with the guts to make it happen, he would not be teaching it. He'd be doing it. Capitalism is not a dirty word in my house, and lame liberal attitudes along with overreaching government officials are something we strive to fight.

Writing this book is another way of getting through to my son. First of all, I can make it mandatory reading for him easily since he has read many books for school. His school requires him to read twenty-five books during the school year, so this one will surely be on his list. The second idea is what if I fell off a cliff tomorrow? My wife would see to the business and raising my son, but only I can communicate to him my theories on real estate as I have written in this book. He would become an owner one day of some real estate, and this book may get him off on the right foot. Go out of your way to be your children's professor of entrepreneurism and help them to develop the much-needed spirit in their hearts.

CHAPTER 62
Overreaching Government Involvement

If I could change anything about the real estate business, it would be the overreaching government involvement that seems to get worse as every year goes by. For starters, wherever your piece of real estate is you will probably find yourself being bombarded with all kinds of business privilege taxes, landlord licenses, use and occupancy permits, and various inspections controlled by the township or city through their vendors providing kickbacks to political positions who arrange for such inspections.

Sooner or later you find yourself with a tenant who doesn't pay the rent and you really get to see how government involvement can give you trouble. The initiation process of an eviction will be on your shoulders to process and cut checks to get everything moving. Your options will be fairly limited while the tenant will have more than their share of avenues to fight you back. The tenant will sit home and enjoy free rent and free water bills. They have the option to appeal the court hearing after decisions were made and drag the process out longer enabling them to live there for free an additional month. They could call the fair housing commission and tell them that the property is unfit for human habitation. This will delay your removal of the tenant from the property for another three weeks while the inspector comes out to look at the miscellaneous issues perceived to be problems with the property. I once had a tenant declare bankruptcy in the middle of the eviction. I had to wait nine weeks for a federal judge to declare the bankruptcy invalid. Everyone including me knew that the bankruptcy would be invalid because she had declared bankruptcy just two years earlier. It doesn't happen often, but when you get a professional manipulator of the system, you're in for a rocky road.

> "Government's view of the economy could be summed up in a few short phrases: If it moves, tax it. If it keeps moving, regulate it. And if it stops moving, subsidize it."
>
> ~ RONALD REAGAN

Just look at how the real estate business has changed in the last five years when it comes to use and occupancy permits for owners of office buildings. I was charged for a standard use and occupancy permit when I purchased my building, which has been the norm for many decades. Then a few years later they came around and decided to charge the use and occupancy permit to every one of my forty-seven tenants totaling over $200 a year. That totals almost $10,000 a year in income for the local government that they can embezzle from my tenants on a regular basis. Part of their extortion fee is an electrical inspection that involves a guy sticking a light in a receptacle plug to ensure that it has power. This was instituted about three years ago, and we already see it's now been expanded to the parking lot as they want to know on their use and occupancy application how many individuals work in every office and how many vehicles those individuals drive.

When one of my tenants was late paying his use and occupancy fee, some crazy woman from the township showed up screaming at my receptionist to evict the tenant now. This is the kind of stuff you're going to have to be prepared to deal with if you want to get into the commercial real estate business as we, the owners of commercial real estate, will become targets of the government, especially the local government when it comes to them requiring a way to generate funds. Just like the liberal professors in colleges who never had to make a payroll and never run a business in their life, these people have no other way to generate funds other than to take it from successful Americans who have built businesses from hard work of their lives. In short, I will say that I find the overreaching of local governments to be an attack on entrepreneurs, capitalism, and America.

CHAPTER 63
Keep It Personal without Corporations

If you ask a group of top real estate investors how they feel about a certain subject, chances are good that you will get a consensus strongly on one side of the argument making it clear which way to go. Whether to hold real estate in your personal name or to hold it in LLC is one of those questions that will not be resolved so easily. I have found over the years that approximately 50 percent of real estate professionals hold the properties in the personal name and the other half in some sort of entity. I happen to be in the camp that believes the best way to hold a piece of real estate is in your personal name and not in the name of the corporation. I would like to spend some time explaining why.

The only reason to hold something in a corporation's name or should I say the main reason is for liability protection. You don't want anyone coming back to sue you in an attempt to take your property from you. I would say that ranks as one of the highest fears that real estate investors have is if somebody will sue them and take their property from them. I once attended a meeting at a real estate group I am a member of called the Diversified Investors Group or DIG for short. The individual speaking was a tax expert and has dealt with this question many times. He was in a room with approximately three hundred people when someone asked this very question. He gave a few reasons why and why not to consider it, and then he said if there was anyone in the room who knew somebody who lost the property because they were sued? I'd say there were as many as three hundred people there who owned dozens of properties, so it's safe to estimate that the owners of one thousand properties were in the room. Not a single person raised their hand proving to me that I have the right position in this argument and never concerned myself with it again. But if that story didn't convince you, let me explain why I feel this way.

If you form a corporation to buy a piece of real estate, you will first have to deal with the legal process of forming that corporation. Depending on how complex the setup needs to be it can cost anywhere between $500 and $5000 to set up a corporation. I have heard a wide range of numbers charged to people depending on whether they use lawyers or depending on whether they do it themselves. You are also going to need any extra items that come along with setting up a corporation such as business cards, letterheads, and signs. As you go to apply for a mortgage, you will find that most financial organizations do not want to lend to a limited liability corporation or to any small company. They will want your personal guarantee that you will repay the money. The best way for them to do that is to have you personally sign the mortgage and have the building in your personal name allowing them to come after you and all your assets for reimbursement. You may find a bank that's willing to lend to a limited liability corporation, but they're going to charge you points and a higher interest rate to do so. Have you ever looked at how much it cost you over the life of a thirty-year mortgage when you're paying a quarter of a percentage point of higher interest rate? You should take a look at it sometime, as the amount of money will astound you.

Now you're going to also have to file separate tax returns from your personal return every year, as you can't merge the two of them. You will incur accounting costs as well as require keeping separate books on your new LLC as well as your personal. You're going to have to open a new bank account under the name of the corporation and order new checkbooks, QuickBooks, and everything else that goes with it.

Now you're finished with all the extra costs associated with starting a new business. But are you really any safer now than you were before? I would direct a question like that to an attorney. I wouldn't ask an attorney who specializes in setting up corporations for people as his ability to give you an honest answer will be tainted. I know at least one real estate attorney who has told me that if you've done something wrong and somebody wants to sue you, it's going to take a hell of a lot more than a limited liability corporation to get in the way of that. If he's right, you could have done all of this work and incurred all of these costs only to still be liable personally anyway. Keep in mind that some of these costs, like filing separate returns, are reoccurring costs annually.

If you have an entity, you need nonconforming or commercial financing. You cannot get FNMA financing for a corporation. Ninety-nine percent of brokers do not have options for entities today as the nonconforming FNMA requirements severely limit them. You will pay a higher rate than residential and will have a higher down payment or lower loan to value. Generally, it will not be fixed rate and there will be a balloon or adjustment, and it will not be for thirty years. I would suggest that buying real estate in a corporation will really make an investment career more difficult.

Another great disadvantage to the LLC is it makes doing at 1031 exchange much more complicated and maybe not possible. I once did a 1031 exchange selling four buildings in three different names taking roughly $100,000 from each of the four buildings. This $400,000 1031 exchange came from two buildings that my wife and I owned together, one building in my wife's name, and one building in my name personally. The building we purchased we purchased together in our personal names allowing this transition to occur. A 15 percent capital gains tax on $400,000 saved my wife and me $60,000 in taxes. Take a moment to think about that. That's a powerful statement I just made. Not only did I not have us paying all the extra fees to leaders to set up corporations and accountants to file additional tax returns, but I also saved $60,000 in taxes. We're talking some serious money here.

You could make the argument that you would form a corporation and roll the money into it. I don't think it's quite that simple. When you get to commercial deals, the amount of money involved gets very large, and you may need a partner to make a deal work. You could try to structure something where the partner buys into your corporation, and people have made this argument to me before. Sorry to say I don't buy the argument any way, shape, or form. It's almost impossible to get a big deal like this done let alone trying to get somebody to buy into a corporation's name. If somebody did buy into a corporation, they would also be buying into any of the problems that that corporation may have gotten into causing more liability for the individual buying into it. Does something sound counterproductive here?

So if everything I'm saying is right, how do you as an investor protect yourself with liability? You can protect yourself with large insurance policies on every property you own backed by a large umbrella policy on the business as well as on yourself personally. Every building I own has $1 million in liability insurance and a $2 million aggregate limit. I also have a $2 million business liability policy and a $3 million personal liability umbrella. This is a massive amount of insurance protection. I would still agree that if I was truly guilty of a major problem I could still be personally liable. But I don't believe that no matter which way you decide to go you will ever be 100 percent protected. My umbrella policies and my insurance policies are all through the State Farm Insurance company. I have been told by some high executives in State Farm's company that if I was ever sued in a large case such as a fire where someone died, State Farm would have serious concerns. With $7 million in insurance policies and umbrella policies on such a building, State Farm would send at no cost to me one of the most talented lawyers in the country to defend this case. Now I don't know about what you think, but that sounds like a pretty good deal to me.

In summary, I can guarantee you if you bring this subject up in a room of educated individuals you will stir up quite a storm. I've tried hard to explain to you what I know about the subject. I feel strongly about this subject as I do about most, and I think I've made the right decision. Until someone convinces me otherwise, I don't plan on making any changes to the way I hold my personal real estate portfolio.

I know of a friend who built a Web of properties in corporations and later decided to undo it. I remember him telling me he spend approximately $6000.00 to set it all up and just as much to tear it down. I don't remember why he wanted to tear it down, but whatever the reason was, it wasn't because it was terrific. I heard a story of a guy who wouldn't buy a dog without owning the dog in an LLC. Vladamir told me that he owned insurance companies for many years and would never have faith that an insurance company would come through for you in the end. Because I respect him so much, his comments have always somewhat haunted me, but they have not been enough to make me change the way I hold my real estate.

CHAPTER 64

Carry Paper to Make It Happen

In April of 2009, I bought a townhome near where I live for the sole purpose of flipping it. The property had gone to sheriff sale and was getting an upset price somewhere in the range of $125,000, but there were no takers. If a property doesn't get sold at a sheriff sale, it then becomes an REO or a real estate offering. This is what a property is called after it is given over to a realtor to move the property through the standard channels using the MLS. I was able to initiate a deal for $118,000 to purchase this property. It was a multiple-story townhome with two bedrooms upstairs and one full bathroom. Downstairs the property had a half bath, a kitchen, laundry room, and living room. The size of the property is 600 sq. ft. on each floor for a total of 1200 sq. ft. It came with an association fee that covered the landscaping costs along with the roof and the parking lot.

I started renovation on the property, and it took six weeks to redo most of the house. I put the house up for sale for $168,900 after sitting on the market for about two months and received a full price offer with a 6 percent sellers assist. This realtor who represented the buyer in this case turned out to be my old friend who sold me my first two properties in 1989. He recognized my name as the listing agent and the owner of this property and knew he would be able to successfully deal with me provided there were problems on this real estate transaction. Since they were giving me a full price offer and I totally renovated the home, there wasn't much to argue about. There wasn't anything for them to demand being fixed, but they did request that I pay for a home warranty.

The problems started when the appraisal was done, and the building was valued at $158,000. Now the buyer was giving my realtor friend a hard time because he felt as if he clearly was directed to massively overpay for building. Furthermore, we had financing issues because the buyer did not have an additional $10,000 to put up to put this deal together. With the buyer threatening to walk if I didn't come up with a solution, I put my thinking cap on between myself and my old friend, the realtor, and we came up with the following solution.

I was planning on making approximately $15,000 off the sale of this property at the original sales price. The deal that we agreed to do was I would carry a second mortgage for $10,000 on a thirty-year amortization at the same interest rate that the original loan the buyer was planning on getting. The only difference would be the second mortgage will be due in five years in full. I wasn't thrilled about only receiving $4349 in profit with a $10,000 second mortgage note, but considering I was in the middle of two other flips, it seemed like the logical solution to the problem. I also went back to my realtor friend and told him that I was taking a huge hit; therefore so was he, as I asked him to take a discounted buyer broker fee for me. I also backed out of my home warranty deal saving myself $400.00.

When you use home equity line of credit money to buy properties and flip them, you need to keep selling those properties and replenishing your line, or you're out of business. Taking $4349 profit is better than being out of business, so I made the deal. If the buyer pays me the $55 a month every month for five years and then pays me the full amount, I actually do rather well. Fifty-five dollars a month turns out to be $660 a year for five years; it turns out to be $3300. At the end of the five years, he owes me almost $9200 anyway because I'm charging interest just like mortgage companies with a small amount of principal being paid off with each payment. If he pays in full, I get the $9200 + $3300 for a subtotal of $12,500 collected on this loan plus the original $4349. So in summary, if he pays everything that is agreed to pay, I will collect $17,500 in profit off this deal by the end of the fifth year. But what happens if he doesn't pay?

Make sure it's legal to have a second mortgage on a deal like this considering it may be in the paperwork for the primary mortgage that no secondary mortgage would exist. If the buyer doesn't pay, as a second mortgage holder, I have limited options. I could file a lien against the house, but I cannot force a foreclosure nor do pretty much anything about it. It also doesn't look likely that the house would even be able to sell for $168,000.

You see his down payment and the seller assist on the appraised figure of $158,000 got them a mortgage somewhere in the range of $148,000. Considering the house was just appraised for $158,000 that would leave little equity in this property to foreclose on anyway. So theoretically in a worst-case scenario, I received my $4349 of profit at settlement and never received another penny. I would have a second mortgage lien on the property in the amount of $10,000, and it is possible that the house would sell ten years from now for $190,000. At that point, I could collect my money.

A much better scenario for me would be to sell the house for full price and walk with the $15,000. However carrying a second mortgage or carrying paper to get the deal done makes sense sometimes. Keep in mind this option as a tool in your toolbox that you one day can pull out to make a deal happen.

CHAPTER 65

Workaholic, OCD and Insomnia

Sometimes your weaknesses can turn out to be the key to your success. In my case, I'm somewhat of a workaholic and I have difficulty sleeping all the time. I don't like to take medication for my sleeping disorder, so I just get up and work in the middle of the night. At first, I would just lie in bed all the time and stare at the ceiling and get aggravated with each passing minute. Now I simply get up and I am productive and efficient in the middle of the night taking care of business such as writing this book. When I get tired during the day, if I had a night where I was up, then I take a nap.

I accomplish an enormous amount of work in the middle of the night mostly related to real estate business. In order to be good at finding deals in the real estate business, you have to do a lot of fishing online for properties. I like doing this in the middle of the night when I can't sleep because if a good deal shows up, I jump on it at the crack of dawn the next morning. The point I am trying to get at is that you can take the things that aren't good about your life and try to find ways to turn them into positives. I can't tell you how many times I lay in bed bitching and moaning about my inability to sleep until it finally occurred to me to get off my ass and use the time productively to make some money.

OCD or obsessive compulsive disorder is just another minor crutch I deal with. Again by turning a possible negative into a positive I embrace my flaws and apply it as best I can to my business. I apologize to people who work for me or with me in advance and explain that these items need to be addressed or else.

My OCD issues won't allow me to go to sleep if there's paperwork on my desk that hasn't been processed. When I say process,

I mean there was a bill on my desk and it would have to be entered into QuickBooks and then put in a folder where bills to be paid would be further processed. I would say I'm a fairly anal guy who is very organized, and I think that's an important characteristic if you're going to run a business.

CHAPTER 66
Twenty-Something-Year Olds

What do you get when you cross a bum with a loser? Your daughter's boyfriend.

I have some serious concerns about the twenty-something-year old generation of young people that I have met as it relates to business. I feel that the new policies of the day create an entitlement atmosphere that ruins the entrepreneurial spirit these individuals may have. Over the summer of 2009, I renovated several different flips in my local area at the same time and required the assistance of young men. Since I was working on all these properties at the same time, it was difficult to keep track of where I needed somebody each day, so I had all the young men working for me call me in the morning to find out what property they'd be working on each day; some of the excuses I got were classic. Here are just a few of my favorites.

- I can't come to work today because it's my girlfriend's birthday.
- One guy called at 11:45 a.m. to ask if we are working today. I told him I had been working since seven, but there's always tomorrow.
- One guy brought a six pack to work because it was Friday. I told him what a coincidence, we fire people on Fridays.
- Another guy quit after he got his first credit card so he could spend his time playing poker professionally online.

When the Obama administration extended unemployment benefits for the fourth time in the spring of 2010, I feel this can do nothing to help the twenty-something generation that already behaves like something is owed to them. Maybe they're lazy and government handouts only make it worse, or maybe I just know a weak batch of young men. I seem to remember when I was that age I had more than my share of issues, but I was interested in business and was trying to formulate a plan how I could start my own business. I may have had many faults, but I always worked hard and had two jobs from my teenage years into my early thirties.

I think business education in this country sucks for young people. They go through twelve years of schooling taught by union teachers who never had to make a payroll in their life. We need to go out of our way to motivate these young people and explain to them how great a life can be when you own your own successful business. I spend a great deal of time trying to show my son who is now twelve the benefits of owning a piece of real estate. It's proving to be much harder than I ever thought it would be. I had delusions that he would see the value in what I've created and desperately want to be a part of it, but it hasn't worked out that way. This summer my son was home while I was working on these flips, and therefore I insisted that he come to work with me for a minimum of four hours a week. I told him it could be any day from breakfast to lunch, and I found him an easy job to do like painting a six-panel closet door. His work was good for a twelve-year-old, but he required constant reminders to stay focused. I'll keep working on him with the hopes that he won't become one of the lazy twenty-something-year olds I saw over the summer.

If you're one of this generation I am bashing here, and you have read this far, you're obviously different. I don't mean to insult young people, but I tell the truth and this is what I see. I hope I am wrong. I also hope that the generation of twenty-something-year-olds is much stronger than the small group of individuals that I worked with. Keep pushing those young people because if this country is ever going to be great again, we're going to need the twenty-something-year old generation to get us there.

CHAPTER 67

Sometimes You Win and Sometimes You Learn

There's probably no way you're going to be a professional real estate investor and not make some pretty big mistakes. The thing about the real estate business is when you screw up, you're going to have to live with it for quite a while as the mistake doesn't just leave your portfolio. The nasty little mistake lingers around in your portfolio dragging down your cash flows and net worth over and over again as every year comes around. Every time you apply for a mortgage or you refinance a property, you have to keep explaining about why the property at 123 Oak Lane hasn't done so well.

Now that I've made it clear that you're definitely going to be making some mistakes, here is a little way that I've learned how to deal with it over the years. Sometimes you win and sometimes you learn helps to soften the blow of the mistakes since at least you're going to be getting something out of it. What you're going to be getting out of it is you're going to learn, and when you will learn from your mistakes, hopefully that will keep you out of the abyss.

Humans are probably programmed to learn from mistakes from the time they are small children. When you are learning how to walk and you lost your balance and fell, no other babies came over to help you up and said this is how you're supposed to walk. You simply banged your head against a coffee table enough times that you finally learned to stay away from the bloody thing. Ultimately after trial and error, you learned how to walk without falling.

My favorite part about sometimes you win and sometimes you learn is when you win. The first delayed flip I ever did I made $125,000 profit. Even though it was my first flip, it was probably my fortieth real estate transaction and a property worth talking about. The property was located between my home and the gym that I drove past at least twice a day. It was a split-level single home sitting on a major road that was zoned for professional use, and it was completely wasted.

This house was twenty-seven years old, and nobody had fixed a single thing since the day it was built. I first found out about it when a friend of mine who is a realtor told me an attorney was going to auction it through an ad in newspaper. The ad required you to place a bid and some other qualifications through the mail to the attorney by a certain date. I did exactly that and later learned that my bid was rejected as the highest bidder got the property and it wasn't me. I couldn't help but notice that month after month had gone by and the property had never been touched. I called the attorney and got him on the phone, and he told me that his deal fell through and he never bothered to do anything else with it. I ended up purchasing this home for $115,000, which at that time even in its dilapidated state was probably worth over $200,000.

The roof had deteriorated to a point where it looked like a pirate ship had shot cannonballs through it. In numerous rooms, there were holes large enough, right through the plywood of the roof, that I could stand on a ladder and poke my head right outside. The holes were covered by a giant blue tarp that was nailed on top of the roof shingles.

The vegetation growing out of the gutters on the roof was over two feet high. There was a shed out back that was so dilapidated that I knocked it down with a screwdriver. The bushes outside were so overgrown and poorly maintained they cost me $1800 just to get them chopped down.

There was a four-foot crawl space underneath half of the split-level where the dining room sat. Centered perfectly in the dining room was not a chandelier but one of these cannonball sized holes in the ceiling that had poured rainwater onto the dining room floor for years to the point where there was a four-foot diameter hole. Since termites love and need wet wood to eat, they decided to take over the dining room years before I got there and eat out everything in sight. Even after I made my presence known to the termites, they decided to continue eating the dining room. I'll never forget standing on the cement base of the house in the crawl space with the dining room floor at about my chest level inside the four-foot diameter hole. I was ripping out the dining room floorboards with the termites simply ignoring me while they just went about their work eating the house.

I used six different thirty-yard dumpsters just to throw out all the things from this house that I no longer needed. A thirty-yard dumpster is about the size of an eighteen-wheeler truck and about six feet high. It took four months to renovate the home, and I had several people help me, but I basically worked there full-time for four months straight. The cost of the renovation was $65,000, and because the property was zoned professional, I had plans to use it as my own office. I had visions of hanging the sign Falcone Real Estate Holding Corporation on Street Road and using it as my daily place of business. I wasn't quite ready to move into it now, so I rented it to a tenant for a year while my business grew to move into such a property. During that year, I ended up buying Executec Suites and I certainly had no more use for this property. I put the property up for sale and sold it for $320,000 making a profit of about $125,000 for four months' work. I wish I had a hundred more like it.

I called this property a delayed flip because I did rent it to somebody for a year before I actually sold it, but the only thing different between this deal and a normal flip would be the extra year I took to sell the home. With sometimes you win and sometimes you learn, this property was definitely a win and a property I learned many great lessons from. Maybe I should change the saying to sometimes you win and learn and sometimes you just learn.

CHAPTER 68

The Difference between Me and Most

Most gurus or authors tell you what you want to hear, which is that you can make $1 million in the real estate business overnight if you just follow their brilliant system they are going to sell you. Most public speakers need to have some kind of hook for you to come out and see them and, more importantly, for you to buy their products at the end of the speech. Everything I say in my public speaking is the truth as well as everything I've written in this book is the truth. I really don't have a whole lot of choice in the matter since I am practically incapable of lying. When you lie to somebody you are compromising the principles of your entire existence because you are altering your character to adjust someone else's opinion of you. Someone else's opinion of you is really none of your business, so you shouldn't waste a moment of effort trying to convince someone what kind of person you are.

The difference between me and most people who talk about real estate is that I'm really out there doing the things that I say. An awful lot of gurus that I've heard speak just talk about how to do things, but I really wonder after reading their books if they've actually done these things or are still doing them. Every deal I told you about in this book is a building that exists that I have either tried to own, owned, or own now. Every story and every idea originated in my own brain or something I heard over the years that I adopted to become my own.

Getting rich slowly may not be the solution to all your problems, and it may not be the plan you were looking for when you purchased this book. But it is a simple basic plan that will work if you follow it and ultimately make you a millionaire. If you're just starting out in the business, the year 2022 sounds like forever to wait to get $1 million in equity in your real estate portfolio. Here is the way I like to think about it; in my own mind it gives me some peace. Getting rich is hard and getting rich fast is even harder, but getting rich slowly the way I described in this book is very possible if you take your time step-by-step to make it happen.

Two weeks ago I went to a real estate meeting, and I had a conversation with a guy I know fairly well. He's a full-time real estate investor who does flips to earn money, and he tries to keep a home as often as he can. He has already built a portfolio in four years of seventeen properties that he is currently keeping and making positive cash flow off of. But after he told me about the seventeen properties, he immediately went into a speech about how that's not enough, and he is disappointed in himself. I'm not sure if he truly believed that or if he was just saying that because he felt somewhat small in the real estate business compared to me. I will tell you as I've told him that I think seventeen properties in four years is an amazing track record; at that pace he's almost guaranteed to be a multimillionaire by the year 2022. I think he's in his mid fifties, so 2022 will make him about seventy years old and ready for retirement. What a beautiful plan this man has and is right on track to accomplish it. There's absolutely nothing to apologize for or nothing he could possibly be disappointed about.

We began to have a discussion about once his portfolio gets to a certain size he's going to have some tough decisions to make about what he's going to do then. In his mind, he was leaning toward paying off the properties as opposed to continuing to build the portfolio. He fears that the size of his portfolio would get so big it would become incredibly difficult to manage. His idea was to stop somewhere around thirty buildings and then simply focus on paying down the mortgage on these buildings as quickly as he could. It's an interesting idea, and I would only say more power to him if he thinks that's the right way to go.

"The quality of your life is always defined by the choices you make."

~ MARSHALL SYLVER

The thing that's great about the real estate business is that no one person has all the ideas. Once you get into this business, you will begin to learn that you can try one hundred different roads and they all get to whatever your goal is, which I assume is to become rich. My strategy has always been to continue to build the real estate portfolio as large is possible because the real money will be made in the increasing real estate prices at the top of the market. If you believe what I just said is true, then you have to say to yourself that the larger the portfolio that you'll own, the more money you will make. If you build a $7 million portfolio and then in the year 2022 there's a 10 percent increase in real estate prices, then you just made your self $700,000 in equity in one year. To me the money you make in just that one year will be far better than paying off mortgages and the properties that you own to make your life simpler. What I'm trying to say is that I don't think the simpler solution is really the way to go but the smarter solution that's going to get you where you want to be.

One of the ideas I had when I was coming up in this business and I began to start thinking about what I would do when I have a large portfolio. For quite a while, I had the plan that I would sell off my buildings to people and carry a mortgage or would become the mortgage company. The only way I could possibly do that was if I had the buildings paid off and I could sell them to people and have these people make payments to me. Did you ever look at a mortgage statement and realize that fifty bucks of your thousand-dollar payment was going to be paid off on principal and on the rest of it was interest.

Imagine that you had even a small portfolio of $2 million worth of buildings and you did the math on the bulk of the money still owed to you. You could sell your entire $2 million portfolio taking a 20 percent down payment for every building in cash. That would mean that you walked from settlement with a $400,000 and you still had a number of people who made payments to you every month, so your cash flow would be terrific. Furthermore, you wouldn't have to repair any of these buildings since you no longer own them. You would reap all the rewards of real estate portfolio without actually doing anything. If somebody doesn't pay your mortgage, you can always foreclose on them and take the property back. If any of the people who you're carrying mortgages were to sell the building or refinance the building, you would get paid off. It doesn't sound like a terrible way to go in my opinion if you can figure a way to pay off your portfolio. Like I said above, for me I don't think this was the way to go as I ultimately changed my mind.

For me the best way is to build the largest portfolio possible and ride the cycle from bottom to top and then do a 1031 exchange into a large commercial building. It's a plan I think is worth repeating, as I've done it through one real estate cycle and plan to do is through a second. When I say it's a plan worth repeating, I don't only mean worth repeating in this book and worth repeating when you're telling your friends and it's worth repeating in reality.

CHAPTER 69

Sell the People Who Are Trying to Sell You

We all have seen signs in the front of office buildings that say no soliciting. The front of my office building has no sign, but I say yes to solicitation because I am going to sell the people who are trying to sell me. I almost always take time to meet the sales people who stop into my office building, and I tell them they have ten minutes to give me their story. Then I turn the tables on them and take ten minutes to tell them about my business and my story. You never know how planting a seed in someone's mind can lead to a deal for an answering service client, a mailbox, or an office rental. I call it selling the people who are trying to sell you or turning the tables on the salesman.

You have got to have a little fun when you're out in the business world working, and I have to admit that this is not only smart but it's very fun. Some of these guys don't know what hit them when they walk into my building and I give them the ten minutes and immediately take them for a tour and show them what I've got to sell. I also offer them commission so they can earn money by telling other people about my building. But it does not stop there.

One of the simplest ways is to tell people about what you do is to create a signature for all the e-mails you send out that directs people to your Web site and tells people about the business you're in. My signature has the name of my office building, the location, e-mail, the phone number, as well as a link to my Web site encouraging people to check me out. How do you expect your friends and family to help you out if they're not even completely sure what you do for a living? It's up to you to educate them on a regular basis about how they can help you succeed in business.

Successful business people are salesmen twenty-four hours a day seven days a week. No matter where I go, no matter what

I'm doing, I always tell people what I do for living every chance I get. I was playing poker the other day with an accountant, and I immediately asked him where his offices were. He told me he saw his clients out of his home in a loft he had above his house. I merely began to tell him about how my receptionist, conference rooms, and offices can be rented on a short-term basis to see his clients during tax season. He didn't seem to have any interest in what I had to offer, but it was always worth doing. Maybe someone else at the table might have overheard what I was saying, and the next day he's had a conversation with someone looking for office space. You have to go out and plant seeds all the time about the business you're in and how people can help you. It's human nature for people to want to help other people. Give them the opportunity to let their human nature assist you in becoming a more successful businessperson.

If you're my friend on Facebook where I have three hundred people who know me, I constantly take time once every month to throw out a video about what kind of business I am doing. The videos are easy to make and inform my friends and acquaintances of how they can help me. I also have an Executec Suites fan page on Facebook where I post the videos regularly. People are always sending me invitations to become a fan of something they feel is important. I always respond with you could become a fan of Executec Suites.

CHAPTER 70

Never Lower the Rent

You don't have to be a landlord very long before somebody tries to negotiate your rental price at lease signing. Sometimes you have to negotiate with people to get them to sign the lease, and dealing with tenants these days is definitely smart. I always have a deal-making attitude when reviewing prospective tenants. What I don't approve of is the lowering of the rent in any scenario. You're building's value will be derived primarily from the amount of income it produces. The value of your rent directly affects the value of your building. So what should you do?

After waiting for six weeks, the prospective tenant you wish to rent to finally shows up at your $895 a month apartment and offers you $850. First of all, I always list my rents with a $495, $595, $695, etc., as I do believe it works on the mind. Many people including me see a $695 rent as a $600 rent and not a $700 rent. Whenever someone offers a deal, I never just say yes. Always counter offer whatever they say no matter how good it is. A technique I use most of my business life is "I'll split it with you." I am renting this unit for $895.00, and you are offering me $850.00. Therefore, I could make a deal to split the difference to $872.50. That's exactly what I do all the time but not on rentals. I prefer the technique below for rental apartments or offices.

Say to them you are asking a $45.00 reduction per month x 12 = $540.00. I will split that amount with you meeting you halfway. Most people can't negotiate past "I will meet you halfway." Both parties just gave up or come up half the amount. Most deals are agreed to right there. But I still will not give them a rent for $872.50. Now I say to them, "I will eat half of the $540.00, a total of $270.00 off of your twelfth month." That usually does not work, so I offer it on the first month lowering their down money required. We have a deal.

So looking back, what did I accomplish? I kept the rent at $895.00 per month except for a $270.00 reduction on the first month, making it $625.00 for the first month only. Because my rent is still $895.00, the building looks stronger to prospective buyers, mortgage companies that I may refinance with, or a bank looking into lending me a home equity line of credit.

Furthermore next year when I raise the rent 3 percent more adding $26.85 on top of the $895.00, the new rent is $921.85. If I lowered the rent during the negotiation, I would be raising the rent from $872.50 + $26.17 = $898.67. Does something sound counterproductive here? When you lower rents, you screw yourself for years to come. Every year the tenant stays on, my negotiating skills reward me as each month and year passes.

The original monies I left on the table of $270.00 dollars were recouped in ten months of rental increase in the second year. I would rather give a tenant half a month's rent off or even a full month's rent before I would lower the rents. You never know how long tenants will be staying in your building, but the longer they stay the better my strategy works. You never know when you're going to sell or need a loan, but when you do, my strategy will help you get the deal done.

Thanks for reading this far and for purchasing Addicted to Real Estate. Would you like a free copy of my residential lease? If so just go to www.addicted2realestate.com/residentiallease and follow the instructions. Thanks again and good luck with your investments.

CHAPTER 71

Barter Services to Keep the Machine Moving

In one of my office buildings, I now use an accountant from our building to do all my returns, the title company to do all my settlements, a Web site designer who does our Web sites as well as my business cards, a marketing guy who does brochures for me and also helps me make wise business decisions, an insurance broker who handles my liability policies, an attorney who helps me with evictions, my real estate broker where I hang my license, and a staffing company that helps fill my temporary needs. I think you get the idea about doing business with the people who do business with your business. Not only does it make your life very efficient when the people you need to talk to every day are only forty feet down the hallway, but it also solidifies the business relationship on both sides of the table. After doing this for several years, I decided to take it to the next level.

I got the idea when a computer company who did repairs and replacements of computer equipment in our building decided to move into retail operation. He owed me $2500 when he left Executec Suites, but we decided just to work it off since I was spending about $4000 a year for them to maintain my computers. I started thinking about offering a deal to vendors who did business with me when I would answer their phones, for example, in exchange for some of their services or allow them to use conference room time in exchange for their services. Today I have barter deals with my HVAC guy, a sign designer, and my roofer. None of these gentlemen are tenants in my building, but by them using some of the services in my building, I guarantee them all the work that comes up in their industry. I often kid around with my roofer that if he did not use my answering service maybe one of his competitors would. So the point being, you can get some of the contractors you are already doing business with to do additional business with you in exchange for you promising them exclusive rights to business. Let's take that idea to the next level.

What about calling a cleaning company that is local to my building and offering them 50 percent of the rent back in cleaning services? What if a stockbroker comes in my building to look at renting office space, and I promise to do a certain amount of investing with him that I'm probably going to do somewhere else anyway? What if a dress designer was to rent an office from me to do her design work, and I promised to purchase a beautiful gown from her that fit me perfectly? I just put that in a see if you were paying attention. Sounds like an interesting concept to me. Let's take a dress designer as an example. Her rent is $9000 a year, and I promise to give back one third in dress designing services. What the hell would I do with $3000 worth of dress designs? I have no idea what I would do with them, but maybe my wife could think of a few things. After the first year is up and she's paid $9000, I would then give her a $3000 credit toward the first third of the second year. That means this dress designer will have been in my building for sixteen months before this deal runs out. I'd like to think there's a good chance that she has become comfortable in my building and has decided to stay for year to come.

"Do business with the businesses that do business with your business."

~ PHIL FALCONE

I realize these ideas are outside the box, but when you have vacancies it takes a crazy idea or two to fill the joint. Even if your building was 100 percent filled, with so many offices you're always going to have people leaving, so to keep it 100 percent filled is almost impossible. With my barter idea of offering a credit for services from the individual, you have a system that may help you close more deals and keep warm bodies coming in the building.

I am always thinking of how to improve my buildings in every way possible. In the past, we had a computer repair company in our building, and it was very convenient for my tenants and for my own business. The worst thing that can happen to a person in my business is for the Internet or telephones to go down. We also have six computers that run the various systems that keep my business operating. With one hundred people working in the building, it's safe to assume there are more than one hundred computers that run either my business or my tenants' businesses. Since I spent $4000 last year on computer work, I offered this deal below to an IT company to move into our building.

I enjoyed our talk today, and I think we will do some big things together. Let's start with this win-win arrangement.

As we agreed today the rate you will charge Executec Suites, Falcone Real Estate Holding Corporation and people in the building will be $95.00 per hour standard or $135.00 per hour on emergencies only after hours.

I will give you the first three months at $695 per month for free, and you will in turn give me twenty-two hours of computer assistance anyway my companies need. The bulk of the 22 hours will be spent on learning the systems we use and working on some of the projects I have for you or just taking care of the issues as myself, my wife, and staff require. I would like to see this time spent during the first three months. I also require new clients to pay first month, last month, and one month security. I will only require from you first month rent at time of lease signing. This can be paid on a credit card if you wish. I will make this e-mail an addendum to the current lease.

The lease I prepare will be fifteen months long, three months as barter, and then twelve months as discussed and outlined below.

We have office space at $695.00 per month for office #118 near the front of the building. You will receive the following for that price.

Receptionists who answer the phone in the name of your company and greet clients in a friendly manner
Fully furnished office any way you prefer
High speed Internet access for as many users as needed
Telephone handsets and all line charges except outgoing calls
Voice mail for each extension with remote message checking capability
Phone numbers and fax numbers if needed
Conference rooms and convenient free parking
Twenty-four-hour secured access to your office
All utilities, janitorial, and maintenance costs included
Mailboxes and package receipts in your absence
And many other additional services

You would pay Executec Suites $695.00 per month for all of the above starting on the fourth month and continue for a year. I will take you around and introduce you to all our companies in the building and recommend that they begin to use you. We will hand out a flyer to all our tenants informing them you have moved into the building as well as give them your brochure with our letter. We will allow you to place an ad on our digital billboard for free. My companies will also begin to use your services. Each time we use your company, you will send us a bill to be paid and charge any people in the building directly to them.

I will guarantee you 50 percent of your yearly rent back to you in gross sales. $695.00 per month is $8340.00 per year, so I will give you directly from my company or indirectly from the clients in my building a combination of at least $4170.00 in business. Any business in the building that gives you business counts toward my required $4170.00 regardless if you know them or have done business in the past. If in one year if I fall short of the $4170.00 goal, I will give you free rent starting after the lease and continue until we have reached the goal. Your cost for the services provided listed above will not exceed $347.50 per month.

I will expect and trust you to keep track of the sales derived from my building and efforts. I also would expect you to be in the building as often as you can and pay for any additional services you may use that are billable such as the following.

Outgoing phone call made on our phones to be billed per usage. Cell phones work great in our facility.
Copier and scanner charges from using our machine at .11 per copy. You may have your own machine.
Patched calls out to you at .35 per patch
Key fobs, $35.00 each.
Use and Occupancy cost from the township with inspections approx. $150.00 yearly.

If you choose to go with any other office, I will still guarantee 50 percent of the rent. I would think by the end of the first fifteen months your gross receipts from this deal will far exceed 100 percent of your rent, but without knowing you, it is hard for me to say. We can reevaluate the deal after the first lease. I look forward to your acceptance of my offer. I am very serious about finding an IT company to make Executec their home and to help keep my business and the tenants businesses running smoothly.

Sincerely,
Phil Falcone

This company did accept this offer and so far it seems to be real great for everyone in the building. If you have vacancies and you are going to be spending this money anyway, it's a win-win for all involved. My tenants gain in more ways than one. We have in-house support for the systems my tenants rely on, and my tenants enjoy in-house support as well. I think it's brilliant if I do say so myself. In a tough economy, you have to think outside the box.

CHAPTER 72

Don't Make Too Much Money

I just met a woman last night at a real estate meeting who wants to become a real estate investor. She said that she had to do it without the support of her husband. When I asked her what kind of real estate investing she would like to do, she told me she wants to flip a home. This of course sent me right into my opinion that flipping is not real estate investing, and as I dug further into her story, I found many more things that she needed to be corrected on. She had a well-paying job and so did her husband and they also have $400,000 in equity in their primary residence and home equity line of credit on that residence already set up. She also has $65,000 in cash to work with if she found the right real estate investment to put the money into.

Flipping homes can be difficult work with very labor-intensive tasks involved, and it takes a confident aggressive person to see one through successfully. If you plan on running one with various contractors without actually picking up a hammer, your chances of issues increase. But considering she's in a situation where she has all the money she needs right now, why does she need to do a flip?

I quickly told her my theory on buying an inexpensive investment property for a buy-and-hold strategy and see if she likes the business. She has enough cash to go out and buy the home for cash followed by doing the repairs and renting the place out and then setting it up for a cash-out refinance. If she bought this book and followed that technique, she might end up owning that home for no money down and completely replenishing the home-equity line of credit allowing her to turn around and do the whole thing again. Her biggest problem with that strategy is my book isn't finished yet. Everything else I laid out in that strategy will be easily accomplished with the help of an experienced person like me, and she already knows me and has my business card.

People often mark the upward surge of a person's financial status by how much money he or she makes, but I don't think that way at all. The more money you make, the more taxes you pay as you get over a certain level of income seems to me more like spinning your wheels than advancing yourself. Just by following the technique that I talk about in this book, you take whatever extra money you have and invest in real estate. Many of the expenses from purchasing a home can become a tax write off as well as the home's mortgage payments' interest can be written off for years to come. Depreciation is one of the greatest imaginary loss items you are legally allowed to take on your tax returns. If you own a number of pieces of real estate, you can write off your entire yearly salary on the grounds of depreciation alone.

A quick explanation of depreciation is if you bought a residential building for $100,000 tomorrow, over the course of a twenty-seven-year period you would be allowed to write off one twenty-seventh of the value of that building. Commercial properties can be depreciated over a thirty-nine year period. You have to account for land value. Most accountants will use 10% for land and depreciate the remaining $90,000 or $3333.33 each year in phantom losses.

Everybody knows that in more years than not real estate values in this country go up, but our brilliant government allows us to depreciate the value of a home each year over the course of twenty-seven years writing the value off to ultimately nothing but land. Of course, the downside to all of this is when you sell that home for $300,000, twenty-seven years later you now owe taxes on the entire $300,000. But of course you can use another government program, the 1031 tax exchange program, to sell the building without paying any taxes on that property.

I try to make my tax returns show a positive income-producing business each year without making too much money. I want to show positive gains so that banks will consider me to be a prudent investor, but I don't want to make too much money to the point that the government will hammer me on taxes. When you get into more sophisticated business deals and large commercial real estate, you will be filing multiple tax returns. What people do when they have a large portfolio like mine is to have a way to tie the tax returns or the businesses together so that you can funnel money from one to another and balance your tax returns properly.

For example, let's say you own a small office building where you run your real estate investment company out of. It was set up so that the business of real estate investing was paying rent back to you personally who owned the building. If the business did extremely well one year and the personal side of your tax returns could use an injection of cash, you simply pay yourself additional rent funneling money from the real estate investment business to the personal side of your returns. If the opposite were true, you pay yourself less rent lowering the expenses of your real estate investment business to a point where it shows a profit. My goal each year is to show a modest profit on each business that I run on my tax returns. If I made too much money and I'm going to be hammered by Uncle Sam, then it's time to go out and buy some more real estate.

PART 5

Wrapping It All Up

CHAPTER 73

How I Run My Operation

I don't advocate a right way or wrong way to run a business. I only have my way, and I'm willing to share with you now. Even though I own office buildings, I don't actually keep an office in any of my buildings. Every possible square foot of space is for rent. When I'm at my largest building, I generally set up shop in the room we call the phone room or the communication center where all the equipment is. It's not exactly a paradise, but I prefer to keep whatever vacant offices we have freshly painted and totally staged for immediate rental. I pride myself on being a sales and service oriented landlord. I insist that the people who work for me have the same attitudes of sales and service, which means that they always put the customer first and they treat the customer as if he or she is the boss. When you view your tenants as your boss, it shows in the way you conduct yourself. Attitude toward your clients is a critical thing, and they need to be completely aware of how you treat all of your tenants. I would like to think there are people in my office building today who could have gone anywhere else but stayed because of me and my staff.

There is a tenant in my building now who complained to me that my receptionist turned down the thermostats from time to time to save energy even though the tenant asked that not happen. I wrote the tenant a note that said that she comes with the coveted Phil Falcone seal of approval and that upon showing this document she would have the power to overrule anyone who works for me at a moment's notice. We all got a good laugh out of it, and the tenant left the situation feeling terrific about any further conflicts over the thermostat. She took the paper or, as we joke around today, the power of attorney document with the coveted Phil Falcone seal of approval and hung it on a wall proudly. She then told me she was considering selling it to some of the other tenants who don't have the power of attorney document as of yet. It's just a cute story to show you an idea and to use your personality to put the tenants above all other things. If you do that, I would predict you'll have a great deal of success in life and in business.

I have a beautiful home office that I work out of, that is made to be as comfortable as possible. I have two lovely desks with three nice windows and the forty-two-inch flat screen TV directly in front of my desk so that my eyes move only a few degrees between seeing the computer and the television set. As I write this paragraph, there is little space in my visual zone between the top of my computer monitor in the bottom of my television set making it possible for me to write this book and watch television at the same time. Across from my desk is a large couch and I sometimes use it to take naps or have a seat for visitors. I think it's really important to have a comfortable office because you will be spending a lot of time in it, and if it's comfortable, you won't mind being there. You have to find a way to enjoy your work because that's probably the key to being good at it. By making the office comfortable, you are just happier and won't mind going upstairs to take care of some paperwork even after working all day.

I use QuickBooks program to track all the financial data from my real estate holdings. I like QuickBooks and I think it works well for the real estate business. Each time a bill comes in or an e-mail, it generally gets piled on top of my desk. As I described earlier I process the bills as soon as possible.

I invoice all my tenants every month professionally just like anyone you owe money to invoices you. Most landlords, when they first start out in the business, just assume that a tenant who owes them $800 a month knows it's due on the first of the month. That is no way to run a business. You should influence your tenants explaining to them exactly what they need to pay you and exactly when they need to pay you every month with the mailing address. How do you expect to get paid if everyone else they owe money to is invoicing them and you're not? I also use the invoices as a communication device, meaning that I want to avoid verbal conversations with my residential tenants as often as possible. If they reach out to me, I will certainly deal with their issues immediately, but I don't want to initiate a conversation. Conversations with your tenants on the residential side will generally lead to something being requested of you, so you want to avoid that if possible. Keep in mind I'm talking about residential tenants here. There's a big difference between the method used for handling my residential tenants and the method used for my office tenants.

Office tenants are impossible to avoid since my office buildings are large enough that we have a staffed management in-house every day. I guess you could say it works both ways because the tenants can't hide from us and we can't hide from them. It makes for a relationship where everybody has to pretty much do what they're expected to or the system just breaks down.

Residential tenants, on the other hand, I meet when I first rent the apartment to them, and then I may not see them again for a year and a half. Some of my tenants I wouldn't even know them if I was sitting next to them in a bar. As long as they're paying the rent, I really don't have an issue with them. I pretty much treat them as if it's their home they rented and I forget about it. I don't worry much about anything as long as that rent check keeps rolling in. Furthermore, I go out of my way to avoid the residential tenants for the reasons I mentioned earlier. The minute you have a conversation with them, they suddenly remember that they wanted you to fix a doorknob or doorbell or whatever. That is why I use the invoices to communicate with my residential tenants. For example, if one of my tenants was short $100.00 dollars on last month's rent, I would add $100.00 to this month's invoice with a note that I need him to clear up this debt as soon as possible. Picking up the phone to call him would not be a good idea, as you'll find your list of items to be repaired growing with every conversation.

When it comes to taking care of the repair list, I have a variety of contractors that I use. It's important to know what you're good at and use contractors to do what you're not good at. I generally hire roofers, HVAC guys, plumbers, electricians, and carpet installers to do work on all my projects. My younger brother Matt works for me and does a great deal of maintenance on the buildings. I choose not to go to contractors for things such as spackling and painting and miscellaneous repair jobs. I usually will take on projects myself if time is available. I'm a handy carpenter and prefer to do projects like kitchen and bathroom renovations. Over the years, I've trained my brother to the point where he's qualified to do a wide variety of jobs that a landlord needs to do. I can't imagine if I didn't know how to fix anything that I would ever survive in this business. Every once in a while I meet a landlord who claims he doesn't fix anything or he doesn't manage his own buildings. The margins in this business are just too tight to have money available to pay people to manage your properties and repair every little thing. I frankly find it hard to believe that you could survive a lifetime in this business without doing any construction work. I have a large portfolio, and I have never hired a manager to handle any portion of it outside of my wife.

My wife quit her job as a nurse three years ago to join me in Falcone Real Estate Holding Corporation. She took over management of our executive suite center. Executec Suites has been running successfully now for over three years. My wife and I are full-time investors who have no other source of income other than our real estate holdings. I think if you ask around, you will find it is rare to find landlords who don't have some other source of income. I suppose if you bought this book you would be helping me have an alternate source of income providing the production of this book ever makes it into the black. I read somewhere that only one out of one hundred landlords ever becomes full-time. I don't know if the number's true, but it certainly feels true. I'm a member of the real estate organization with eight hundred members, and I currently only know of a few individuals who are full-time. I am sure there are more than a few, but I just haven't met them.

So when using QuickBooks to keep track of real estate investments, I will list every income and expense based on what they call a class. A class in QuickBooks is the name of the piece of real estate in question. For example, if the property is located on Shelmire Avenue, in QuickBooks I call the property Shelmire. So the end of the year, I will clearly be able to see how much money each individual property made as well as my entire portfolio. I spend time looking at these numbers because the only way to improve a business is to understand exactly what's going on with it now.

One thing QuickBooks does not keep track of is the equity in your buildings. I have a download of my **"equity tracker chart"** that I wrote specifically to do this. It's a multipage chart used to maintain all the pertinent information you'll need to know about your real estate business. There are sections to track all the data about your tenants, the lease structure, all down money paid, as well as security deposits paid at the time they moved in and other important information about your tenants. The **"equity tracker chart"** and other helpful tools are available at the Web site listed below.

www.addicted2realestate.com

I have all kinds of other information available for you—such as the application I use when I first meet tenants, the lease I use to sign the tenants for residential apartments as well as for office space, charts I use to calculate the potential profit to be earned on the flip. I also have personal financial statements that will be needed every time you go to borrow money from a bank as well as other miscellaneous information you will be required to know in the real estate business.

In summary, I would say that the real estate business is a simple business, and it can be run easily if you continue to think that way. Don't make something complicated that doesn't have to be.

CHAPTER 74

From Rags to Riches, and Maybe Rags Again

One of things that has always scared me about making big commercial moves is you have to get yourself into a danger zone sometimes in order to make it happen. The idea of going from rags to riches and maybe rags again has crossed my mind more than once as it nearly happened when I purchased the 1600 Building for the second time. At forty-four years old and now in my second cycle, I don't think I am willing to take the chance to go to rags again. So how do you make that big commercial move without taking the big chances that come with it? Maybe you try to strike a lease option like I did for Bucks County Suites. I can't be sure that that's going to be the solution to many future deals since that particular deal had so many characteristics that made it workable under that kind of scenario. As I write this paragraph in January 2010, the owner still hasn't signed my lease option agreement, and I'm beginning to get concerned that he is stalling. That being said the lease option isn't the solution to all your problems either.

If I follow my own advice, then every market has a condition that tells you what you should invest in this market, and right now it is telling me to invest in foreclosed homes and to build up a portfolio of homes that I can purchase cheaply and rent out. Those kinds of deals are not as sexy as a large commercial deal like Bucks County Suites, but it certainly is a move in a positive direction building my portfolio as well as doing flips to earn income. I'll always keep looking for that big commercial deal, but I think following my own advice to get rich slow and ride the cycle from the bottom to top if it's the only option I have right now and if I can't find that killer commercial deal. If I did not find another terrific commercial deal and all I did was build up a portfolio of thirty or so homes that I bought dirt cheap and made a few million bucks off of, I could think of worse things in life.

The way I look at it is if plan A was to buy a hugely successful commercial building and plan B was to buy foreclosed residential homes and build up a portfolio, I probably will find myself bouncing from plan A to plan B, back and forth dozens of times. My dream was always to be a full-time real estate investor who supported his family from his real estate holdings in the business I love. As long as I continue to do that, I don't think you'll ever catch me complaining.